GONE WITH THE WIND

THE SCREENPLAY

GONE WITH THE WIND

THE SCREENPLAY

Sidney Howard

Based on the novel by
Margaret Mitchell

Edited and with an Introduction by
Herb Bridges
and Terryl C. Boodman

DELTA

A Delta Book
Published by
Dell Publishing
a division of
Bantam Doubleday Dell Publishing Group, Inc.
666 Fifth Avenue
New York, New York 10103

Design by Richard Oriolo

Library of Congress Cataloging in Publication Data
Howard, Sidney Coe, 1891–1939.
Gone with the wind : the screenplay / by Sidney Howard : based on the novel by Margaret Mitchell : edited and with an introduction by Herb Bridges and Terryl C. Boodman.
p. cm.
Updated ed. of: GWTW, the screenplay. 1980.
ISBN 0-385-29833-1
1. United States—History—Civil War, 1861–1965—Drama. I. Bridges, Herb, 1929– . II. Boodman, Terryl C. III. Howard, Sidney Coe, 1891–1939. GWTW, the screenplay. IV. Mitchell, Margaret, 1900–1949. Gone with the wind. V. Gone with the wind (Motion picture) VI. Title.
PN1997.G888 1989
791.43'72—dc20 89-11713
CIP

Printed in the United States of America
Published Simultaneously in Canada

December 1989

10 9 8 7 6 5 4 3

BVG

SELZNICK INTERNATIONAL
presents

GONE WITH THE WIND

from the novel by
Margaret Mitchell

starring
CLARK GABLE
VIVIEN LEIGH
LESLIE HOWARD
OLIVIA DE HAVILLAND

Screenplay by
SIDNEY HOWARD

Produced by
DAVID O. SELZNICK

Directed by
VICTOR FLEMING

Final Shooting Script
January 24, 1939

THE PLAYERS
in the order of their appearance:

BRENT TARLETON	FRED CRANE
STUART TARLETON	GEORGE REEVES
SCARLETT O'HARA	VIVIEN LEIGH
MAMMY	HATTIE MCDANIEL
ELIJAH	ZACK WILLIAMS
BIG SAM	EVERETT BROWN
GERALD O'HARA	THOMAS MITCHELL
PORK	OSCAR POLK
ELLEN O'HARA	BARBARA O'NEIL
JONAS WILKERSON	VICTOR JORY
SUELLEN O'HARA	EVELYN KEYES
CARREEN O'HARA	ANN RUTHERFORD
PRISSY	BUTTERFLY MCQUEEN
JOHN WILKES	HOWARD HICKMAN
INDIA WILKES	ALICIA RHETT
ASHLEY WILKES	LESLIE HOWARD
MELANIE HAMILTON	OLIVIA DE HAVILLAND
CHARLES HAMILTON	RAND BROOKS
FRANK KENNEDY	CARROLL NYE
CATHLEEN CALVERT	MARCELLA MARTIN
RHETT BUTLER	CLARK GABLE
MAYBELLE MERRIWETHER	MARY ANDERSON
AUNT "PITTYPAT" HAMILTON	LAURA HOPE CREWS
DOCTOR MEADE	HARRY DAVENPORT
MRS. MERRIWETHER	JANE DARWELL
MRS. MEADE	LEONA ROBERTS
RENÉ PICARD	ALBERT MORIN
FANNY ELSING	TERRY SHERO
OLD LEVI	WILLIAM MCCLAIN
UNCLE PETER	EDDIE ANDERSON
PHIL MEADE	JACKIE MORAN

REMINISCENT SOLDIER . . . . CLIFF EDWARDS
BELLE WATLING . . . . ONA MUNSON
THE SERGEANT . . . . ED CHANDLER
A WOUNDED SOLDIER . . . . GEORGE HACKATHORNE
A CONVALESCENT SOLDIER . . . . ROSCOE ATES
A DYING SOLDIER . . . . JOHN ARLEDGE
AN AMPUTATION CASE . . . . ERIC LINDEN
A MOUNTED OFFICER . . . . WILLIAM BAKEWELL
THE BARTENDER . . . . LEE PHELPS
A COMMANDING OFFICER . . . . TOM TYLER
THE YANKEE DESERTER . . . . PAUL HURST
THE CARPETBAGGER'S FRIEND . . . . . . ERNEST WHITMAN
A RETURNING VETERAN . . . . WILLIAM STELLING
A HUNGRY SOLDIER . . . . LOUIS JEAN HEYDT
EMMY SLATTERY . . . . ISABEL JEWELL
THE YANKEE MAJOR . . . . ROBERT ELLIOTT
HIS POKER-PLAYING CAPTAINS . . . . . . GEORGE MEEKER
WALLIS CLARK
THE CORPORAL . . . . IRVING BACON
A CARPETBAGGER ORATOR . . . . ADRIAN MORRIS
JOHNNY GALLEGHER . . . . J. M. KERRIGAN
A CARPETBAGGER BUSINESSMAN . . . . . OLIN HOWLAND
A RENEGADE . . . . YAKIMA CANUTT
HIS COMPANION . . . . BLUE WASHINGTON
TOM, A YANKEE CAPTAIN . . . . WARD BOND
BONNIE BLUE BUTLER . . . . CAMMIE KING
BEAU WILKES . . . . MICKEY KUHN
BONNIE'S NURSE . . . . LILLIAN KEMBLE COOPER

STAFF

The Production designed by	WILLIAM CAMERON MENZIES
Art direction by	LYLE WHEELER
Photographed by	ERNEST HALLER, A.S.C.
Technicolor Associates	RAY RENNAHAN, A.S.C. WILFRID M. CLINE, A.S.C.
Musical Score by	MAX STEINER
Associate	LOU FORBES
Special Photographic effects by	JACK COSGROVE
Associate: Fire effects	LEE ZAVITZ
Costumes designed by	WALTER PLUNKETT
Scarlett's hats by	JOHN FREDERICS
Interiors by	JOSEPH B. PLATT
Interior decoration by	EDWARD G. BOYLE
Supervising Film Editor	HAL C. KERN
Associate Film Editor	JAMES E. NEWCOM
Scenario Assistant	BARBARA KEON
Recorder	FRANK MAHER
Makeup and hair styling	MONTY WESTMORE
Associates	HAZEL ROGERS BEN NYE
Dance Directors	FRANK FLOYD EDDIE PRINZ
Historian	WILBUR G. KURTZ
Technical Advisers	SUSAN MYRICK WILL PRICE
Research	LILLIAN K. DEIGHTON
Production Manager	RAYMOND A. KLUNE
Technicolor Co. Supervision	NATALIE KALMUS
Associate	HENRI JAFFA

Assistant Director	ERIC G. STACEY
Second Assistant Director	RIDGEWAY CALLOW
Production continuity	LYDIA SCHILLER
	CONNIE EARLE
Mechanical Engineer	R. D. MUSGRAVE
Construction Superintendent	HAROLD FENTON
Chief Grip	FRED WILLIAMS
In Charge of Wardrobe	EDWARD P. LAMBERT
Associates	MARIAN DABNEY
	ELMER ELLSWORTH
Casting Managers	CHARLES RICHARDS
	FRED SCHUESSLER
Location Manager	MASON LITSON
Scenic Department Superintendent	HENRY J. STAHL
Electrical Superintendent	WALLY OETTEL
Chief Electrician	JAMES POTEVIN
Properties:	
Manager	HAROLD COLES
On the set	ARDEN CRIPE
Greens	ROY A. MCLAUGHLIN
Drapes	JAMES FORNEY
Special properties made by	ROSS B. JACKMAN
Tara landscaped by	FLORENCE YOCH
Still photographer	FRED PARRISH
Camera Operators	ARTHUR ARLING
	VINCENT FARRAR
Assistant Film Editors	RICHARD VAN ENGER
	ERNEST LEADLEY

GONE WITH THE WIND
THE SCREENPLAY

INTRODUCTION: LIGHTS DOWN, CURTAIN UP

Gone With the Wind is a classic, a film whose images are indelibly imprinted on the inner eyelid of every generation since the one that first witnessed its premiere in December 1939. The problems and personalities of its characters, their view of their world, its gripping realities and fiery romanticism are all a part of our own world, no matter how many years stretch down the long road between us and the time the movie was made.

We feel that we know as much about Rhett and Scarlett, from the major theme of their tempestuous relationship to the minor chords of their favorite refrains, as we do about our own grandparents.

"Frankly, my dear, I don't give a damn" is immediately attributable to Rhett Butler (and to Clark Gable) in everyone's mind, as "Fiddle-dee-dee" and "I'll think about it tomorrow" are inextricably linked to Scarlett O'Hara.

THE BACKSTORY

Gone With the Wind was a book before it was a movie. Written by Margaret Mitchell, a big-eyed, small-boned, fifth-generation Atlantan, *GWTW* (as it soon became known) was a megahit blockbuster of a book, sold out from the moment it hit the stores.

Except for the fact that it weighed in at a hefty 1,037 pages, there was nothing at first glance to suggest it was any more than a typical romance novel, the kind of sweeping saga of power and passion now found in supermarket checkout lines. Even its author described it as essentially Victorian.

But *GWTW* was far different from the norm. The first thing it had going for it was the writing style—tightly plotted, evocative of time and place, with a charming ability to get beneath the skin of its characters, feel what they felt, and understand them even when they didn't understand themselves. And not only to understand but also to like them, even when their actions were unlikable.

The second was its heroine, Scarlett O'Hara.

Gone With the Wind debuted in June 1936, at the height of the Great Depression. The Fates, in the guises of Economy, Dust Bowl, and Drought, had dealt out a poor hand. Life was going from bad to worse. People were frightened.

Then along came the enchanting Scarlett O'Hara, an iron-willed, indomitable spirit who refused to be knocked down by the blows of war, poverty, death, or despair. She determined that, come hell or high water, *she* would triumph over disaster and privation, and she did. With hard work, a quick mind, and sheer force of will she wrested her life back from the brink, steering it unswervingly from radishes to riches. Scarlett was not only a survivor but a winner.

On some level of consciousness the message was transmitted to *GWTW*'s readers—there is no hardship that cannot be overcome. Scarlett O'Hara had become a role model—and a perfect candidate for a movie career.

TRANSFORMATION—FROM NOVEL TO SCREENPLAY

Selznick International Pictures, in the person of David O. Selznick, bought the movie rights to *Gone With the Wind* at the tail end of July 1936. The purchase price of $50,000 was astronomical for a first-time author with an as yet untried book, but Katharine Brown, head of Selznick's New York story department, was confident of its future success when she first saw it in May, a month before the book's release to the general public.

"I beg, urge, coax and plead with you to read it at once," she wired David in Hollywood. ". . . I know that after you do you will drop everything and buy it."

Selznick, however, did not drop everything and buy it. First, it was common knowledge at all the studios that Civil War pictures were box-office losers. And second, if he had a female star on hand who was right for the part of Scarlett, he said (never dreaming that this would be the major refrain of his life for the next two years) he might be interested. But he didn't have one and he wasn't interested—at the moment.

Then something—divine inspiration, Kay Brown's repeated urgings, his own creative instincts—piqued his business flair. David changed his mind and bought the story.

Margaret Mitchell thought he'd made a mistake. She didn't see how it could possibly be made into a film. If David Selznick wanted to try, fine, she said, but he had no idea what he was getting into.

She knew, and she refused to have anything to do with it.

Immediately obvious was the fact that there was way too much book to be covered in the course of an average eighty- or ninety-minute film. And it would be difficult to cut. Millions of moviegoers across the country had already clutched *GWTW* close to their hearts and would recoil in horror at any changes made to their beloved story.

And it *was* a good story. Selznick was smart enough to see that, and to realize that cutting out pieces here and grafting on new scenes there would only transmogrify it into a Frankenstein's monster of a film that would do justice to neither the novel nor Selznick International.

When a moviemaker sets out to translate a novel to the screen, he has to decide the thrust of the film. He can choose to use only the bare bones of the story, replacing skin and muscle with something else entirely. He may decide to use the body of the story but change the personality to suit his own philosophy, as Walt Disney did in *Mary Poppins,* transforming the homely, crotchety nanny into a lovely creature of sweetness and light. Or he may decide to be faithful and leave the original story intact.

David Selznick generally chose the last option. He had already successfully brought *David Copperfield, The Prisoner of Zenda,* and *A Tale of Two Cities* to life on-screen, and all had achieved both critical and popular success.

But none of them were as long as *Gone With the Wind.* The one that came closest, *David Copperfield,* he had taken up to midpoint in the novel, and then ended the movie. Selznick considered doing the same with *GWTW* but dismissed it. He thought about making it into two separate films, one ending at Scarlett and Rhett's honeymoon and the next beginning on their arrival back in Atlanta. This idea, too, was dismissed.

Somehow the book would have to arrive on-screen radically cut down from the book, yet with the appearance of having not been touched. This called for a screenwriter with the delicate skills of a plastic surgeon.

Selznick invited Margaret Mitchell to do the job. She refused, saying she knew nothing about birthing movies, and besides, it would only bring her grief.

He thought of and discarded various other writers, finally settling on Sidney Howard, a Broadway playwright, Hollywood screenwriter, and Tyringham, Massachusetts, farmer—the last of which interested David not in the least.

Howard had made his mark in Hollywood penning such films as *Dodsworth* (from his own Broadway hit), *Bulldog Drummond,* and *Raffles,* but he was best known, in Selznick's eyes, as a constructionist.

A good script, like a good novel, hinges as much on plot construction as on character. The ability of the screenwriter to balance one aspect of a story against another, each dependent upon the next and yet each crucial to the integrity of the whole, is much like that of an architect designing the roof beams of a house. If he fails, the house falls in and the story falls apart. If he sticks to the textbook basics, the house stands, sturdy but chunky and dull; the story is workmanlike but uninspired—the audience can see the end coming ten minutes into the show. But if the architect or writer is a master, the house, while still sturdy, becomes an airy, graceful work of art, and the script weaves plot points and character together into an inseparable piece of magic.

Sidney Howard repaired to Tyringham, preferring as a background to his labors the gentle lowing of his cows to the fevered racket of Hollywood.

This drove Selznick crazy. He liked his writers to work at the studio, in a nearby hotel, or at the very farthest, in a bungalow in the Hollywood hills, but always within reach. Selznick was not the type of producer who sat, at far remove, in an ivory-tower office commanding only finances; he was a tireless contributor to the entire picture, demanding daily (or hourly) script conferences with his writers.

To be denied this crucial interaction simply because Sidney was a gentleman farmer was almost more than Selznick could bear. But Howard would not be budged, and David had to content himself with voluminous memos on his thoughts and ideas for the project.

Meanwhile Sidney Howard was putting together his own ideas. The first stage in a screenwriter's work is usually to write a *treatment,* a third-person, present-tense, scene-by-scene "book report" of the movie-to-be. What Howard eventually sent off to Hollywood, however, was only a preliminary treatment, a handbook of what he felt should stay in, what would go out, and how the subject matter (for example, racial stereotypes and the Ku Klux Klan) should be handled.

He erased, as with a cosmic hand, Wade Hampton Hamilton, Scarlett's child by her first husband, Scarlett's stuffy Charleston and Savannah relatives, and the pre-Tara lives of her parents. He suggested adding in a few scenes, nonexistent in the book, to show the excitement of Rhett's shipping activities during the blockade. This preliminary was a masterful beginning to a difficult treatment.

But despite its thoroughness, Howard soon found himself shipped out to Hollywood for the inevitable script conferences with Selznick and George Cukor, the film's director. He next found himself ensconced in Hollywood, writing the actual script.

Howard worked sixteen hours a day for six weeks to complete the screenplay. When it was finished, he had pared down the 1,037-page book to a 400-page script, which, although mercifully shorter, would still use up five and half hours of screen time. But Selznick decided it was good enough for a jumping-off point, and Sidney Howard thankfully returned to the peace of the Massachusetts countryside.

Now Selznick began using writers like rags to mop up the excess script and wring out the overflow. Among them were Jo Swerling, Charles MacArthur (husband of Helen Hayes and coauthor of *The Front Page*), John Van Druten, Oliver H. P. Garrett, and F. Scott Fitzgerald.

Selznick had decreed that the characters would speak with the words Margaret Mitchell gave them in every possible instance, and original dialogue by a screenwriter could be substituted only if and when absolutely nothing else worked. This frustrated Fitzgerald no end, and he complained that he was constantly having to search through the book for scraps of similar conversations to force into his new scenes.

Fitzgerald's greatest contribution to the script was a taut spareness of style, demonstrating that a few short sentences, worded properly, spoke worlds more than a seemingly more descriptive long-winded passage, as in a scene where Ashley goes into great detail about the harsh conditions facing the Confederate soldiers. As amended by Fitzgerald, Ashley merely stated (with words from the novel), "When our shoes wear out—well, some of the men are barefooted now and the snow is deep in Virginia."

He also reworked the scene where Ashley, closely watched by Scarlett, goes up to bed with Melanie. As originally written, the three parted for the evening in a flurry of "good nights." Fitzgerald saw that the words detracted from the tone of the scene. In his more eloquent version, Ashley and Melanie walk upstairs in silence, eyes only for each other, and Scarlett is left in the shadows, staring at their retreating figures, alone.

Despite his brilliance, Fitzgerald was let go after only two weeks, a massive ego blow that did nothing to derail him from the careening track to drink, depression, and death only eighteen months later.

But he was not the only writer given short shrift on the project. No one else worked more than a week or two before being thanked and sent on his way, each time perforce leaving the screenplay more jumbled and disjointed than it had been before.

By this time, two and a half years had surged away like floodwaters under a bridge. It was January 1939, and filming was about to begin. "Don't get panicky at the small amount of final revised script . . ." Selznick wrote to Jock Whitney, a principal backer of the production. He still believed he could make a movie out of the morass of revisions piled upon revisions upon rewrites.

The cameras started rolling and kept on for two weeks, during which time shooting script appeared day by day like manna from heaven.

And then the ax fell on George Cukor, just as it had on Fitzgerald and so many others. Selznick unseated him as director of *Gone With the Wind,* replacing him with Victor Fleming, fresh off the set of *The Wizard of Oz.*

Fleming, asking to see *GWTW*'s script, was horrified by the undisciplined mass of pages. He refused to film a single scene until presented with a workable final draft. Time (i.e., money) was of the essence. Selznick coerced Ben Hecht, (Charles MacArthur's writing partner on *The Front Page* who was long since tried and dismissed), into revising the massive tome one more time.

Hecht had never read the novel and was completely unfamiliar with the story, and though Selznick and Fleming spent several hours relating it to him, he still didn't understand it, claiming it was entirely too long and complicated.

Sidney Howard's screenplay (the only version with a coherent plot line) was resurrected and used as a guide, and Selznick, Fleming, and Hecht spent five grueling days and nights in labor. After much discussion of each scene, producer and director now acted out the whole thing for their audience of one. Selznick played Scarlett and Ashley, Fleming took over Rhett and Melanie, and Hecht, playing the parts of writer, reviser, and typist, hunched over his clattering machine.

On the fifth day a blood vessel burst in Fleming's right eye, and Selznick collapsed on the sofa in a coma that merely turned out to be a thirteen-hour sleep. But the final script was finished, at least in essence.

Changes were still being made up to the final day of shooting, including the last scene of the film, where Rhett leaves Scarlett. As originally written by Sidney Howard, the scene, and thus the film, ended with the distraught Scarlett telling Mammy that they're going home to Tara, and ". . . I'll think of some way to get him back" for "Tomorrow is another day." Fade out.

Selznick felt this version ended the film on a "terrifically depressing note." What he wanted was an ending that packed a punch—that would leave viewers with a sense of hope. He himself came up with the device actually used: Scarlett remembering (and the audience hearing) the voices of the men in her life, Gerald and Ashley and Rhett, telling her that it is really Tara she loves. She decides to go home to Tara and "think of some way to get him back. After all, tomorrow is another day." The scene then dissolves to Scarlett at Tara, before a flaming sunset, thus tying it into the warm scene with her and Gerald at Tara at the beginning of the film.

Another Selznick touch was the addition of the word *frankly* to Rhett's "My dear, I don't give a damn." Although it wasn't in the novel, the two-syllable adverb adds a chilling note of indifference to the phrase, revealing in one word as much of Rhett's feelings as ten sentences could do.

Too many cooks seem not to have spoiled the broth of *GWTW*'s screenplay. Not only is one contributor's work undetectable from the next in the final tally, but surprisingly, there is seemingly little difference between the book and the script.

The Tarleton twins become the Tarleton boys (although this had nothing to do with the script; it was because the makeup people couldn't make the two unrelated actors look similar enough). But the changes are mainly in the elimination of characters. Dilcey, the only house slave loyal enough to work the fields without complaint, has completely disappeared from the script. Gone, too, is Ella, Scarlett's colorless second child.

Will Benteen, Tara's caretaker after the war, has been deleted, and along with him Suellen's longed-for marriage. And of Carreen's love for the dead Brent Tarleton and subsequent retreat to a convent, there is no mention.

Also erased are the richly painted county neighbors: the twins' horse-mad mother; tart-tongued Grandma Fontaine and her daughter Young Miss; the Calverts' Yankee stepmother and their contemptuous overseer. Although Scarlett's world was densely populated with intriguing characters, there were far more than the screenplay could handle.

And even with this long list of those stricken from the script, the movie stays surprisingly faithful to the book. A viewer who watches the film and then turns immediately to the novel will be hard put to find a missing sequence that detracts from the original story.

Most of these omissions were planned into the script. Others, such as various barbecue scenes and Scarlett's wedding night with Charles Hamilton, were weeded out during the marathon editing work, which finally reduced the film to its final length of three hours and forty-two minutes.

CASTING

Casting is as intrinsic to a good film as the script. The right actor can bring a certain flair, a nuance to the story that no amount of writing alone can accomplish.

And the casting of *GWTW,* like the writing, was an ordeal in itself.

A large part of the problem was that seemingly everybody in America had his or her own idea of who should play what role, and no one was hesitant about letting Selznick in on it.

From the outset everyone was agreed on Rhett—his part should go to Clark Gable. (There were backers for Ronald Colman and Gary Cooper, too, but there was really no contest with Gable.)

But Scarlett posed a greater challenge, since every *GWTW* reader pitched for a different actress. Miriam Hopkins, Margaret Sullavan, Katharine Hepburn, Joan Crawford, Paulette Goddard, Bette Davis . . . the list ran on and on, and yet Selznick felt that not one of the contenders was quite right. In each, an indefinable something was missing. When asked to define what it was, David would say he didn't know but he'd recognize it when he saw it.

What he did recognize was that the melding of an actor's personality and looks with that of the screen character must be complete.

(Even though we know that Han Solo, starship jockey, is played by the same person as Indiana Jones, ace archaeologist/adventurer, and that both are in reality Harrison Ford, a mere mortal carpenter, within the constraints of the movie we must be convinced that Ford is singularly and totally the one character we are watching.)

And this was Selznick's problem. Gable was easy to cast—he *was* Rhett Butler, as much as Harrison Ford and no one else could ever be Indy Jones. Scarlett, however, was a world unto herself. No actress was quite like her, and Selznick feared that any well-known star would bring with her to the part the accumulated public memory of past roles, thereby dimming Scarlett's lights.

Selznick screen-tested every actress in Hollywood. He sent out search parties to the far corners of the country to find a new star, an unknown quantity to fill Scarlett's dainty Moroccan slippers. But, like Prince Charming's hunt for the girl to fit Cinderella's glass slipper, none could be found.

And like Cinderella, the search for Scarlett had a fairy-tale ending.

In December 1938, the first scene was about to be shot, even though Scarlett, who appeared in it, still had not been cast. The old sets on the studio back lot, themselves cast in the role of Atlanta, were set on fire. As David Selznick, bundled up against the cold night air, watched the filming, his brother, Myron, presented to him English actress Vivien Leigh. Selznick always maintained that from the moment he laid eyes on her, the flames highlighting her face, he knew he had found Scarlett O'Hara. He later gave her a screen test but only for form's sake. The part was already hers.

And Vivien wanted the role of Scarlett fiercely.

Gable, on the other hand, resisted being cast as Rhett, fearing that he couldn't possibly live up to the individual fantasies of everyone who had ever read the book. Oddly, out of millions of moviegoers, he was the only one who couldn't see himself in the part.

Something seems to have turned the male leads against their fictional alter egos, for Leslie Howard fought against being cast as Ashley Wilkes, claiming that he had "played enough ineffectual characters already." And again, despite his distaste for the role and the fact that he was at least twenty years older than Ashley, he fit it as no one else could.

Only the lures of a generous bonus to Gable (so he could divorce his wife and marry Carole Lombard) and the position of producer on another film (*Intermezzo*) to Howard secured their services.

Olivia de Havilland, as Ashley's gentle wife, Melanie, made the role her own. She had spent much of her movie career up to this point smiling beatifically on Errol Flynn (as in *Captain Blood, The Adventures of Robin Hood,* etc.), but in Melanie she was able to demonstrate the strength of character that can lie beneath a soft smile.

Selznick's casting of *Gone With the Wind* was flawless. From Mammy (Hattie McDaniel, who won an Oscar for her work) to plantation owner Gerald O'Hara (Thomas Mitchell, who won an Oscar that same year for his role in *Stagecoach*) to brothel madame Belle Watling (Ona Munson as the prostitute with the proverbial heart of gold), each actor added another layer of shading to the finished film.

THE DIRECTOR

If the actor is a brilliant brush stroke on the canvas of the screenplay, the director is its guiding light. It is the director who determines the inner essence of the story and prompts the actors along that route. He also decides how the audience will view the story: whether from a safely framed distance of long shots; or more intimately, with close shots of the actors; or with sweeping vistas or confining interiors. The director's vision gives the story its final, cohesive look.

Gone With the Wind, remaining true to its spirit of tribulations in progress, had three different directors.

George Cukor was the first. He had an excellent reputation, having worked on masterpieces such as *Little Women* and *Dinner at Eight* with Selznick. He and David were friends.

But two weeks into filming, Selznick let him go. His reasoning was that Cukor's softly pitched directorial style was better suited to more intimate films than to one with the full-throttle scope of *GWTW.*

Cukor, understandably, was disappointed. Vivien Leigh and Olivia de Havilland were distraught. But no amount of tearful pleading would change Selznick's mind. Cukor was gone, replaced within days by Victor Fleming.

Fleming, a hale and hearty he-man who had tracked tigers and raced cars in earlier years, was considered a "man's director." He and Gable, already longtime pals, got along famously.

Vivien Leigh fared not as well. She longed for the sensitive, thoughtful Cukor, as Scarlett longed for Ashley, and could not reconcile herself to the brusque Fleming. He was no more enamored of Vivien than she was of him, and their spats were frequent.

She got around him, however, by spending secret Sundays at Cukor's home under his tutelage. By accident, she discovered that Olivia de Havilland was receiving the same clandestine guidance.

So now the film had two directors.

The third, Sam Wood, was brought aboard when Fleming mutinied after one too many arguments with Selznick.

Selznick, the producer, could almost be counted as a fourth director, since he insisted on complete creative control of the entire picture. (He had had run-ins with Cukor on this subject too.) David, who exhaled memos as others do air, fired off one instruction after another to the more and more irate Fleming.

Fleming finally stormed off the set, claiming he had had a nervous breakdown, and refused to come back. David refused to ask him back—for the requisite Selznick period of about two weeks, during which time he hired Sam Wood.

Wood was a workmanlike, if uninspired, director who kept things going until Fleming allowed himself to be wooed back. And after his return Selznick kept Wood on, with Victor filming one scene in the morning and Sam filming another in the afternoon, until the movie was finished.

Amazingly, with three directors of entirely different temperaments, *Gone With the Wind* suffered not at all, and in fact looks virtually seamless from one man to the next. Something of this is due to the expertise of all three; something more to Selznick's tyrannical but omniscient vision; still more to the power of the script to sweep the viewer headlong into the story and hold him there.

PRODUCTION VALUES

Production values play as large a part as directing in transforming a script from words on a page to magic on a screen.

The set and costume designers, special-effects director, and art director are each in their own way screenwriters, for without them the story cannot be true to time and place. Minus their skills, a film lacks the feel that makes it real.

Through the magic of special effects, 800 extras lying on a studio back lot become 1,600 wounded soldiers outside the Atlanta train station. (Each man was responsible for the manipulation of a dummy lying beside him.) Rhett and Scarlett race through the flames of the burning of Atlanta in a rickety wagon, even though the scene was filmed before Vivien Leigh got the part. (This is done through *process shots,* where later footage of the actors is shot onto the background footage.)

And matte (background) paintings and hanging miniatures (scale models of buildings dangled in front of full-size set pieces) add lavish detail to a place that doesn't really exist.

It is hard to believe that almost all of *Gone With the Wind* was shot on the back lot. Tara, Aunt Pittypat's house, and all of Atlanta that we are allowed to see were built from scratch. Red dirt from Arizona was shipped in by the truckload to recreate Georgia's ruddy soil. Architects and interior designers (including a gentleman borrowed from *House & Garden* magazine) worked diligently on the homes, not only to make them historically accurate but to have them reflect the characteristics of their fictional owners and the tone of the film.

And this is where it gets interesting, where we see that making a movie is like being in an orchestra: All the individual players have to work together to make a cohesive, smoothly humming whole.

The mansion Scarlett builds after she marries Rhett in the book is hideously garish and opulent and tasteless. First, the screenwriter has to put a clue into the script for the set designer; perhaps one character remarking upon the total tackiness to another or a visual description that the movie audience will never read. Next the set designer has to furnish it so that we can see and judge the tastelessness for ourselves.

Now the art director, the person responsible for the overall look of the film, must decide what tone to use. *GWTW* has a rich, textural Technicolor look, full of flaming sunsets, rich red earth, silks and velvets, to reflect the rich, heady, fiery feel of the film. In another film, the sets and players may be dressed in muted browns to reflect the more somber thoughts of the characters.

This is where the costume designer comes in. His job is to bring reality to the clothes of the period and, just as importantly, to set the tone of the film and give us a ready reference for each character.

In her porch scene with the Tarleton boys, for example, Scarlett was originally dressed in the same green sprigged muslin she wore to the barbecue. This was later changed to a dress of demure white ruffles to clue us in to her (at this point) younger, more girlish personality. Fast-forwarding several years in the film, the figure-hugging burgundy gown Rhett forces her to wear to Ashley's birthday party is lavishly studded with garnets, as brazen and flashy as Scarlett herself.

Then there is the music. Movie music tells us when to laugh, when to cry, when events are about to take a thrilling turn. Like set and costume design, it determines the tone of the film with a deep somber theme; a light, airy motif; or, as with *GWTW,* a rich, vibrant orchestral blend of original music and old Southern standbys such as "Dixie."

Music also contributes to an audience's understanding of the screenplay. Max Steiner, the movie's composer, wrote a theme for each of the major characters, as well as for Tara itself. The interweaving of music and visuals tells as much as words ever can about the story.

Between popcorn and perfume, music and magic—of actors and actresses, sets and costumes and color—it is difficult to imagine how

GWTW's screenplay would read if one had not already seen the movie. For, having done so, the mind's eye fills in the white space around the printed words with all the Technicolor brilliance remembered from the screen.

Perhaps, without first having seen the film, the script would seem hollow or lackluster. Perhaps it would only hint at the richness of the story to be unreeled.

But we think not. For what is the purpose of words on a printed page—whether in the form of a screenplay, poem, or novel—if not to fill in the blank space in the mind, give it an idea to grab hold of, an emotion to soar on, a philosophy to clasp with both hands.

Gone With the Wind has fulfilled this function admirably. The book that started out as a Victorian romance novel became a symbol of courage for a Depression-weary world, then a screenplay, and from that a film that is still a synonym for fire and passion and faith, proving itself down the years to be truly a classic. Read it with your heart, see it in your mind, and experience it.

GONE WITH THE WIND

FADE IN:
FOREWORD
TITLE:

There was a land of Cavaliers and
Cotton Fields called the Old South . . .

Here in this pretty world
Gallantry took its last bow . . .

Here was the last ever to be seen
of Knights and their Ladies Fair,
of Master and of Slave . . .

Look for it only in books, for it
is no more than a dream remembered,
a Civilization gone with the wind . . .

FADE OUT.

1 *FADE IN:*
EXT. FRONT OF TARA—EXTREME LONG SHOT

A little pickaninny chases a turkey across the lawn toward the verandah.

2 *EXT. FRONT OF TARA—LONG SHOT*

CONTINUED:

2 CONTINUED

The turkey runs past CAMERA—the pickaninny after it. In the b.g., on the verandah, Scarlett O'Hara, in her billowing skirts, forms the apex of a triangle of which the sides are the Tarleton twins—handsome, long-legged, high-booted, lounging on either side of her with their mint juleps. Brent is standing with his back to CAMERA, blocking Scarlett's face from view.

BRENT What do we care if we *were* expelled from college, Scarlett? The *war's* going to start any day now, so we'd have left college anyhow!

STUART War! Whee! Isn't it exciting, Scarlett? Those fool Yankees actually *want* a war! We'll show 'em!

CAMERA MOVES IN unobtrusively as Brent moves aside and no longer blocks her from view, to a LARGE CLOSE UP OF SCARLETT.

SCARLETT Fiddle-dee-dee! War, war, war! This war talk's spoiling all the fun at every party this Spring! I get so bored I could *scream!*

She makes a motion to indicate in affected fashion just how annoyed she is by this boring subject. The twins look uncomfortable and embarrassed. Scarlett sees this and speaks with all the superiority of ignorant youth.

SCARLETT Besides, there isn't going to be any war.

BRENT *(indignantly)* Not going to be any war!

STUART Of course there's going to be a war!

SCARLETT Great balls of fire! If either of you boys say war *just once again,* I'll walk in the house and slam the door!

BRENT But, Scarlett honey!

STUART Don't you *want* there to be a war?

Scarlett rises indignantly and starts toward the door. Brent and Stuart call to her, both rising:

together

BRENT
Scarlett honey, please. We're sorry.

STUART
We'll talk about something else. I promise we will.

SCARLETT *(looks at them)* Well—
(considers a moment, pouting)
All right. But remember—

(looks from one to the other)
—I warned you.

The boys, delighted, take the coquette by her arm and propel her back to where they were, talking as they go and as they sit:

STUART I've got an idea—let's talk about the barbecue the Wilkeses are giving over at Twelve Oaks tomorrow.

BRENT Yes, that's a *good* idea! You're eating barbecue with us, aren't you, Scarlett?

SCARLETT *(who has been arranging herself and smoothing her skirt coquettishly)* Oh, I haven't really thought about *that* yet. I'll think about that tomorrow.

STUART But you're giving us all your waltzes at the ball tomorrow night, aren't you?
(nodding to his twin, then to himself, in succession)
First Brent, then me, then Brent again, and so on.

BRENT Promise?

SCARLETT *(leading them on)* Why, I'd just love to—

The twins are delighted and let out a yell:

TWINS *(together)* Whoopee!

SCARLETT *(smiling demurely)* If only—if only I didn't have every one of them taken already.

Catastrophe! The boys are terribly let down.

BRENT *(dismayed)* Why, honey!

STUART But, Scarlett, you can't do that!

BRENT How about if we tell you a secret?

SCARLETT *(snorting)* A secret!
(her curiosity overcomes her)
Who about?

STUART Well—
(hesitates, then plunges ahead)
You know Melanie Hamilton from Atlanta—

CONTINUED:

2 CONTINUED

Scarlett is immediately disappointed.

BRENT Ashley Wilkes' cousin? Well, she's visitin' the Wilkeses at Twelve Oaks—

SCARLETT Melanie Hamilton! That goody-goody! Who wants to know a secret about her!

STUART Well, anyway, they say—we heard—

Scarlett looks up interested.

BRENT *(unable to withhold his anxiety to tell the secret, breaks in on his brother)* Ashley Wilkes is going to marry her!

CAMERA MOVES IN TO A BIG CLOSE UP OF SCARLETT.

SCARLETT *(incredulously)* Ashley! It isn't so!

3 BACK TO SCENE

The boys are unaware of the blow this has been to Scarlett and simply go on talking excitedly:

STUART Why, Scarlett, of course it's so!

BRENT You know the Wilkeses always marry their cousins.

STUART *Now* do we get all the waltzes?

SCARLETT *(automatically, stunned, quietly)* Of course.

The boys jump up, elated, and whirl around in a dance, a little away from Scarlett:

BRENT *(as they dance)* Whee-ee! I'll bet the other boys will be hoppin' mad.

STUART *(as they dance)* We two can handle 'em!

They haven't noticed that Scarlett has risen to her feet and started away. Suddenly they are aware of this and step to the edge of the verandah, calling after her:

BRENT Scarlett!

STUART Where're you going?

4 MEDIUM SHOT—SCARLETT (COSGROVE)

Scarlett, her face a study in pain and shock, walks swiftly, determinedly away from the verandah toward CAMERA.

SCARLETT *(with passionate intensity, to herself as she goes)* It isn't true! It can't be true! Ashley loves *me!*

5 CLOSER SHOT—THE TWINS

—still gazing after Scarlett.

BRENT Now what do you suppose has gotten into her?

STUART Do you suppose we said something that made her mad?
(turns to his brother)
Look . . . Don't it look to you like she would have asked us to stay to supper?

6 CLOSE SHOT—MAMMY

She sticks her head out of an upper window and calls:

MAMMY Miss Scarlett! Miss Scarlett! Where you goin' widout yo' shawl, and the night air fixin' to set in? And huccome you didn' ask the gempmum to stay for supper? You ain' got no more manners dan a fiel' han'—and after Miss Ellen and me done labored wid you. Come on in de house. Come on in before you get your death o' dampness.

7 CLOSE SHOT—SCARLETT

She stops and looks back.

MAMMY'S VOICE Miss Scarlett, you come on in de house!

SCARLETT *(calling back impatiently)* No! I'm going to wait for Pa to come home from the Wilkeses.

8 CLOSE SHOT—MAMMY—IN WINDOW

MAMMY Come on in heah! Come on! Umph, umph, umph!

DISSOLVE TO:

9 EXT. BELL TOWER—TARA (SUNSET)

Two little pickaninnies are on the huge wheel above the ground, forcing it to revolve, throwing their weight from one side to the other. This causes the quitting bell to ring—which is the message to the field hands that the day's work is finished.

10 COTTON FIELD

Slaves at work plowing furrows. The quitting bell is heard faintly. One of the slaves, Elijah, stops.

ELIJAH Quittin' time.

Another huge black slave, known as Big Sam, turns on Elijah sharply.

BIG SAM Who said?

ELIJAH I sez.

BIG SAM You can't sez. I'se de foahman. I'se de one dat sez when it's time to quit.
(he calls to the other slaves)
Quittin' time.

The other slaves stop work. The bell stops ringing.

11 SERIES OF CUTS OF QUITTING TIME AT THE PLANTATION

12 LONG SHOTS—GERALD O'HARA

—on his finely bred big white horse riding at breakneck speed toward direction of the plantation. He jumps his horse across a narrow stream to a glade where a half dozen fine saddle horses are pastured. They stampede as Gerald gallops in and out of the scene, ducking expertly under the low-hanging branch of a tree as he passes.

13 GERALD

He enters scene, on his hunter, riding TOWARD CAMERA. He jumps the fence to the road, crosses the road at an angle, heading directly for the fence at the opposite side of the road. As the horse takes off for the second jump, Cut to

13 A THE OTHER SIDE OF THE FENCE—ON THE PLANTATION GROUNDS

As the horse clears it easily and lands.

14 CLOSE SHOT—GERALD

Gerald pulls up his reins, pats his mount.

GERALD *(to his horse)* There's none in the county can touch you, nor in the state.

He sets about smoothing his hair and his cravat. Scarlett's laughter is heard off scene. Gerald looks in her direction.

15 LONG SHOT

Scarlett, laughing, runs alongside a pond, toward Gerald.

SCARLETT *(calling)* Pa! So it's proud of yourself you are!

16 CLOSE SHOT—GERALD

Embarrassed, he dismounts, slips the reins over his arm and starts toward Scarlett, as she enters to him. He pinches her cheek.

GERALD Well, Katie Scarlett O'Hara. So you've been spying on me!
(with indignation)
And like your sister, Suellen, you'll be telling your mother on me—that I was jumping again.

SCARLETT Oh, Pa. You know I'm no tattle-tale like Suellen. But it does seem to me that after you broke your knee last year jumping that same fence . . .

GERALD I'll not have me own daughter telling me what I shall jump and not jump. It's my own neck, so it is.
(he slaps his horse, and the horse starts out alone)

SCARLETT All right, Pa. You jump what you please.

Scarlett links her arm in his and they start to walk by the water's edge toward the house.

SCARLETT How are they all over at Twelve Oaks?

GERALD The Wilkeses? Oh, in the stew you'd expect with the barbecue tomorrow, and talking nothing but war—

SCARLETT *(interrupting)* Bother the war! Was . . . Was anyone else there?

GERALD Oh . . . their cousin Melanie Hamilton from Atlanta, and her brother Charles.

A shadow passes over Scarlett's face, which darkens with anger and dislike.

SCARLETT *(contemptuously)* Melanie Hamilton! A pale-faced, mealy-mouthed ninny—and I hate her!

CONTINUED:

16 CONTINUED

GERALD Ashley Wilkes doesn't think so.

SCARLETT *(flaring)* Ashley Wilkes *couldn't* like anyone like her!

GERALD What's your interest in Ashley and Miss Melanie?

SCARLETT Oh, it's—it's nothing. Let's go in the house, Pa.

GERALD Has he been trifling with you? Has he asked you to marry him?

SCARLETT No.

GERALD No, nor will he! I had it in strictest confidence from John Wilkes this afternoon that Ashley's going to *marry* Miss Melanie. It'll be announced tomorrow night at the ball.

Scarlett takes the news badly. Tears come to her eyes. Involuntarily she blurts out:

SCARLETT I don't believe it!
(she flies off on a run)

GERALD *(calling after her)* Here . . . Here! Where are you off to? Scarlett!

The authority of his voice stops her.

GERALD What are you about?
(he catches up with her and takes her by the arm, with dawning realization)
Have you been making a spectacle of yourself? Running about after a man who's not in love with you when you might have any of the bucks in the county?

SCARLETT I haven't been running after him. It's—
(she turns away from him)
—it's just a surprise, that's all.

GERALD Now don't be jerkin' your chin at me.
(he follows her, puts his arm around her)
If Ashley wanted to marry you, t'would be with misgivings I'd say "yes." I want my girl to be happy . . . and you'd not be happy with him.

SCARLETT I would, I would!

GERALD But what difference does it make who you marry, so long as he's a Southerner and thinks like you?

Tears of frustration come into Scarlett's eyes. She bows her head. Gerald takes her arm; they start walking again, turning toward a rise of ground.

GERALD And when I'm gone—
(observes she is paying no attention)
I'll leave Tara to you—

SCARLETT I don't want Tara! Plantations don't mean anything when—

GERALD *(stops in his tracks, indignant)* Do you mean to tell me, Katie Scarlett O'Hara, that Tara—that land doesn't mean anything to you?

Scarlett doesn't answer. They have stopped near the top of the hill that commands a view of the surrounding countryside. Gerald gestures off with his arm.

17 PROLONGED PANNING SHOT OF THE RICH, BEAUTIFUL LAND OF TARA FROM THEIR VIEWPOINT

GERALD'S VOICE *(continued)* Why, land is the only thing in this world worth working for, worth fighting for, worth dying for—because it's the only thing that lasts.

18 BACK TO TWO SHOT—GERALD AND SCARLETT

SCARLETT *(disgusted)* Oh, Pa, you talk like an Irishman.

GERALD 'Tis proud I am that I'm Irish, and don't you be forgettin', Missy, that you're half Irish, too—

19 BACK TO PANORAMIC SHOT

GERALD'S VOICE *(continues)* —And to anyone with a drop of Irish blood in them, why, the land they live on is like their mother. Oh, but there, there now, you're just a child. It will come to you, this love of the land—There's no getting away from it if you're Irish.

20 REVERSE SHOT ON THE BACKS OF GERALD AND SCARLETT

Looking at the land. Gerald puts his arm around her. CAMERA RETREATS BACK, BACK, BACK, until we have the tiny, silhouetted figures of Gerald O'Hara and his daughter gazing over the lands of Tara,

CONTINUED:

20 CONTINUED

beautiful in the sunset, to the thematic musical accompaniment which we will use for Tara throughout the picture.

FADE OUT

21 *FADE IN:*
EXT. TARA—LONG SHOT—(COSGROVE)—NIGHT

Ellen O'Hara's carriage drives up the driveway, approaching the house.

22 *INT. TARA HALL—STAIRCASE—MAMMY—NIGHT*

Mammy is discovered on the landing looking out of the window. She turns, excited, having seen Ellen's carriage approaching.

MAMMY Yon she come! Miss Scarlett! Miss Suellen! Miss Carreen! Your ma's home.
(she hurries down the stairs, muttering to herself, CAMERA FOLLOWING WITH HER)
—Actin' lak a wet nurse to dem low-down, po' white trash Slatterys 'stead o' bein' here eatin' her supper!
(calls off toward the back of the house)
Cookie! Stir up de fiah—Miss Ellen's home!
(she continues down the stairs, muttering)
Miss Ellen got no business wearin' herself out . . .

She crosses through the hall, passing Pork at the table in the hall.

MAMMY Pork!

PORK Yas'm.

MAMMY Take de lamp out on de porch—

She passes by the open door to the study and calls in to Gerald, who is sitting there:

MAMMY Mist' Gerald, Miss Ellen's home—
(hurries on toward the front door, still muttering)
Wearin' herseff out waitin' on dem po' white trash—

Mammy is now at the front door. In a corner beside it are a couple of dogs who are barking in excitement, and a little, sleeping, colored boy.

MAMMY Shut up, dogs! Barkin' in de house lak dat! Git up from dere, boy! Doan you hear Miss Ellen's come? Git out dere an git her medicine chist!

The pickaninny scrambles to his feet and he and Pork go out to the verandah.

23 EXT. VERANDAH

The carriage has drawn up in front of the steps. Pork hurries forward with the lamp and holds it to light the way as Mrs. Ellen O'Hara gets out. Several hound dogs swarm on the verandah and leap about her delightedly.

PORK We wuz gettin' wuh'ried 'bout you, Miss Ellen. Marse Gerald—

ELLEN *(wearily)* It's all right, Pork, I'm home.

As she starts up the steps to the verandah, Jonas Wilkerson steps out from the shadows where he has obviously been waiting. He is nervous, twirling his hat in his hand.

WILKERSON Mrs. O'Hara, we finished plowing the creek bottom today. What do you want me to start on tomorrow?

ELLEN *(pausing)* Mr. Wilkerson . . .
(regarding him with obvious distaste)
I've just come from Emmy Slattery's bedside. Your child has been born . . .

WILKERSON *(pretending astonishment)* My child, ma'am? I'm sure I don't understand—

ELLEN *(coldly, completely disregarding his performance)* Has been born and—mercifully—has died. Goodnight, Mr. Wilkerson.

24 REVERSE ANGLE

Featuring Wilkerson's silhouetted head in the f.g., a look of hatred on his face as Ellen passes by him through the open door into the house. Pork follows her, carrying the lamp. The door closes.

25 INT. MAIN HALL

Ellen inside the front door. Mammy has come back into the hall and is taking Ellen's hat and coat. Pork sets the lamp down on the opposite end of the hall table from its mate. They start down the hall toward Ellen's study.

MAMMY Ah'll fix yo' supper for yo' mahseff.

CONTINUED:

25 CONTINUED

ELLEN After prayers, Mammy.

MAMMY Yas'm.

CAMERA precedes Ellen as she walks into the study, where Gerald is waiting. Ellen goes to him.

ELLEN Mr. O'Hara, you must dismiss Jonas Wilkerson.

GERALD Dismiss him, Mrs. O'Hara? He's the best overseer in the county.

ELLEN He must go tomorrow morning the first thing.

GERALD But—
(Ellen whispers into his ear)
—No!

ELLEN *(nods)* Yes.
(she goes to the other end of the room to pick up her prayer book)

GERALD The Yankee Wilkerson and the white trash Slattery girl—
(laughs)
Ho!

ELLEN *(on her way out the door)* We'll discuss it later, Mr. O'Hara.

GERALD Yes, Mrs. O'Hara.
(he follows her out into the hall)

26 INT. HALL

Ellen's daughters, Suellen and Carreen, fly down the stairs toward their mother, screaming and gurgling. Scarlett follows them a little more slowly.

GIRLS *(together)* Mother!
There's Mother!
Good evening, Mother!

SUELLEN Scarlett's new dress is prettier than mine! I look a fright in my pink! Why can't she wear my pink and let me wear Scarlett's green dress!

CARREEN Mother! Can't I stay up for the ball?

They meet Ellen at the foot of the stairs.

SUELLEN I want to wear Scarlett's green dress!

ELLEN I don't like your tone, Suellen. Your pink gown is lovely.
(she turns to Carreen)

CARREEN Oh, Mother—can't I stay up for the ball tomorrow night?

ELLEN *(over her shoulder to Suellen)* But you may wear my garnets with it.

Suellen gurgles delightedly.

Ellen looks over and sees Scarlett, who has hung back and who is standing silently at the foot of the stairs.

CARREEN Why can't I stay up for the ball tomorrow night?

Ellen, not answering, goes to Scarlett and takes her hand.

ELLEN Scarlett, you look tired, my dear. I'm worried about you.

SCARLETT Oh, I'm all right, Mother.

CARREEN *(insisting)* Oh, why can't I stay up for the ball tomorrow night? I'm thirteen now.

ELLEN Now, you may go to the barbecue and stay up through supper.

She continues on into the living room for prayers. Suellen comes near to Scarlett.

SUELLEN I don't want to wear your tacky green dress anyhow, stingy!

Scarlett's hand darts out and she gives Suellen's hair a vicious yank.

SCARLETT Oh, hush up!

Suellen gasps, but before she can retaliate, Ellen's voice calls:

ELLEN *(off scene)* Prayers, girls.

Suellen assumes a demure expression and goes toward the parlor. Scarlett follows slowly.

DISSOLVE TO:

27 INT. PARLOR—NIGHT

A circle of yellow light. Ellen is on the floor on her knees, the open prayer book on the table before her and her hands clasped upon it. Gerald is

CONTINUED:

27 CONTINUED

kneeling beside her; Scarlett and Suellen on the opposite sides of the table, their voluminous petticoats in pads under their knees; Carreen kneeling facing a chair, her elbows on the seat. The house servants are kneeling by the doorway: Mammy; Pork, straight as a ramrod; two maids, graceful in spreading bright calicoes; the cook, gaunt and yellow beneath her snowy head-rag; Prissy; and a little colored house boy, very sleepy. Their dark eyes are gleaming expectantly.
Ellen's eyes are closed, her voice rises and falls, lullingly and soothingly. The Negroes sway as they respond.

ELLEN —and to all the saints that I have sinned exceedingly in thought, word, and deed through my fault, through my fault, through my most grievous fault—

ELLEN AND ALL —therefore I beseech Blessed Mary, ever Virgin—

28 CLOSE SHOT—SCARLETT

Her face has come up as though to show the Deity the depths of her suffering. She does not respond with the others.

ALL *(except Scarlett) (O.S.)* —Blessed Michael, the Archangel, Blessed John the Baptist—

Then a bright light seems to turn on suddenly within Scarlett and an ecstatic smile spreads over her face.

SCARLETT *(as she looks up with sudden revelation, gasps to herself)* But Ashley doesn't know I love him.
(a sudden thought)
I'll tell him. And then he *can't* marry her!

29 CLOSE SHOT—ELLEN

She looks over severely at Scarlett as she continues the prayer.

ELLEN AND ALL —the holy Apostles Peter and Paul—

30 CLOSE SHOT—SCARLETT

She realizes her mother's eyes are on her and bows her head with the others.

SCARLETT *(joining with others)* —and all the Saints to pray to the Lord our God for me.

On the portrait of the pious Scarlett, we

FADE OUT.

31–34 FADE IN:
INT. SCARLETT'S BEDROOM—CLOSE SHOT—SCARLETT—DAY

—standing in her underclothes and stays, clinging to the bedpost.

SCARLETT *(gasping as if in pain)*
(suddenly, as o.s. Mammy pulls her tighter)
Oooh!

CAMERA PULLS BACK to a LONG SHOT of the room to show that Mammy is lacing Scarlett's stays. On the bed lies a long clothesbox with Scarlett's dress for the ball.

MAMMY Jus' hole on an' suck in.

At this moment, Prissy comes in the room with a tray full of food. She starts to set it down. Scarlett sees her.

SCARLETT *(over her shoulder)* You can take all that back to the kitchen! I won't eat a bite!

Prissy, scared, starts to turn away with the tray.

MAMMY Oh, yas'm, you is! You'se gwine ter eat eve'y mouffull of dis!

Mammy wins. Prissy sets down the tray and beats a hasty retreat.

SCARLETT No, I'm not!
(she glares at Mammy)
So put on the dress because we're late already.

MAMMY *(giving the last tug)* Whut mah lamb gwine wear?

SCARLETT *(points to a fluffy dress)* That.

MAMMY *(in arms)* No, you ain'! You kain show yo' buzzum befo' three o'clock.
(Scarlett grabs up the dress)
Ah's gwine to speak ter yo' ma 'bout you!

SCARLETT If you say one word to Mother I won't eat a bite.

Mammy, who has been on her way out, suddenly stops dead on this. She admits defeat by coming back to Scarlett and carefully dropping the
CONTINUED:

31–34 CONTINUED

twelve yards of green sprigged muslin over the mountainous petticoats and hooks up the top of the tight, low-cut basque.

MAMMY *(muttering)* Keep yo' shawl on yo' shoulders. Ah ain' aimin' fo' you to git all freckled after de buttermilk Ah done put on you all dis winter, bleachin' dem freckles—

The dress on—and to Scarlett's satisfaction—Mammy turns back to the tray.

MAMMY An' now, Miss Scarlett, you come on an' be good an' eat jes' a lil'.

SCARLETT *(belligerent and determined)* No! I'm going to have a good time today and do my eating at the barbecue.

MAMMY *(squares off)* Ef yo' don't care whut folks says 'bout dis fambly, Ah does! Ah has tole you an' tole you dat you kin allus tell a lady by de way dat she eats in front o' folks lak a bird! An' Ah ain' aimin' fer you to go ter Mist' John Wilkes an' eat lak a fiel' han' an' gobble lak a hawg.

SCARLETT Fiddle-dee-dee!
(she picks up her parasol and goes toward the door)
Ashley Wilkes told me he *liked* to see a girl with a healthy appetite.

MAMMY *(shakes her head)* Whut gempmums says an' whut dey thinks is two diffunt things. An' Ah' ain't noticed Mist' Ashley axin' fer ter mahy you.

This stops Scarlett. She turns, throws down her parasol viciously, and sits down to the tray, starting to throw the food down hastily and distastefully.

MAMMY Now don't eat too fas'! No use havin' it come right back up agin.

Scarlett, eating, now discovers that she can take nourishment after all.

Gerald's voice is heard calling impatiently from outside.

GERALD'S VOICE *(o.s.)* Scarlett! Scarlett O'Hara!

Scarlett is on her feet and hastily prepares to leave.

GERALD'S VOICE If you're not here before I count ten, Katie Scarlett, we'll be going without you!

Scarlett gets up, runs to the window, and looks out as she calls in answer.

SCARLETT *(calls down)* I'm comin', Pa!

Scarlett turns back into the room, gets on her knees to recover the parasol, which has landed under a dresser.

SCARLETT Oh, oh dear, my stays are so tight, I know I shall never get through the day without belching.

She is out the door, and as Mammy, who has gathered up the clothesbox from the bed, starts to follow, we

DISSOLVE TO:

35 EXT. COUNTRY ROAD—TWELVE OAKS IN DISTANCE (COSGROVE)—EXTREME LONG SHOT

The O'Hara carriage and Gerald on horseback. In the distance ahead of the O'Haras, we see other carriages on the road going toward Twelve Oaks. Pork is driving the O'Hara carriage. Mammy is on the seat beside him with the long clothesboxes containing the girls' dresses for the evening. Suellen, Carreen, and Scarlett sit in back. Gerald, riding alongside, pays little attention to his daughters. He is singing: "Peg in a Low-Backed Car."

DISSOLVE TO:

36 EXT. VERANDAH TWELVE OAKS—DAY

John Wilkes, silver-haired, erect, and radiating hospitality, stands on the verandah steps greeting arriving guests. Around them the hubbub and activity of swarming guests.

The O'Hara carriage has just arrived and WE FOLLOW GERALD as he comes up the last step toward John Wilkes.

GERALD Well, John Wilkes, it's a grand day you'll be havin' for the barbecue.

They shake hands.

JOHN WILKES So it seems. But why isn't Mrs. O'Hara with you?

GERALD Oh, she's after settling accounts with the overseer. She'll be along for the ball tonight.

India Wilkes comes up alongside her father and greets Gerald, too.

CONTINUED:

36 CONTINUED

INDIA Welcome to Twelve Oaks, Mr. O'Hara.

GERALD Thank you kindly, India.
(turns to Wilkes as he exits)
Your daughter's getting prettier every day, John.
(he pinches her cheek)

Wilkes and India laugh appreciatively. Gerald passes on toward the entrance to the hall, calling "Good morning" to someone as he leaves. John Wilkes turns to India, who is starting away.

JOHN WILKES India, here are the O'Hara girls. We must greet them.

INDIA *(with a toss of the head)* I can't stand that Scarlett. If you'd see the way she throws herself at Ashley—

JOHN WILKES Now, now, that's your brother's business, India— You remember your duties as hostess.

He starts down the steps and helps the girls out of their carriage.

JOHN WILKES Good morning, Miss Carreen—you're looking lovely. Good morning, Scarlett.

Scarlett and her sisters reach the steps where India is waiting.

SCARLETT Why, India Wilkes, what a lovely dress!

SUELLEN Perfectly lovely, darling!

CARREEN Just *lovely!*

SCARLETT *(not looking at the dress, but looking around for Ashley)* I just can't take my eyes off it.

She moves on into the HALL, CAMERA FOLLOWING HER IN, still looking around anxiously for sight of Ashley.

The hall is crowded with guests, most of the young belles and bloods of the county being present. The girls in crinoline and the laughing young men in fawn and grey trousers. Colored maids are hurrying up the stairs bearing the long boxes containing their mistresses' gowns for the evening. The Wilkes' butler and his assistants hurry through the halls, bowing and grinning and offering tall, mint-topped, frosted glasses.

Young men greet Scarlett eagerly as she moves through the crowd, scarcely noticing their greetings, her mind on Ashley alone.

FEMININE VOICES	MASCULINE VOICES
Scarlett, honey!	You're looking mighty fine this morning, Miss Scarlett.
Miss Scarlett, good mornin'.	Good mornin', Miss Scarlett.
Where you goin', Scarlett?	Wait a minute, Scarlett!
Scarlett, honey! Where you going?	It's a pleasure to see you, Miss Scarlett.

SCARLETT *(scarcely turning her head)* Good mornin' . . . Mornin' . . . Mornin' . . .

37 CLOSE SHOT—SCARLETT

Suddenly her face lights up as she sees Ashley!

SCARLETT Ashley!

She starts to run toward the staircase.

38 CLOSE UP—ASHLEY—(ON STAIRS)

—as he reaches the lower step—a filmy scarf in his hand. He looks up at sound of Scarlett's voice.

ASHLEY Scarlett, my dear!

39 TWO SHOT

Scarlett stops a few paces away from him.

SCARLETT I've been looking for you everywhere. I've got something I must tell you— Can't we go someplace where it's quiet?
(she is smiling and beaming)

ASHLEY Yes. I'd like to. But I—I have something to tell you, too. Something I—I hope you'll be glad to hear.

Scarlett's face is a mixture of fright and hope. Ashley takes her arm and starts to lead her down the hall.

ASHLEY But come say "hello" to my Cousin Melanie first.

SCARLETT Oh, do we have to?

ASHLEY She's been so looking forward to seeing you again.

Scarlett's face is a sullen mask. By now they have come upon Melanie, whose back is to them and to the CAMERA.

ASHLEY Melanie, here's Scarlett.

40 CLOSE UP—MELANIE

She turns toward the CAMERA on hearing Ashley's voice and her face lights up with the greatest friendliness.

41 THREE SHOT—SCARLETT, MELANIE, ASHLEY

MELANIE *(advances toward them)* Scarlett! I'm *so* glad to see you again!

SCARLETT *(gushing insincerely)* Melanie Hamilton! What a surprise to run into you here! I hope you're going to stay a few days with us at least.

During Scarlett's line Ashley has been tenderly adjusting the scarf over Melanie's shoulder—almost as if in caress. Scarlett watches, jealous and resentful.

Throughout the remainder of the scene, Ashley grows increasingly embarrassed and annoyed at Scarlett's cattiness.

MELANIE I hope I'll be able to stay long enough for us to become real friends, Scarlett. I do so want us to be.

ASHLEY *(quite lightly)* We'll keep her here, won't we, Scarlett?

SCARLETT Oh, we'll just have to make the biggest fuss over her, won't we, Ashley?
(links her arm through Ashley's; to Melanie:)
And if there's anybody knows how to give a girl a good time, it's Ashley. Though I expect our good times here will seem terribly silly to you because you're so serious.

MELANIE *(laughs)* Oh, Scarlett, you have so much life. I've always admired you so. I wish I could be more like you.

SCARLETT You mustn't flatter me, Melanie, and say things you don't mean.

Melanie is embarrassed, and Ashley comes to her rescue.

ASHLEY Nobody could accuse Melanie of being insincere—
(to Melanie)
Could they, my dear?

SCARLETT Oh, well, then she's not like you, is she, Ashley?
(with a fake laugh)
Ashley never means a word he says to any girl.

She turns straight to Charles Hamilton, Melanie's brother, who has come up beside them.

SCARLETT Why, Charles Hamilton, you handsome old thing, you!

CHARLES But . . . oh . . . Miss O'Hara . . .

Scarlett turns back to Melanie as Charles attempts to say more.

SCARLETT Do you think that was kind to bring your good-looking brother down here just to break my poor, simple, country girl's heart? *(she has extended her two hands to Charles in a manner that is neither poor nor simple)*

42 CLOSE SHOT—SUELLEN AND INDIA WILKES

who stand apart. They have observed the scene between Scarlett and Charles Hamilton, and India looks like a thundercloud.

SUELLEN Look at Scarlett! She's never even noticed Charles before. Now, just because he's your beau, she's after him like a hornet!

43 BACK TO GROUP

SCARLETT *(gushing)* Charles Hamilton, I want to eat barbecue with you, and mind you don't go off philandering with any other girl, 'cause I'm mighty jealous!

CHARLES Oh, I *won't,* Miss O'Hara! How could I!

Scarlett starts up the stairs, looking back toward Ashley to see what impression she is making.

44 SCARLETT ON STAIRS

She accosts Frank Kennedy, who is coming down, still casting glances over her shoulder, hoping that Ashley is noticing.

SCARLETT I do declare, Frank Kennedy, if you don't look dashing with that new set of whiskers!

FRANK *(flattered)* Thank you . . . thank you, Miss Scarlett.

SCARLETT You know, Charles Hamilton and Rafe Calvert asked me to eat barbecue with them, but I told them I couldn't because I promised you.

44A CLOSE SHOT—SUELLEN AND INDIA WILKES

CONTINUED:

44A CONTINUED

Still glaring off at Scarlett's antics.

INDIA You needn't be so amused, Suellen. Look at her! She's after *your* beau now.

Suellen takes one look, then starts to exit scene, determined to recover her property.

45 STAIRS—SCARLETT AND FRANK

—with other guests passing them in a continuous stream.

FRANK Oh, that's mighty flattering of you, Miss Scarlett . . .

Suellen marches in and drags Frank away by the arm.

FRANK *(calling back over his shoulder, flustered)* I'll see what I can do, Miss Scarlett.

CAMERA MOVES WITH SCARLETT as she starts up the stairs. Another girl, Cathleen Calvert, comes from the bottom of the steps to walk beside her.

CATHLEEN What's your sister so mad about, Scarlett? You sparkin' her beau?

SCARLETT *(with a toss of her head)* As if I couldn't get a better beau than that old maid in britches!

They continue on up the stairs and find the Tarleton twins in their path —a Georgia belle hanging to the arm of each.

SCARLETT Brent and Stuart Tarleton, you handsome old things, you!— Oh no, you're not! I'm not going to say that! I'm mad at you!

BRENT Why, Scarlett, honey!

STUART What have we done, honey?

SCARLETT *(coquetting)* You haven't been near me all day—and I wore this old dress just because I thought you liked it . . . I was counting on eating barbecue with you two.

BRENT Well, you are, Scarlett.

STUART Of course you are, honey.

SCARLETT Oh, I never can make up my mind which of you two is the handsomer. I was awake all last night trying to figure it out.

BRENT *(embarrassed)* Oh, shucks!

Scarlett starts up the stairs again as the twins' companions come back into scene, annoyed at being forsaken for Scarlett, and drag them away.

Scarlett catches up with Cathleen. Suddenly she stops and stares at someone below. She catches Cathleen's wrist.

SCARLETT Cathleen—who's that?

CATHLEEN Who?

SCARLETT That man looking at us and smiling—that nasty, dark one.

46 CLOSE SHOT—RHETT BUTLER (FROM THEIR ANGLE)

He lounges at the foot of the stairs, a mint julep glass in his hand, smiling up at them.

47 CATHLEEN AND SCARLETT

—continuing up the stairs.

CATHLEEN *(whispering)* My dear, don't you know? That's Rhett Butler. He's from Charleston—and he has the most terrible reputation!

SCARLETT *(in the same guarded voice as before, casting another look downward)* He looks as if—as if he knows what I look like without my shimmy!

CATHLEEN *(shocked)* Scarlett!
(in a voice only a little above a whisper)
Why, my dear, he isn't received! He's had to spend most of his time up North because his folks in Charleston won't even speak to him. He was expelled from West Point, he's so fast. And then there's that business about that girl he didn't marry.

SCARLETT *(eagerly)* Tell! Tell!

CATHLEEN Well, he took her out buggy riding in the late afternoon—without a chaperone! And then—
(the most incredible thing in the world)
And then he refused to marry her!

Cathleen's voice drops even lower, and she whispers in Scarlett's ear. By this time they have reached the top of the stairs. Scarlett whispers something back.

CONTINUED:

47 CONTINUED

CATHLEEN *(aloud)* No—but she was ruined just the same.

DISSOLVE TO:

48 INT. HALL AT TWELVE OAKS

Ashley and Melanie are walking to a door leading to a side verandah. Ashley opens the door for Melanie and as they go out, we see:

49 EXT. TWELVE OAKS LAWNS (FROM THEIR ANGLE ON VERANDAH)

A scene of gaiety and wild charm. The barbecue—a furbelow feast—is spread over the lawn. Children run under the trees. Black Mammies tag after them. Gallants and their ladies are eating, drinking, laughing—and Negroes, grinning and shiny-eyed, wander over the grass, holding aloft great trays of food and drink.

There is a long table stretching down the center of the lawn at which many guests sit.

50 BACK TO ASHLEY AND MELANIE ON VERANDAH

Melanie's lips part as if overcome for a moment by a sense of rapture as she and Ashley look at the scene.

MELANIE Ashley!

ASHLEY Happy?

MELANIE So happy.

ASHLEY You seem to belong here—as if it had all been imagined for you.

MELANIE *(tenderly)* I like to feel that I belong with the things you love.

ASHLEY You love Twelve Oaks, as I do.

MELANIE Yes, Ashley—I love it as more than a house. It's a whole world that wants only to be graceful and beautiful.

ASHLEY *(with a sad smile)* It's so unconscious that it may not last—forever.

MELANIE *(takes his arm, her voice grows softer)* You're afraid of what may happen if the war comes, aren't you? But we don't have to be afraid—for us. No war can come into our world, Ashley. Whatever comes, I'll love you—just as I do now—until I die.

Ashley raises her hand and kisses it.

51 EXT. BARBECUE—GROUP SHOT UNDER A TREE

Where Scarlett on a high rosewood ottoman is surrounded by a circle of young men. Scarlett is laughing.

SCARLETT Now isn't this better than sitting at an old table? A girl hasn't only two sides to her at a table!

Laughter and hearty approval as Scarlett beams around her at the circle. Brent and Stuart Tarleton and Charles Hamilton jump to their feet.

BRENT I'll get her dessert.

STUART She said me.

CHARLES Allow me, Miss O'Hara.

Scarlett looks the three over judiciously and makes her selection.

SCARLETT I think—mmmm—
(as a great favor)
I think Charles Hamilton may get it.

CHARLES Oh, thank you, Miss O'Hara! Thank you.

He hurries away; the other beaux greatly impressed.

STUART Go get it! Isn't he the luckiest—

Scarlett's face suddenly falls as she sees:

52 LONG SHOT—(FROM SCARLETT'S ANGLE)—MELANIE AND ASHLEY

Arm in arm, walking across the lawn under the trees, absorbed in each other, coming from direction of the house.

53 CLOSE UP—SCARLETT

Watching, jealous. Charles Hamilton's face comes into the close up, bending over to whisper to Scarlett. He has returned with her dessert.

CHARLES *(whispers in Scarlett's ear)* Miss O'Hara, I love you!

Scarlett looks at the food, shakes her head, distracted.

CONTINUED:

53 CONTINUED

SCARLETT I don't guess I'm as hungry as I thought.

DISSOLVE TO:

54–56 INT. BEDROOM—TWELVE OAKS—DAY

Mammy is just helping Scarlett off with her dress. In the b.g. are other Mammies and other girls in stages of undress. As the scene progresses, the Mammies leave and the girls go to lie on the beds and sofas. Babble of voices interrupted by girlish laughter. Mammy is muttering to Scarlett, who, we observe, is in none too pleasant a frame of mind.

SCARLETT Why do I have to take a nap? I'm not tired!

MAMMY Well-brought-up young ladies takes naps at parties. And it's high time you started behavin' lak you wuz Miss Ellen's daughter.

SCARLETT When we were at Saratoga, I didn't notice any Yankee girls taking naps.

MAMMY No. An' you won't see any Yankee girls at de ball tonight, neither.

By this time Mammy has Scarlett's dress in her hands and exits with it as Suellen comes into the scene, also in her pantalettes.

SUELLEN *(cattily to Scarlett)* How's Ashley today, Scarlett? He didn't seem to be paying much attention to you.

SCARLETT *(gives a little look around to be sure no one has heard and speaks in an enraged undertone)* You mind your own business! You'll be lucky if you don't lose old Whisker-Face Kennedy.

Scarlett is removing her shoes.

SUELLEN *(trembling with rage)* You've been sweet on Ashley for months! And his engagement's going to be announced tonight. Pa said so this morning!

Scarlett takes this for a moment, then covers up hastily.

SCARLETT That's how much you know!

She sticks out her tongue at Suellen. Suellen sticks out her tongue in return. Mammy has come back into the scene in time to see this, and stands aghast, looking on.

MAMMY Miss Scarlett! Miss Suellen! Behave yourseffs! Actin' lak pore white trash chillen! If you'se old ernuff to go to parties, you'se old ernuff to ack lak ladies!

During this speech Scarlett has stretched out on the nearby divan or mattress, which has been unoccupied until now, although there is room for two. On a little table next the divan is a photograph of Charles Hamilton.

Scarlett affects a yawn and stretches back with the elegant indifference of a woman of the world. Then reaches her arm around and scratches her back.

MAMMY *(indicating Scarlett's bed)* Miss Suellen, you lie down there!

SUELLEN I don't want anything to do with her!

She flounces out to find a bed in the next room. Mammy looks after her a moment, enraged, then exits after her.

57 CLOSE SHOT—SCARLETT ON BED, VERY WORRIED, HER THOUGHTS ON ASHLEY

We hear the whispering voices of Maybelle Merriwether and another girl as they approach Scarlett:

GIRL Now, you didn't really! What did he say?

MAYBELLE MERRIWETHER He said, "Will you take a walk with me later?"

GIRL *(impressed)*
And what did you say *then?*

The girls have now come up almost to Scarlett's side.

MAYBELLE MERRIWETHER I dropped my eyes and I said, "Mr. Calvert, sir, I should be honored."

The other girl spies Charles Hamilton's picture on the table, goes to it, and picks it up.

GIRL Scarlett, look! There's a picture of that cute Charles Hamilton—and in India's room, too!

Scarlett turns, casually looks at the picture, and snorts in disgust.

MAYBELLE MERRIWETHER I heard in Atlanta that India's going to *marry* Charles!

CONTINUED:

57 CONTINUED

SCARLETT *(with disgust)* Who cares!
(she turns over)

58–60 INT. ADJOINING BEDROOM AT TWELVE OAKS—LATE AFTERNOON

It is the quiet of late afternoon. The shutters are closed, and through the half-open slats the sunlight streams. A door is open between this room and the adjoining room in the b.g. The beds and couches in both rooms are crowded with young ladies who are resting for the evening gaiety, three or four to a bed. Their stays are loosened, their hair let down, and they are asleep. Little Negro girls sit next each bed, fanning the young ladies to keep them cool while they nap. CAMERA PANS ACROSS the array of sleeping girls in one bed, to the doorway from the adjoining room, where we pick up Scarlett, fully dressed, tiptoeing out. She motions the little Negro girl to silence, leans over to make sure that Melanie and Suellen, who are side by side in one of the beds, are still asleep. Then, first taking a quick look into the mirror and pinching her cheeks to bring the color into them, she noiselessly opens the door, peers out, and slips out into the hall, closing the door softly behind her.

61 INT. UPPER HALL—AT HEAD OF STAIRS—(SHOOTING UP FROM HALLWAY BELOW AT SCARLETT)

Scarlett enters scene and starts down the stairs on tiptoe. Men's voices come from the dining room below.

GERALD'S VOICE We've borne enough insults from the meddling Yankees. It's time we made them to understand we'll keep our slaves with or without their approval. 'Twas the sovereign right of the State of Georgia to secede from the Union!

AD LIB That's right—

GERALD'S VOICE The South must assert herself by force of arms. After we've fired on the Yankee rascals at Fort Sumter, we've got to fight!

Scarlett has reached the turn in the staircase. She looks over and down into dining room as she continues down—CAMERA PANNING WITH HER.

GERALD'S VOICE There's no other way!

AD LIB Fight! That's right. Fight!
Let the Yankees be the ones to ask for peace!

KENNEDY'S VOICE We'll have Abe Lincoln on his knees.

BRENT'S VOICE They can't start this war too quick to suit me.

A chorus of approval from the other men in the dining room. By this time Scarlett has descended to a point from which she can see into the dining room. She pauses, drawing closer to the banister.

62 INT. DINING ROOM—(FROM SCARLETT'S ANGLE)

Through the uprights of the banister, a portion of the dining room is visible. Here all the gentlemen of the party have gathered and are drinking.

GERALD The situation is very simple. The Yankees can't fight and we can.

STUART There won't even be a battle—that's what I think. They'll just turn and run every time.

CHARLES One Southerner can lick twenty Yankees.

STUART We'll finish them off in one battle. Gentlemen always fight better than rabble.

KENNEDY Yes—gentlemen always can fight better than rabble.

GERALD *(to Ashley; his voice booming higher than any of the others)* And what does the Captain of the Troop say?

ASHLEY Well, gentlemen, if Georgia fights, I go with her. But, like my father, I hope that the Yankees will let us leave the Union in—in peace.

A babble of protest from the Tarletons and the others.

STUART But, Ashley . . . !

BRENT Why, Ashley, they've insulted us!

CHARLES You can't mean that you don't want war!

ASHLEY Most of the misery of the world has been caused by wars. And when the wars were over, no one ever knew what they were about.

More protests from the young men.

63 CLOSE SHOT—RHETT BUTLER

standing aloof and a little apart from the other men, who are grouped

CONTINUED:

63 CONTINUED
around the punch bowl. As he smokes his cigar quietly, he glances from one to another of the excited men with cynical amusement.

AD LIBS *(o.s.)* Why, Ashley—if it wasn't that I knew you!
I can't believe . . .
I'm sure disappointed in you, Ashley Wilkes!

64 GROUP SHOT

GERALD Now, gentlemen, gentlemen. Mr. Butler's been North, I hear. Don't you agree with us, Mr. Butler?

RHETT *(takes a step forward)* I think it's hard winning a war with words, gentlemen.

CHARLES What do you mean, sir?

RHETT I mean, Mr. Hamilton, that there's not a cannon factory in the whole South.

BRENT What difference does that make, sir, to a gentleman?

RHETT I'm afraid it's going to make a great deal of difference to a great many gentlemen, sir.

CHARLES Are you hinting, Mr. Butler, that the Yankees can lick us?

RHETT No, I'm not hinting. I'm saying very plainly that the Yankees are better equipped than we. They've got factories, shipyards, coal mines, and a fleet to bottle up our harbors and starve us to death. All we have is cotton . . . and slaves . . . and arrogance.

There is a moment of consternation and tense silence, then:

STUART That's treachery!

CHARLES Sir, I refuse to listen to any renegade talk.

RHETT I'm sorry if the truth offends you.

CHARLES Apologies aren't enough, sir!
(he walks up to him and speaks slowly)
I hear that you were turned out of West Point, Mr. Rhett Butler, and that you aren't received by any decent family in Charleston—not even your own.
(a moment's silence)

RHETT *(smiling)* I apologize again, sir, for all my shortcomings.

(to Ashley)
Mr. Wilkes, perhaps you won't mind if I walk about and look over your place. I appear to be spoiling everybody's brandy and cigars and dreams of victory.
(he bows and exits)

65 HALLWAY

Scarlett, on the stairs, having heard Rhett's exit speech, crouches back out of sight so that he may not see her. (Her position is such that she cannot see Rhett's direction, either, when he exits from this angle. Rhett comes out of the dining room and starts across the hall.) The voices continue from inside:

MEN'S VOICES Well, that's just about what you could expect from somebody like Rhett Butler.
I did everything but call him outside.

Rhett looks over his shoulder toward direction of the dining room, smiles a little, and walks on across the hall out of scene.

66 INT. DINING ROOM—GROUP ABOUT PUNCH BOWL

All except Ashley, evidently in an ugly temper.

BRENT A Yankee coward, that's all he is!

CHARLES He refused to fight.

ASHLEY Not quite that, Charles. He just refused to take advantage of you.

CHARLES Take advantage of me?

ASHLEY *(smiling)* Yes—he's one of the best shots in the country. As he's proved a number of times, against steadier hands and cooler heads than yours.

CHARLES I'll show him!
(moves as if to start after Rhett)

ASHLEY *(puts out a detaining hand)* Now, now, now, please. Don't go tweaking his nose any more. You may be needed for more important fighting, Charles. Now, if you'll excuse me, Mr. Butler is our guest—I think I'll just show him around.

67 INT. HALL

CONTINUED:

67 CONTINUED

As Ashley comes out of the dining room, Scarlett runs noiselessly down the stairs and follows right in back of him until she comes to the open door of the library. She slips into the doorway, unseen by Ashley, and calls after him:

SCARLETT *(whispering)* Psst! Psst!

68 CLOSE SHOT—ASHLEY

He turns, startled.

69 CLOSE SHOT—SCARLETT—(FROM HIS ANGLE)

Peeking out of the partly opened door, she beckons him eagerly.

SCARLETT Ashley—Ashley—

70 INT. LIBRARY—SHOOTING THROUGH DOOR INTO HALL, HOLDING SCARLETT IN F.G.

Ashley appears outside door.

ASHLEY *(amused)* Scarlett! Who you hiding from in there?

Scarlett takes him by the sleeve, pulls him into the room, closes the door.

ASHLEY *(smiling)* What are you up to? Why aren't you upstairs resting like the other girls?
(as she shakes her head, unable to speak; still with his amused, paternal air)
What is it, Scarlett—
(Scarlett tries to speak—as if she had something wonderful to tell)
A secret?

SCARLETT *(blurts it out)* Oh, Ashley—Ashley—I love you.

ASHLEY *(in a predicament, distressed)* Scarlett!

SCARLETT *(moves closer, eyes on his)* I love you. I do.

ASHLEY *(trying to maintain the paternal note)* Well, isn't it enough to have collected every other man's heart today? You've always had mine. You cut your teeth on it.

SCARLETT *(moves even closer, with desperation)* Oh, don't tease me now. Have I your heart, my darling? I love you! I love you!

ASHLEY *(his hand closes over her lips; moved, fearful)* You mustn't say such things. You'll hate me for hearing them.

SCARLETT *(jerks her head away)* Oh, I could never hate you! And—and I know you must care about me, because . . . Oh, you *do* care, don't you?

ASHLEY *(her vehemence sobers him; in spite of himself, he says more than he intended)* Yes. I care.
(then)
Oh, can't we go away and forget that we ever said these things?
(he walks a little away from her)

SCARLETT But how can we do that? Don't you want to marry me?
(follows him)

ASHLEY I'm going to marry Melanie.

SCARLETT But you can't. Not if you care for me.
(her hands are gripping his arms)

ASHLEY *(he frees himself to hold her hands in his. Genuinely touched)* Oh, my dear, why must you make me say things that will hurt you?
(as she doesn't answer)
How can I make you understand—you're so young and unthinking. You don't know what marriage means.

SCARLETT I know that I love you and I want to be your wife. You don't love Melanie!

ASHLEY *(hesitates; then gravely, reaching for words)* She's like me, Scarlett—she's part of my blood—and we understand each other.

SCARLETT *(unable to understand any of his explanations and persisting in her obsession)* But you love *me!*

ASHLEY How could I help loving you? You, who have all the passion for life that I lack! But that kind of love isn't enough to make a successful marriage when two people are as different as we are. You see, Scarlett, you—

SCARLETT *(passionately)* Well, why don't you say it, you coward! You're afraid to marry me! You'd rather live with that silly little fool who can't open her mouth except to say—

CONTINUED:

70 CONTINUED

(in sarcastic mimicry)

"Yes" and "no" and raise a passel of mealy-mouthed brats just like her!

ASHLEY *(rises, his tone sharp)* You mustn't say things like that about Melanie.

SCARLETT Who are you to tell me I mustn't? You led me on— You—you made me believe you wanted to marry me—

ASHLEY *(shocked)* Now, Scarlett! Be fair. I never at any time—

SCARLETT *(going all out, shanty Irish)* You did! It's true. You did. And I'll hate you till I die! I can't think of anything bad enough to call you—

Ashley extends a placating, soothing hand. She slaps him full across the face with all her strength. Horrified and grief-stricken, he stands a moment, stunned; then sadly bows and exits.

Scarlett watches him go as though watching the end of her life. Her rage returns and she looks around her with the fury of thwarted and humiliated love. Her hand drops to a little table beside her, and she is fingering the tiny china rose bowl on which two Chinese cherubs smirk. She is suddenly aware of it and looks at it. She picks it up and hurls it viciously across the room toward the fireplace.

71 CLOSE SHOT AT FIREPLACE

The back of a sofa in the f.g., facing the fireplace. The china piece crashes, and as the sound of the crash ends, we see Rhett's arms raised from the back of the sofa, as if to avoid being hit.

He lets out a long, drawn-out whistle and rises from the sofa, faces Scarlett.

RHETT Has the war started?

72 FULL SHOT—LIBRARY

Scarlett is too frightened for a moment to even utter a sound. She catches hold of the back of a chair, her knees going weak.

Rhett strolls smilingly across the room toward Scarlett.

73 TWO SHOT—RHETT AND SCARLETT

SCARLETT *(grasping at dignity as best she can)* Sir, you—you should have made your presence known!

RHETT In the middle of that beautiful love scene? That wouldn't have been very tactful, would it? But don't worry, your secret is safe with me.

SCARLETT Sir, you are no gentleman!

RHETT And you, miss, are no lady.

SCARLETT Oh!

RHETT Don't think I hold that against you. Ladies have never held much charm for me.

SCARLETT First you take a low, common advantage of me, then you insult me!

RHETT I meant it as a compliment . . . and I hope to see more of you when you're free of the spell of the thin-blooded Mr. Wilkes. He doesn't strike me as half good enough for a girl of your . . . What was it? . . . Your passion for living.

SCARLETT How dare you! You aren't fit to wipe his boots!
(she starts to run out of the room in a rage)

RHETT *(laughs and calls after her)* And you were going to hate him for the rest of your life!

Scarlett flings out of the room, slamming the door behind her.

74 FRONT HALL—TWELVE OAKS—BY THE STAIRS

Scarlett, angry, insulted, her heart pounding, is walking toward the stairs, when suddenly she hears voices and stops, shrinking back in the shadow of the banister.

INDIA'S VOICE Well, she certainly made a fool of herself running after all the men at the barbecue.

MELANIE'S VOICE That's not fair, India. She's so attractive, the men just naturally flock to her.

75 TRUCKING SHOT

with India, Suellen, Melanie, and another girl, who is a little behind them, as they descend the stairs.

SUELLEN Oh, Melanie, you're just too good to be true. Didn't you even see her going after your brother Charles?

CONTINUED:

75 CONTINUED

INDIA Yes . . . and she knows Charles belongs to me!

MELANIE You're wrong, India. Scarlett is just high-spirited—and vivacious.

ANOTHER GIRL *(leaning over from behind them)* Well, men may flirt with that kind of girl, but they don't marry them.

INDIA If you ask me, there's only one person she really gives a rap about—and that's Ashley.

MELANIE Ashley! You know that's not true. I think you're being very mean to her.

By this time the girls have come all the way down the stairs and are starting to cross the hall toward the front door.

76 CLOSE SHOT—SCARLETT

The girls have disappeared from Shot. Scarlett, shamed and horrified, raises her fists as if to pound at the stair rail.

Suddenly from outside we hear a wild, shrill cry—the Rebel yell. The cry is picked up by twenty or thirty other male voices and grows to a deafening roar. A couple of male guests appear in the hall and race past Scarlett. Others start swarming through the hall, running toward outside. She pays no attention to the commotion. Dazed, she picks up her skirts and starts to race up the stairs toward the landing, against the tide of girls and women who start pouring down the stairs.

Ad lib voices of both men and women from outside and inside:

WOMEN *(running downstairs)*
What is it?

It's war! It's come!
Isn't it wonderful!
A war—with battles and everything?
Let's go see!

MEN
At last we can fight Yankee thieves!
We'll leave tonight!
Send for the horses!

77 INT. HALL—CHARLES HAMILTON

Charles, running in from outside, sees Scarlett on the landing above him and calls to her:

CHARLES Miss O'Hara!

78 CLOSE SHOT—SCARLETT—ON LANDING

CHARLES' VOICE Miss O'Hara!

Scarlett stops and turns, annoyed. Charles bounds up the steps to her.

CHARLES Isn't it thrilling? Mr. Lincoln has called for soldiers—volunteers to fight against us.

SCARLETT Oh, fiddle-dee-dee! Don't you men ever think about anything important?

CHARLES But it's war, Miss O'Hara! And everybody's going off to enlist. They're going right away. I'm going, too!

SCARLETT *(thinking of Ashley)* Everybody?

She runs to the window and looks out, searching for Ashley. Charles follows her, but she pays scant attention to him.

CHARLES Oh, Miss O'Hara, will you be sorry? To see us go, I mean?

SCARLETT *(sarcastically)* I'll cry into my pillow every night.

Charles, misunderstanding, takes her hand. Scarlett still searching through the window.

CHARLES Oh, Miss O'Hara, I've been wanting to ask you—but I was scared. But I thought perhaps now—now that we're going and you say that you'll be sorry—Oh, Miss O'Hara, I told you I loved you. I think you're the most beautiful girl in the world . . . and the sweetest, and the dearest. I know I couldn't hope that you could love *me* . . .

79 EXTERIOR—SHOOTING FROM INSIDE THROUGH THE WINDOW (FROM SCARLETT'S VIEWPOINT)

Amid the confusion of horses being saddled; of men and women running in all directions; Ashley, on his horse in the driveway in front of the house, lifts Melanie off the ground into his arms and kisses her.

CHARLES' VOICE I'm so clumsy and stupid . . . not nearly good enough for you. But if you *could* . . . if you could think of marrying me, I'd do anything in the world for you—just anything, I promise.

80 TWO SHOT—CHARLES AND SCARLETT—AT WINDOW ON LANDING

CONTINUED:

80 CONTINUED
Stricken, Scarlett turns back to Charles.

SCARLETT What did you say?

CHARLES *(abashed)* Miss O'Hara, I said would you marry me?

SCARLETT *(looks at him slowly, waits a moment, then speaks with determination)* Yes, Mr. Hamilton. I will.

CHARLES *(delirious with joy)* You will? You'll marry me! You'll wait for me?

SCARLETT *(lowering her eyes)* Oh, I—I don't think I'd want to wait.

CHARLES *(scarcely daring to believe his ears)* You mean you'll marry me before I go?
(she nods, avoiding his eyes)
Oh, Miss O'Hara . . . Scarlett!
(just to call her by her name is an effort and a thrill. He takes her hand.)
When may I speak to your father?

SCARLETT The sooner the better.

CHARLES *(grinning all over his face with joy)* I'll go now. I can't wait. Will you excuse me . . . dear?
(the excitement of saying "dear" is almost too much for him—he lifts her hand to his lips, kissing it again and repeats:)
—dear?

He runs down the stairs and off, three steps at a time.

81 ANGLE SHOT THROUGH WINDOW—WITH SCARLETT IN CLOSE UP IN THE FOREGROUND

Scarlett, looking out the window, sees Ashley riding away, waving back to Melanie, who gazes sorrowfully after him, her hands over her mouth.

CHARLES' VOICE *(exuberant o.s.)* Mr. O'Hara! Mr. O'Hara!

Scarlett is wretched, heart-broken.

SCARLETT *(in a forlorn whisper)* Oh, Ashley, Ashley—

FADE OUT.

82 FADE IN:
INT. PARLOR AT TARA—NIGHT

The reception after Charles and Scarlett's marriage. The room is lighted by many candles. Scarlett, in her mother's wedding dress and veil, stands in the receiving line in front of the mantelpiece between Charles on one side and her mother and father on the other, receiving congratulations from the guests. Charles is in the uniform of his troop.

The impression of a great many guests should be gained from the babble of voices, from silhouetted figures on the wall behind the receiving line—and from the people immediately ahead of and immediately behind Ashley and Melanie, who, as we pick up the scene, are the ones congratulating Scarlett and Charles.

(Some of the men we see are in uniforms of their troops. Ashley, too, in uniform.)

MELANIE *(kissing Scarlett)* Scarlett, I thought of you at *our* wedding yesterday and hoped yours would be as beautiful. And it was.

SCARLETT *(like a sleepwalker)* Was it?

MELANIE *(nods emphatically)* Now we're really and truly sisters.

Melanie moves a step forward to Charles. Ashley, coming up behind her, bends to kiss Scarlett on the cheek without a word. He is embarrassed and avoids Scarlett's eyes. He takes Melanie's arm and moves off with her. Scarlett turns to look after them, tears coming to her eyes. Charles sees this, but mistakes the cause. He looks at Scarlett lovingly, presses her hand, and whispers:

CHARLES Don't cry, darling. The war will be over in a few weeks and I'll be coming back to you.

Scarlett now really starts to cry and sob as she looks at him, and we

FADE OUT.

83 FADE IN:
SWORD ON TABLE—CAMERA SHOOTING FROM ABOVE

A sword in its scabbard lies beside an open, handwritten letter. CAMERA MOVES DOWN into CLOSE UP of letter. The paper is of an inexpensive type of Confederate grey, faintly ruled. CAMERA IRISES DOWN to the lines:

Head Qrs.
Hampton's Legion

CONTINUED:

83 CONTINUED

Columbia, S.C.
14 June, 1861

My dear Madam

I would have advised you of Capt. Hamilton's illness had he not requested otherwise.

Herewith I send you his sword. May it console you that Captain Hamilton made the great sacrifice for our glorious Cause.

CAMERA PANS DOWN

Though he was not vouchsafed a hero's death upon the field of glory, he was nonetheless a hero, dying in camp here of pneumonia, following an attack of measles.

I am, Madam, very respectfully

Your obt. servt.
Wade Hampton
Col. Cmdg.

DISSOLVE TO:

84 *INT. SCARLETT'S BEDROOM—CLOSE SHOT—SCARLETT AT MIRROR—DAY*

She is trying on a widow's bonnet. She regards her own image with disgust, takes off the bonnet, and reaches out of scene. CAMERA PANS A LITTLE to include what she is reaching for. It is a modish hat of brilliant hue. CAMERA PANS BACK as she tries it on and regards herself in the mirror with satisfaction.

Reflected in the glass may be seen a door behind her, which opens, and Mammy appears.

MAMMY Miss Scarlett!

SCARLETT Well, I don't care—I'm too young to be a widow!

MAMMY *(sternly)* Miss Scarlett!

Scarlett takes off the gay bonnet and picks up the black one again.

SCARLETT *(coldly)* Oh—oh—I'd just go around scaring people in that thing.

MAMMY You ain't supposed to be around people. You'se in mourning.

SCARLETT For what!
(throws herself down on the bed and cries)

SCARLETT I don't feel anything. Why do I have to pretend and pretend?

Ellen enters.

ELLEN *(quietly)* What is it?

Ellen comes forward to Scarlett and sits down on the bed, speaks tenderly.

ELLEN Baby, what is it?

SCARLETT *(crying)* My life's over—Nothing will ever happen to me any more.

ELLEN *(patting Scarlett)* Darling . . .

SCARLETT *(sitting up and looking strickenly at her mother)* Oh, Mother, I know you'll think I'm horrible. But I just can't bear going around in black. It's bad enough not being able to go to any parties—but looking this way, too—
(throws herself back on the bed and sobs)

ELLEN *(patting Scarlett's head)* I don't think you're at all horrible. It's only natural to want to look young and be young, when you are young.
(she has put her arm around her)
Oh, Baby, how would you like to go visiting somewhere? Savannah, perhaps?

SCARLETT *(sobbing)* What would I do in Savannah?

ELLEN Well, Atlanta, then. There's lots going on there, and you could stay with Melanie and her Aunt Pittypat—

Scarlett stops sobbing—after a moment of silence, sits up.

SCARLETT Melanie! Yes. Yes, I could, couldn't I?

85 CLOSE UP—MAMMY

CONTINUED:

85 CONTINUED

She realizes what Scarlett is up to, turns away with a gesture of knowing disgust, and busies herself with something on the bureau.

86 BACK TO SCENE

SCARLETT *(jumps up and throws her arms around her mother, accepting the idea)* Oh, Mother, you're sweet to me, sweeter than anybody in the world.

Scarlett sees Mammy's face over Ellen's shoulder, looking at her knowingly.

ELLEN You'd like it, really?
(Scarlett nods slowly)
All right, then. Now stop your crying and smile. You can take Prissy with you.
(rises and turns to Mammy)
Start packing Miss Scarlett's things, Mammy. I'll go write the necessary letters.
(she exits)

SCARLETT *(sitting on the bed, staring rapturously ahead of her—whispers:)* Atlanta . . . !

MAMMY *(grimly)* Savannah would be better for you. You'll jus' git in trouble in Atlanta . . .

SCARLETT *(guiltily)* What trouble are you talking about?

MAMMY You know what trouble Ah's talkin' about. I'se talkin' about Mistuh Ashley Wilkes. He'll be comin' to Atlanta when he get his leave —and you sittin' there waitin' fo' him—
(hisses it)
—jes' like a spider. He belongs to Miss Melanie and . . .

SCARLETT *(who has risen and walked slowly to Mammy. She speaks grimly and icily.)* You go pack my trunks like Mother said.

DISSOLVE TO:

87 EXT. ATLANTA ARMORY—(COSGROVE)—NIGHT—AUTUMN, 1862

A huge banner strung across the building, reading:

MONSTER BAZAAR
FOR THE BENEFIT OF ATLANTA'S
OWN MILITARY HOSPITAL

DISSOLVE TO:

88 INT. BAZAAR—LONG SHOT

The great armory drill room is decorated for the occasion. Around the walls are little booths with pretty Atlanta girls in attendance on their customers. The floor is filled with dancers in bright evening dresses, convalescing officers of the Home Guard and of the Georgia militia in their bright uniforms. The room is lit by candles in donated candlesticks. The walls are decorated with flag bunting, and ivy vines.

At one end of the hall is the musicians' platform, decorated with palms. On the wall behind it, draped in flags, are the portraits of Jefferson Davis and Alec Stephens.

89 LOW CAMERA ANGLE—ON DANCERS' FEET

—as they whirl in the dance.

SWING CAMERA TO:

90 CLOSE SHOT—MELANIE AND AUNT PITTYPAT

—standing in front of their booth.

AUNT PITTYPAT They're all whispering, and I just know it's about her.

MELANIE What's it matter what they say, Aunt Pittypat?

AUNT PITTYPAT But Scarlett is living under my roof. So they all think I'm responsible for her.
(she shudders)
And for a widow to appear in public at a social gathering! Every time I think of it I feel faint!

MELANIE *(patiently)* But, Aunt Pitty, you know that Scarlett only came here to help raise money for the Cause. It was splendid of her to make the sacrifice.

THE CAMERA STARTS TO PAN, as Melanie continues to talk, to a CLOSE SHOT OF SCARLETT, who is leaning on the counter of the booth, from inside, looking very demure. CAMERA PASSES HER FACE and starts to move down to her feet.

CONTINUED:

90 CONTINUED

MELANIE'S VOICE *(continuing)* From the way you're talking, anyone would think she came here to dance instead of sell things!

By this time the CAMERA HAS REACHED Scarlett's feet, peeping out from under the skirt of her widow's mourning. She taps them in time to the music.

91 AUNT PITTYPAT AND MELANIE—AT BOOTH

Aunt Pittypat starts to turn away, befuddled and upset.

AUNT PITTYPAT Well, I'd better go and explain to everybody so they don't think we're all fast.

She exits . . . as a bugle blows a fanfare off scene and Melanie and Scarlett look up, and Scarlett starts out of the booth.

92 MUSICIANS' PLATFORM

The bugler finishes. Dr. Meade steps forward from the side of the platform. The little darky drummer boy gives a long roll on his drum. The murmur from the dancers quiets down. Dr. Meade raises his hands for attention:

DR. MEADE I have important news—*glorious* news. Another triumph for our magnificent men in arms.
(reads from the slip of paper in his hand)
General Lee has completely whipped the enemy and swept the Yankee army northward from Virginia!

93 LONG SHOT—CROWD

Cheers and excitement and applause from crowd.

94 DR. MEADE

Dr. Meade puts his hand up for silence and the cheers die down.

DR. MEADE And now—a happy surprise for all of us . . . We have with us tonight that most daring of all blockade runners, whose fleet of schooners, slipping past the Yankee guns, have brought to us here the very woolens, silks, and laces we wear tonight. I refer, ladies and gentlemen, to that will-o'-the-wisp of the bounding main—

95 FULL SHOT—THE BAZAAR (SHOOTING OVER MEADE)

DR. MEADE *(continuing)* —none other than our friend from Charleston—
(gestures grandiloquently)

There is a general stir as everyone turns and gazes in the indicated direction—toward the side of the hall where Scarlett and Melanie's booth stands. The crowd applauds.

96 CLOSE SHOT—SCARLETT

—who now stands next to Melanie in front of booth. She has been applauding mechanically. While the applause continues, interspersed with women's cries of approval and Rebel yells from the men, she looks off scene and suddenly stops clapping, as she sees:

97 CLOSE SHOT—RHETT BUTLER (FROM SCARLETT'S ANGLE)

DR. MEADE'S VOICE *(continuing as the applause subsides)* —Captain Rhett Butler!

Rhett smiles arrogantly, almost contemptuously.

98 LONG SHOT—CROWD APPLAUDING

They cheer madly as Rhett steps forward, clicks his heels, and bows. He takes a step nearer Scarlett's booth.

99–101 CLOSE SHOT—SCARLETT—(MELANIE IN B.G., AT FURTHER END OF BOOTH)

Scarlett looking up in amazement and fright. Rhett steps in close to her.

Scarlett, alarmed, tries to escape through the entrance into the booth. Her dress catches on the boards. Rhett leans over to release her skirt.

RHETT Permit me.
(releases her skirt)

Scarlett, still looking for an avenue of retreat, tries almost childishly to get away. Melanie comes over to Rhett, holding out her hand.

MELANIE Captain Butler, it's such a pleasure to see you again. I met you last at my husband's home—

RHETT *(takes her hand gravely)* It's kind of you to remember, Mrs. Wilkes.

CONTINUED:

99–101 CONTINUED

MELANIE *(with a half gesture of introduction)* Did you meet Captain Butler at Twelve Oaks, Scarlett?

SCARLETT *(sharply, not knowing what to say)* Yes. I—I think so.

RHETT Only for a moment, Mrs. Hamilton. It was in the library. You—er . . . had broken something.

SCARLETT *(glaring at him, but trying to control her voice)* Yes, I remember you, Captain Butler.

RHETT May I offer you my sympathy on your bereavement? I heard of your marriage. As brief as it was—sudden.

SCARLETT *(sensing his mockery, and livid)* Thank you.

RHETT *(begins fingering the various wares on the counter)* And now, what are you ladies selling for the Cause?

Before Scarlett or Melanie can reply, a one-armed officer in uniform comes into scene carrying a split-oak basket over his unwounded arm. It is full of trinkets of jewelry.

BASKET CARRIER *(holding out the basket)* Ladies, the Confederacy asks for your jewelry . . . on behalf of our noble Cause.

SCARLETT We're not wearing any. We're in mourning.

BASKET CARRIER Oh, I beg your pardon.
(he bows and starts to turn away)

MELANIE *(sincerely regretful)* I'm so sorry.

RHETT *(noticing Melanie's distress)* Wait!
(takes from his pocket a large gold cigar case and, as the man turns back with the basket, drops it in.)
On behalf of Mrs. Wilkes and Mrs. Hamilton.

BASKET CARRIER Thank you, Captain Butler.
(starts to turn away again)

MELANIE Just a moment—please.
(she removes the wedding ring from her finger and drops it gently into the basket)
Here.

BASKET CARRIER But it's your wedding ring, ma'am.

MELANIE It may help my husband more—off my finger.
(she turns aside to hide her tears)

BASKET CARRIER Thank you.

RHETT *(sincerely)* That was a very beautiful thing to do, Mrs. Wilkes.

Scarlett, not to be outdone, yanks off her own wedding ring.

SCARLETT Here—you can have mine, too—for the Cause.
(throws ring into basket; she watches Rhett, waiting for approbation)

RHETT And you, Mrs. Hamilton. I know just how much that means to you.

DR. MEADE *(hurries up to booth)* Melanie!

MELANIE *(turns)* Yes, Dr. Meade . . .

DR. MEADE I need your approval for something we want to do that's rather shocking.
(to Rhett and Scarlett, taking Melanie by the arm)
Will you excuse us, please?
(leads Melanie out)

Rhett bows. When they are out of earshot, he turns on Scarlett:

RHETT Well, I'll say one thing—the War makes the most peculiar widows.

SCARLETT I wish you'd go away! If you'd had any raising, you'd know I never wanted to see you again.

RHETT Now, why be silly—you've no reason for hating me. I'll carry your guilty secret to my grave.

SCARLETT *(sarcastically, but slightly relieved and a shade more friendly, she speaks like a silly child)* Oh, I guess I'd be very unpatriotic to hate one of the great heroes of the war, Captain Butler. I do declare, I was surprised that you should turn out to be such a noble character.

RHETT *(laughs)* I can't bear to take advantage of your little-girl ideas, Miss O'Hara. But I'm neither noble nor heroic.

SCARLETT *(surprised)* But you *are* a blockade runner—

RHETT For profit—and profit only—

CONTINUED:

99–101 CONTINUED

SCARLETT Are you trying to tell me you don't believe in the Cause, Captain Butler?

RHETT I believe in Rhett Butler. He's the only Cause I know. The rest doesn't mean much to me.

102 MEDIUM SHOT—PLATFORM

The bugler steps back, and Dr. Meade comes to the center of the platform.

DR. MEADE And now, ladies and gentlemen, a startling surprise for the benefit of the hospital.
(He laughs. The crowd laughs with him. Then, as if announcing the most startling thing in the world, Dr. Meade springs it)
Gentlemen, if you wish to lead the opening reel with the lady of your choice—you must *bargain* for her!

103–105 SERIES OF CLOSE UP REACTIONS

Young girls—giggling, delighted.

Group of young men—extremely pleased.

Over the hubbub from the hall, young officers giving the Rebel yell: "Ee-ya-ee!"

DR. MEADE'S VOICE *(over hubbub)* The roll of the drum will open the bidding.

106 CLOSE UP—SCARLETT

—as the drums roll. She is eager, intrigued, and trying to hide it.

107 CHAPERONE'S CORNER

Mrs. Merriwether comes up and accosts Mrs. Meade, who is sitting next to Aunt Pittypat.

MRS. MERRIWETHER Caroline Meade, how can you permit your husband to conduct this—this slave auction?

MRS. MEADE Dolly Merriwether, how dare you criticize me. Melanie Wilkes told the doctor that if it's for the benefit of the Cause, it was quite all right.

MRS. MERRIWETHER She did!
(glares at Aunt Pittypat)

AUNT PITTYPAT Oh dear, oh dear. Where are my smelling salts? I think I shall faint. I—

MRS. MERRIWETHER Don't you dare faint, Pittypat Hamilton. If Melanie says it's all right, it is all right.

AUNT PITTYPAT *(confused)* Oh—

108 FULL SHOT—ARMORY—(DR. MEADE IN F.G., SHOOTING FROM MUSICIANS' PLATFORM)

DR. MEADE Come, gentlemen. Do I hear your bids? Make your offers. Don't be bashful, gentlemen.

RENÉ PICARD Twenty dollars—twenty dollars for Miss Maybelle Merriwether.

ANOTHER OFFICER Twenty-five dollars for Miss Fanny Elsing!

DR. MEADE Only twenty-five dollars for giving your favorite lady the outstanding honor of leading the reel?

RHETT'S VOICE *(from crowd)* One hundred and fifty dollars *in gold!*

Gasps of surprise from the crowd, then a cheer.

DR. MEADE For what lady, sir?

RHETT *(walking toward the platform)* For Mrs. Charles Hamilton.

The general laughter and murmur of voices ceases abruptly. There is a gasp of surprise. All those about Rhett turn and stare at him.

109 CHAPERONE'S CORNER

They all gasp.

110 CLOSE UP—SCARLETT

—reacting in amazement.

111 CLOSE SHOT—DR. MEADE

DR. MEADE *(shocked)* For *whom,* sir?

112 CLOSE SHOT—RHETT IN CROWD

Those about him are gazing at him in amazement and disapproval. Only a slight curl of his lips betrays his inner amusement. He casually strolls a little nearer the platform.

CONTINUED:

112 CONTINUED

RHETT Mrs. Charles Hamilton.

113 LONG SHOT

Including Dr. Meade on platform and Rhett advancing slowly toward him.

DR. MEADE Mrs. Hamilton is in mourning, Captain Butler. Any of our Atlanta belles would be proud . . .

RHETT *(his glance sweeps the crowd coldly)* I *said* Mrs. Charles Hamilton.

DR. MEADE *(annoyed)* She will not consider it, sir.

114 CLOSE SHOT—SCARLETT

SCARLETT *(tossing her head back)* Oh, yes, I will!

She throws open the trap of the booth defiantly, and CAMERA FOLLOWS HER AS—her black dress in striking contrast as she walks through the blaze of color, her head high, not looking at any of the shocked faces as the women draw their skirts away from her—she makes her way toward Rhett.

115 REACTIONS OF SHOCK FROM GUESTS

116 AUNT PITTYPAT

—in group with other dowagers.

Aunt Pittypat faints.

117 TWO SHOT—RHETT AND SCARLETT

—as they meet on the floor.

Rhett advances a step or two to meet her, smiles, and bows low. Scarlett curtsies and throws her head back defiantly.

118 CLOSE SHOT—LEVI, THE COLORED ORCHESTRA LEADER

—trying to save the situation, he calls:

LEVI Choose yo' partners fo' de Verginny reel!

119 TWO SHOT—RHETT AND SCARLETT

—couples forming behind them for the dance.

RHETT Well, we've sort of shocked the Confederacy, Scarlett.

SCARLETT It's a little bit like blockade running, isn't it?

RHETT It's worse—
(grabs her)
But I expect a very fancy profit out of it—

SCARLETT *(as they start to dance)* I don't care what you expect and I don't care what they think. I'm going to dance and dance. I wouldn't mind dancing tonight with Abe Lincoln himself!

As the reel starts,

DISSOLVE TO:

120 LONG SHOT—WALTZERS ON FLOOR

121 CLOSE TWO SHOT—RHETT AND SCARLETT (WAIST FIGURES)—WALTZING

RHETT You're the most beautiful dancer I've ever held in my arms.

SCARLETT *(coquettishly, with something of her old manner from her barbecue scene)* Oh, Captain Butler, you shouldn't hold me so close. I'll be mad if you do!
(Rhett holds her even closer and whirls her around.)

122 MEDIUM SHOT—DANCERS WALTZING

123 CLOSE TWO SHOT—RHETT AND SCARLETT

Waltzing.

SCARLETT Another dance and my reputation will be lost forever.

RHETT If you've enough courage, you can do without a reputation.

SCARLETT Oh, you do talk scandalous!

124 LONG SHOT—DANCERS ON FLOOR—LOW CAMERA SETUP

125 CLOSE TWO SHOT—RHETT AND SCARLETT

SCARLETT You do waltz divinely, Captain Butler.

RHETT Don't start flirting with me. I'm not one of your plantation beaux. I want more than flirting from you.

CONTINUED:

125 CONTINUED

SCARLETT *(coquettishly)* What *do* you want?

RHETT I'll tell you, Scarlett O'Hara, if you'll take that Southern belle simper off your face.
(she drops her expression and looks at him, embarrassed)
Someday I want you to say to *me* the words I heard you say to Ashley Wilkes . . .
(she looks up at him, gasping with fury at the shamelessness of the reminder)
"I love you."

Scarlett, aghast at his brazen attack and at the revelation of his interest, narrows her eyes when she realizes that at last she has the upper hand over this man whose insults she has been unable to cope with in their two meetings.

SCARLETT *(triumphantly)* That's something you'll never hear from me, Rhett Butler, as long as you live!

126 LONG SHOT—DANCERS

—including Rhett and Scarlett.

DISSOLVE TO:

127 INSERT: HAND UNFOLDING LETTER

"Dear Mrs. Wilkes:

The Confederacy may need the life-blood of its men, but it does not yet demand the heart's blood of its women. I have redeemed your ring at ten times its value.
Please accept its return as a token of my reverence for the courage and sacrifice of a very great lady.

Captain Rhett Butler"

MELANIE'S VOICE How sweet, how kind. He is a thoughtful gentleman.

CAMERA PANS DOWN to postscript. Hand holding letter holds two wedding rings on thumb.

"P.S. I also enclose Mrs. Hamilton's ring."

SCARLETT'S VOICE Fiddle-dee-dee, why doesn't he say something about my sacrifice?

DISSOLVE TO:

128–135 INT. AUNT PITTYPAT'S LIVING ROOM—CLOSE UP OF PARIS HAT BOX—(JULY, 1863)—DAY

The lid is being taken off, revealing a green bonnet.

As we PULL BACK we hear Scarlett's voice:

SCARLETT'S VOICE Oh . . . oh, the darling thing!

CAMERA is now back and reveals Rhett in a chair, watching Scarlett as she looks delightedly at the bonnet she has taken out of the box.

SCARLETT Oh, Rhett, it's lovely—lovely. You didn't really bring it all the way from Paris just for me? Oh—

RHETT Yes, I thought it was time I got you out of that fake mourning. Next trip I'll bring you some green silk for a frock to match it.

SCARLETT Oh, Rhett!

He takes out a cigar from a new case as he talks:

RHETT It's my duty to the brave boys at the front to keep the girls at home looking pretty.

Scarlett runs toward the mirror with the bonnet, talking as she goes:

SCARLETT Oh, it's so long since I've had anything new!
(she stands on a hassock to more easily see herself in the mirror, gurgles with delight, then to play a trick on Rhett, puts the bonnet on backwards and turns to him)
How do I look?

Rhett looks up from lighting his cigar.

RHETT *(dismayed)* Awful, just awful!
(gets up and goes to her)

SCARLETT *(looks herself over as Rhett approaches)* Why, what's the matter?

Rhett yanks the bonnet off her head, readjusts it.

RHETT This war's stopped being a joke when a girl like you doesn't even know how to wear the latest fashions.

SCARLETT Oh!

CONTINUED:

128–135 CONTINUED

Rhett catches the mischievous look on her face and realizes what she has been up to. He laughs and Scarlett laughs with him.

SCARLETT Oh, Rhett, let me do it.

She turns, looks again into the mirror, and finishes tying the bow.

SCARLETT *(turns back, suddenly remembering)* But, Rhett, I don't know how I'll dare to wear it!

She lifts her skirts to get down from the hassock, exposing a little of her pantalettes.

RHETT *(eyeing her pantalettes)* You will, though. And another thing . . . those pantalettes.
(shakes his head)
I don't know a woman in Paris that wears pantalettes any more.

SCARLETT *(eagerly and impulsively)* Oh, what do they—
(stopping herself)
You shouldn't talk about such things!

RHETT *(laughs aloud)* You little hypocrite! You don't mind my *knowing* about them—just my *talking* about them.

SCARLETT *(examining the bonnet again)* But, Rhett, I can't keep on accepting these gifts from you.
(looks at bonnet lovingly, her resolution weakening)
Although you *are* awfully kind—

RHETT I'm not kind. I'm just tempting you. I never give anything without expecting something in return. I always get paid.

SCARLETT Well, if you think I'll marry you just to pay for the bonnet, I won't!

RHETT *(dropping his arms, laughs and strolls away)* Don't flatter yourself! I'm not a marrying man.

SCARLETT *(following him)* Well, I won't kiss you for it, either.

She looks at him provocatively and flirtatiously. Rhett catches her by the arm. She closes her eyes and looks as if ready to be kissed. Rhett puts his arms about her then, when it looks as though we were about to go into a hot love scene:

RHETT Open your eyes and look at me.

Scarlett opens her eyes. Rhett studies them, shakes his head.

RHETT No . . . I don't think I will kiss you.
(he releases Scarlett, to her embarrassment and rage)
Although you need kissing—badly. That's what's wrong with you. You should be kissed—and often—and by someone who knows how.

SCARLETT *(piqued)* And I suppose you think you're the proper person!

RHETT *(judiciously)* Mmm . . . I might be . . . if the right moment ever came . . .

SCARLETT You're a black-hearted, conceited varmint, and I don't know why I let you come to see me.

RHETT I'll tell you why, Scarlett. Because I'm the only man over sixteen and under sixty who's around to show you a good time. But cheer up—the war can't last much longer.

SCARLETT *(eagerly)* Oh, really, Rhett? Why?

RHETT There's a little battle going on right now that ought to pretty well fix things—
(soberly for a moment)
—one way or the other.

SCARLETT *(anxious)* Oh, Rhett . . . Rhett . . . tell me . . . Is Ashley in it?

RHETT *(wearily)* So you still haven't gotten the wooden-headed Mr. Wilkes out of your mind?

Picking up his hat, disgustedly:

RHETT Yes, I suppose he's in it.

Rhett starts for the door.

SCARLETT *(running after him)* Oh, but tell me, Rhett . . . *please* . . . where is it?

RHETT *(turning at the door)* Some little town in Pennsylvania—called Gettysburg.

He exits, closing the door after him.

DISSOLVE TO:

136 EXTERIOR STREET—OUTSIDE EXAMINER *OFFICE—LONG SHOT—ATLANTA—DAY*

A tense, silent crowd waits outside the newspaper office for news of the Battle of Gettysburg.

Over this DISSOLVES in the title:

TITLE: Hushed and grim, Atlanta turned painful eyes toward the far-away little town of Gettysburg . . . and a page of history waited for three days while two nations came to death grips on the farm lands of Pennsylvania . . .

As the title DISSOLVES OUT, we pick out anxious, worn faces in the crowd—all eyes turned toward the Examiner *office where casualty lists are being printed.*

A boy appears at the top of the steps leading to the newspaper office, waving a sheaf of the lists in his hands.

As the boy starts running down the stairs, the crowd surges forward in one movement, fighting its way to get the lists, and frantic hands reach up for the news that will break their hearts. We see Uncle Peter, Aunt Pitty's Negro coachman, in the scrambling crowd at the foot of the steps.

137 SCARLETT AND MELANIE'S CARRIAGE

Scarlett and Melanie are seated. Uncle Peter comes up to them, handing them the list which is in two pieces.

UNCLE PETER Heah yo' is, Miss Melanie. Dey was fightin' fo' dem so hard it jus' got tore in half.

Melanie passes it to Scarlett, her fingers trembling violently.

MELANIE Please, Scarlett—you look—the W's at the end.

Scarlett takes the sheet nervously, her emotion as strong as Melanie's.

SCARLETT *(hunting on the torn sheets)* Wellman—Wendell—White—Whitner—Wilkins—Williams—Woolsey—Workman—

MELANIE *(with a gasp of excited relief)* Scarlett, you've passed him!

SCARLETT He isn't there! He isn't there!

MELANIE *(laughing and crying at the same time)* Ashley's safe! He isn't listed.

SCARLETT He's safe! He's safe!

Melanie looks at Scarlett, realizes the depth of her emotion, takes her hand and presses it.

MELANIE Oh, Scarlett, you're so sweet to worry about Ashley like this for me.

Scarlett turns away in embarrassment. Melanie hears a sob from off scene and looks in that direction.

138 THE MEADE CARRIAGE—MRS. MEADE AND DR. MEADE

—with their small son, Phil, about fifteen, seated opposite them. Mrs. Meade is sobbing, rocking herself distractedly.

139 SCARLETT AND MELANIE

MELANIE *(looks—gasps as she realizes that Mrs. Meade has lost someone)* I must go to her.
(she exits scene)

140 MEADE CARRIAGE

DR. MEADE *(to his wife)* Don't, my dear—not here. Let's go home.

Melanie comes into the scene, opens the carriage door.

MELANIE Mrs. Meade, not . . . ?

DR. MEADE Yes. Our boy . . . Darcy.

MRS. MEADE *(picking up a piece of knitting from her lap)* I was making these mittens for him. He won't need them now.

PHIL *(standing abruptly)* Mother, I'm going to enlist! I'll show them! I'll kill *all* those Yankees!

MELANIE *(climbing into the carriage and taking Mrs. Meade in her arms)* Phil Meade, you hush your mouth! Do you think it will help your mother to have you off getting shot, too? I never heard of anything so silly.

She comforts Mrs. Meade.

CUT BACK TO:

141 SCARLETT—

CONTINUED:

141 CONTINUED

Alone in her carriage staring at the torn casualty list. Her eyes are wide and a little blurred with tears. Rhett rides up on horseback.

RHETT It's a black day, Scarlett. You haven't had bad news, have you?

SCARLETT Ashley's safe.

RHETT *(sincerely)* I'm glad . . . for Mrs. Wilkes' sake.

SCARLETT *(genuinely moved)* But, Rhett, there are so many others . . .

RHETT Many of your friends?

SCARLETT Just about every family in the county. The Tarleton boys. Rhett—
(her voice breaks)
—both of them.

RHETT *(sincerely sympathetic, turns, and looks at the crowd and speaks more softly)* Look at them—all these poor, tragic people! It's the South sinking to its knees. It will never rise again. The Cause—the Cause of living in the past—is dying right in front of us.

SCARLETT *(looking at him in surprise)* I've never heard you talk like that before.

RHETT I'm angry. Waste always makes me angry! And that's what all this is.
(looks around again)
Sheer waste.
(then, rallying himself he looks at her)
But don't you be downcast.

She looks at him, not knowing quite what he means. He returns her look and speaks with rather bitter jealousy:

RHETT Ashley Wilkes is still alive to come home to the women who love him—both of them.

Scarlett sharply turns her head away, angry and hurt. Rhett, with his cynical smile making its first appearance of the day, turns his horse and rides off, as we

DISSOLVE TO:

142 INSERT: NOTICE OF FURLOUGH HELD IN MAN'S HANDS

Head Qrs. Cav. Corp.
Nr. Orange Court House, Va.
23 Dec. 1863

Special Orders
No. 169

Three days Christmas furlough is hereby granted to Maj. Ashley Wilkes of Cobb's Legion in consideration of meritorious service during the Pennsylvania campaign.

E. V. White
Maj. & A. A. Genl.

Approved
J. E. B. Stuart
Maj. Gen. Comdg.

DISSOLVE TO:

143 *EXT. ATLANTA RAILROAD STATION—(DECEMBER, 1863)—DAY. MIST. FOG.*

A military train—terribly nondescript and ramshackle—made up of boxcars, flats, and coaches, is just clanking its way out of the station through the fog. Wisps of wood-smoke in the fog and the banging of a couple of flat wheels, the chugging of the engine and the tinny ringing of the bell fade under the crowd noises.

On the platform, soldiers on leave, a few wounded on stretchers and convalescents, being greeted by their sobbing, laughing women-folk. The soldiers' uniforms are ragged and dirty, and they are carrying their gear in everything from regulation knapsacks to bandanna handkerchiefs.

A band comprised of small boys and playing foully out of tune is on hand to welcome the wounded and furloughed men. Their music blares weakly through the crowd noises.

We see the embraces of mothers and sons, husbands and wives, sweethearts—of all classes and conditions . . . with much calling of the familiar phrase.

VOICES *(ad libs)* Merry Christmas!
Chris'mus gif! Chris'mus gif!
Oh . . . son . . . son!

CONTINUED:

143 CONTINUED

And now you're . . . home . . .
Oh, my darling!
Etc. . . .

The CAMERA MOVES THROUGH THIS until it stops upon Ashley and Melanie, in each other's arms. Slow and painful tears are crawling down Melanie's cheeks, while she tries to smile with a bright anguish of happiness. She touches Ashley's face, almost timidly, with her fingertips, as if her fingers must learn the new hollows in his cheeks.

Ashley's uniform—that of a Major of Cavalry—is patched and faded, with badly mended ravels hanging down from the cuffs. It is no longer Confederate grey, but butternut; and he is wearing a shabby old overcoat over it. He carries a bedding roll. He is tanned and very lean, with desperately tired eyes; he wears a pistol in a shabby holster; a battered scabbard slaps against his boots; and his spurs are brightly polished over run-over heels. The uniforms of the other returning men are similarly changed, many of them even worse. CAMERA MOVES UP TO CLOSE SHOT of Ashley and Melanie, as she comes out of the embrace to speak:

MELANIE *(rising inflection, rather unsteady)* Oh, you're . . . here . . . you're really here! At last! Oh—my dear, I've waited so long.

ASHLEY *(kissing her again, and smiling a little with his eyes; with new wrinkles at the corners of his eyes)* Melanie! My dear—my darling wife.

She touches his face again and puts her head on his chest for a moment —then comes out of it sharply with a sudden thought.

MELANIE Oh—but we're forgetting Scarlett.

CAMERA MOVES QUICKLY to reveal Scarlett, standing a little aside. Her face is almost blank—frozen with the steely repression of her internal conflict between happiness at seeing Ashley again and agony at having to watch Melanie's hands upon his face. She is in the green bonnet Rhett has given her, and under her coat is the dress made of the green silk Rhett promised to bring her. Pinned to her coat she is wearing a sprig of holly; and with it her fingers are unwittingly betraying her desperate restraint. She isn't aware of it, but her fingers, quite rigid but very casually, are plucking one by one the berries from the sprig, and dropping them one by one.

As Ashley and Melanie move into the same scene, with Scarlett, Ashley speaks, reaching for her hand, the last berry slips between her fingers; and she tries to smile.

ASHLEY Scarlett, dear—

Scarlett tries to smile with her eyes, at least; a tear interferes, but she winks it away and manages a too-bright smile with her lips.

ASHLEY Well, is this any way to greet a returning warrior?

SCARLETT *(as another tear gets away and rolls down her cheek)* Ashley —I—I—
(her lips quiver once, uncontrollably)

Then Scarlett sets her jaw with determination, smiles again, quite gently:

SCARLETT —Merry Christmas, Ashley.

QUICK DISSOLVE TO:

144 EXT. BARNYARD—AUNT PITTYPAT'S HOUSE—DAY

Uncle Peter is in the yard, hatchet in his hand. He is in pursuit of a large frightened rooster.

UNCLE PETER *(during the chase)* Come on, ol' gentlemen . . . We'se et all yo' wives. We'se et all yo' little chicks. You'se got nobody to worry yer head about fer leavin'. Come on . . . Now you jus' stand still so you can be Chris'mus gif' fer dey white fo'ks. Now hol' on . . . hol' on . . . don't go gettin' so uppity even if you' is the las' chicken in Atlanta . . .
(he pounces on the rooster)

QUICK DISSOLVE TO:

145 INT. DINING ROOM—AUNT PITTYPAT'S—CHRISTMAS DAY

Open on CLOSE UP of CARCASS—the remains of the poor old rooster. We hear Scarlett's voice as CAMERA STARTS TO PULL BACK:

SCARLETT'S VOICE *(petulantly)* Oh, let's not hear about the war. It's Christmas . . .
(softly and reminiscently)
Let's talk about Twelve Oaks and Tara and the times before there was any old war . . . Can we have the wine, Aunt Pittypat?

CONTINUED:

145 CONTINUED

Now CAMERA has pulled back to reveal Aunt Pittypat, Scarlett, Melanie, and Ashley about the table. In b.g. a sad little holly wreath and holly decorating the table. Aunt Pittypat is carefully dividing the contents of a Madeira bottle among four glasses. Uncle Peter stands at her side.

AUNT PITTYPAT *(pouring the wine)* Why did you say there wasn't enough, Uncle Peter? There's plenty.
(she takes the tray from Uncle Peter and carries it to the others)
This is the last of my father's fine Madeira that he got from his uncle, Admiral Wilbur Hamilton of Savannah, who married his cousin, Jessica Carroll of Carrollton, who was his second cousin once removed and kin to the Wilkeses, too. And I saved it to wish Ashley a Merry Christmas. But you mustn't drink it all at once, because it *is* the last.

DISSOLVE TO:

146 INT. AUNT PITTYPAT'S HALLWAY

Melanie and Ashley climbing the stairs to the second floor, arm in arm. Uncle Peter is lighting the way for them, holding aloft a fine silver candelabra.

Ashley is walking with studied casualness, glancing down at Melanie's fingertips on his sleeve; she is walking with downcast eyes.

ASHLEY *(tenderly, but at the same time giving the impression that he's saying it as a safe sort of thing to fit into his casual air—just as if they had walked upstairs together like this every evening for all these months)* I meant it, my dear. It *was* a lovely Christmas gift—really. Only generals have tunics like this nowadays.

MELANIE *(still not looking at him)* I'm . . . so happy you like it, dear.

ASHLEY *(strokes the tunic and continues a little too brightly, so that he sounds slightly affected)* Where *did* you get the cloth?

MELANIE *(hesitating)* It was sent me by a Charleston lady. I nursed her son while he was in the hospital, Ashley—before he died—and—
(she looks at him imploringly at her own reminder of the danger to her beloved)
Oh, you will take care of it, won't you? You won't let it get—torn? Promise me!

ASHLEY You mustn't worry—
(lightly)

I'll bring it back to you without any holes in it.
(tenderly)
I promise.
(they have reached the top of the stairs. Melanie turns)

147 LONG SHOT—(FROM THEIR ANGLE)

—shooting diagonally across the stairs.

Scarlett standing in the doorway to the living room, her hand on the drape, watching Ashley and Melanie off scene. The scene is lighted by a candle on a table beside Scarlett and by Uncle Peter's candle o.s.

148 TWO SHOT—ASHLEY AND MELANIE

—looking back at Scarlett.

On Ashley's face we read his realization of Scarlett's emotions. His eyes flicker a little and he glances quickly again at his wife's hand on his new sleeve. But immediately he forces a smile and calls to Scarlett.

ASHLEY Goodnight, my dear.

Melanie tenderly throws a kiss to Scarlett.

MELANIE Goodnight, Scarlett, darling.

149 CLOSE UP—SCARLETT

Still gazing upward after Melanie and Ashley. She opens her lips to mumble a wretched goodnight to them, but fails and closes her lips again with a long breath. Standing there completely motionless for a moment, she hears their footsteps going into their bedroom, a slight, embarrassed cough from Ashley and then the sound of the door closing softly but decisively. At that, her fingers, holding the drape, clench into a fist for an instant, and then slowly and hopelessly relax and slip down the drape. The light effect on Scarlett's face has been changing for the past moment or two as Uncle Peter's candle vanishes, but her face remains lit by the wan light of the candle beside her.

DISSOLVE TO:

150 INT. HALL—AUNT PITTYPAT'S—MORNING—MIST

Uncle Peter is coming down the stairs carrying Ashley's blanket roll. Scarlett enters the scene hastily as he reaches the bottom step.

CONTINUED:

150 CONTINUED

SCARLETT Is it time yet, Uncle Peter? Is it time for Mr. Ashley to leave?

UNCLE PETER Pretty quick now, Miss Scarlett.

SCARLETT Miss Melanie isn't going to the depot with him? She hasn't changed her mind?

UNCLE PETER No, ma'am, she's layin' down. She's so upset, Mist' Wilkes tole her she cain't even come downstairs.

He exits out the front door with Ashley's blanket roll. Scarlett turns distracted and desperately unhappy, and walks a few steps away from the bottom of the stairs. Then she hears Ashley's footsteps on the stairs and turns back hastily.

151 MEDIUM SHOT—ASHLEY

Coming down the stairs. He is miserable at the farewell scene he has just been through with Melanie. Stops as he sees Scarlett.

152 CLOSE UP—ASHLEY

His face reveals his nervousness as he sees Scarlett waiting for him. He wishes he did not have to face what is going to be a difficult scene, in view of the last time they were alone together at Twelve Oaks.

153 CLOSE SHOT—SCARLETT (FROM ASHLEY'S ANGLE)

She runs toward the bottom of the stairs, looking eagerly up.

SCARLETT Ashley!

154 TWO SHOT

As Ashley reaches the lower steps, Scarlett runs up two steps to meet him, speaking as she runs:

SCARLETT Ashley, let me go to the depot with you?

ASHLEY *(dodging)* Oh, Scarlett, I'd rather remember you as you are now—not shivering at the depot.

SCARLETT *(lowering her head in disappointment)* All right.

Ashley, in kindly fashion, takes her hands. Scarlett looks at him. Suddenly her face brightens slightly.

SCARLETT Ashley, I've got a present for you too!

She starts into the living room, Ashley following.

155 INT. LIVING ROOM

Scarlett comes into the living room, picks up a yellow silk sash from the table, and holds it up to Ashley. He takes it.

ASHLEY Why, Scarlett, it's beautiful! Tie it on me, my dear.

He unbuckles his sword belt and Scarlett ties it around him.

SCARLETT While Melly was making your new tunic, I made this to go with it.

ASHLEY You made it yourself? Then I'll value it all the more.

SCARLETT You know there's nothing I wouldn't do for you.

ASHLEY There's something you can do for me.

SCARLETT *(eagerly)* What is it?

ASHLEY Will you look after Melanie for me? She's so frail and gentle, and she loves you so much. You see, if I were killed and she had—

SCARLETT Oh, you mustn't say that! It's bad luck. Say a prayer, quickly.

ASHLEY You say one for me. We shall need all our prayers now the end is coming.

SCARLETT The end?

ASHLEY The end of the war. And the end of our world, Scarlett.

SCARLETT But, Ashley, you don't think the Yankees are beating us!!
(she sits down on settee)

ASHLEY The Yankees have beaten us. Gettysburg was the beginning of the end, only people here don't know it yet.
(moves away from her to the window)
Oh, Scarlett, my men are barefooted now, and the snow in Virginia is deep. When I see them, and I see the Yankees coming and coming, always more and more—
(turns back to Scarlett)
Well, when the end does come, I shall be far away. Even if I'm alive. Too far to be able to look out for Melanie.
(sits beside Scarlett)

CONTINUED:

155 CONTINUED

It'll be a comfort to me to know that she has you. You will promise, won't you?

SCARLETT *(dully)* Yes. Is—is that all, Ashley?

ASHLEY All except—good-bye.
(stands up)

SCARLETT *(standing)* Oh, Ashley—I can't let you go!

ASHLEY You must be brave—

SCARLETT No!

ASHLEY You must—

SCARLETT No!

ASHLEY How else can I bear going? Oh, Scarlett—you're so fine and strong and beautiful. Not just your sweet face, my dear, but you—

Sound of chimes off scene.

They look off. Ashley starts as if to go. Scarlett takes a step after him.

SCARLETT Kiss me. Kiss me good-bye.

He bends his head to her forehead. But she turns her face so that his lips meet her lips and her arms are about his neck in a strangling grip. For an instant he presses her body close to him. Then, suddenly, he reaches up, detaches her arms from his neck, and stands holding her crossed wrists in his two hands.

ASHLEY No, Scarlett. No.

SCARLETT Oh, Ashley, I love you! I've always loved you! I've never loved anyone else! I only married Charles just to hurt you. Oh, Ashley, tell me you love me. I'll live on it all the rest of my life!

He looks at her almost stupidly for a moment, then in his face she sees his love for her and his joy that she loves him and, battling with both, his shame and his despair. Then he turns to take up his hat.

ASHLEY Good-bye.
(he goes out)

Scarlett stands looking after him a moment, watching him leave. We hear the sound of the front door closing after Ashley. A sob, and Scarlett runs to the window to look after him.

156 EXT. SHOOTING FROM INT. THROUGH THE WINDOW—OVER SCARLETT'S SHOULDER

Scarlett watches Ashley as he goes quickly down the walk and is lost in the mist. The last Scarlett and the audience see of Ashley being the glitter of his sword.

SCARLETT *(in a whisper)* When the war's over, Ashley! When the war's over!

FADE OUT

FADE IN:

TITLE: Atlanta prayed while onward surged the triumphant Yankees . . .

Heads were high but hearts were heavy, as the wounded and the refugees poured into unhappy Georgia . . .

157 INT. HOSPITAL IN CHURCH—NIGHT

CAMERA, TRUCKING, enters the front door of the church, and, as a worshiper would in times of peace, comes slowly down the center aisle: toward a light which burns at the far end of the aisle, illuminating the altar and two women's figures who are bending, motionless, over an indistinct vagueness in the shadows under the altar. Their attitudes are queerly religious—macabre and pitiful in that place. Slowly we reveal that the center aisle of the church is lined and crowded with beds, now: beds of all descriptions commandeered from the homes of Atlanta—from the sagging, ugly iron bedsteads with cracked and peeling paint taken from the shacks of Negroes and poor white trash to one enormous and baronial canopied bed from a mansion.

The whole scene of the beds is dimly lit from unseen sources, and enormous, looming shadows move vaguely on the walls. From somewhere, a man's voice, high-pitched and terribly tense, is saying—almost chanting—words which, as the CAMERA enters and trucks slowly, are indistinct. And from the beds, continuously, come the awful night sounds of that place, running underneath that one voice in a litany of pain.

As CAMERA comes steadily down the aisle, nearer and nearer to the pulpit, the light there is revealed as the wavering flame of an old kerosene

CONTINUED:

157 CONTINUED

lamp, the figures become Melanie and Scarlett; and they are bending over a bed, from which that high-pitched, chanting voice is coming. Scarlett is busy with bandages. Melanie has a towel pinned around her head, like a coif.

THE VOICE *(gradually becoming more and more distinct)* —and there's a place back home where a wild plum tree comes to flower in the springtime . . . Down by the creek, you know.

MELANIE *(soothingly, like trying to quiet a fretful child in the night)* Yes, I know—I know—

CAMERA is now there and has stopped, very close, making a TWO SHOT of Melanie and Scarlett against the altar. Their shadows are enormous against the altar. They look at each other as the voice goes on. Melanie bites her lip, and then looks down again at the unseen man in the bed. Scarlett is watching Melanie's face curiously.

THE VOICE *(beginning to wander a little in delirium)* When we were little, my brother, Jeff, and I used to . . . I told you about my brother, Jeff, didn't I, ma'am? . . . I *know* I did. He . . . we don't know where Jeff is, now, ma'am. Since Bull Run, we haven't heard anything and . . .
(his voice breaks)

MELANIE Please . . . we *must* have your temperature now. Please do just take this in your mouth and not talk any more. Not just now.

She stoops, with the thermometer in her hand, and finally straightens up, looking again at Scarlett.

SCARLETT *(finishing ravelling the bandages)* Melanie—I'm so tired. I've *got* to go home. Aren't you tired, Melanie?

MELANIE *(smiling a little with anguish)* No . . . I'm not tired. This could be . . . Ashley. And only strangers here to comfort him. I'm not tired, Scarlett.

Tears come to Scarlett's eyes. Melanie turns and looks out, over all the beds, from which the night sounds are coming.

MELANIE They could all—be Ashley, Scarlett . . . And . . .

The two women look at each other for a moment. Then Melanie stoops again, followed by her shadow on the altar, and takes the thermometer from the mouth, now silent except for the breathing.

As she straightens up, holding the thermometer in both hands to read it, bowing her head a little to read it, CAMERA PANS UPWARD, and her shadow on the pulpit's face is like that of a saint, bowing its head over folded hands.

DISSOLVE TO:

158 EXT. HOSPITAL STEPS—NIGHT

LOW CAMERA SET UP, shooting up hospital steps at an angle. Two carriages at the curb in f.g. The horses facing away from CAMERA.

Melanie and Scarlett are coming down the hospital steps. Uncle Peter stands waiting beside Miss Pittypat's carriage. The other carriage standing at the curb is a handsome open vehicle. Suddenly, a loudly dressed woman steps out of it, her back to us. She runs up the steps to the two girls, the CAMERA MOVING in with her. As she gets near them Scarlett stops, horrified. Melanie stops a second or two later.

At the time the dialogue starts, we are in a CLOSE SHOT OF THE THREE, shooting over woman's shoulder at the two girls.

WOMAN *(Belle)* I've been sitting by this curb one solid hour waiting to speak to you, Miz Wilkes.

Uncle Peter enters on the run.

UNCLE PETER Go on, you trash, don't you be pesterin' these ladies!

SCARLETT *(sharply)* Don't talk to her, Melly.

MELANIE *(frightened, but seeing it through)* It's all right, Scarlett.
(to Belle)
Who are you?

BELLE My name's Belle Watling, but that doesn't matter.
(to Scarlett)
I expect *you* think I've got no business here.

MELANIE Hadn't you best tell me what you want to see me about?

BELLE First time I come here, I said, "Belle, you're a nurse." But the ladies didn't want my kind of nursing. Well, they was more than likely right. Then I tried giving them money. My money wasn't good enough

CONTINUED:

158 CONTINUED

for them either, old peahens! But I know a gentleman who says *you're* a human being. If you are, which they ain't, you'll take my money for the hospital.

Mrs. Meade emerges from the hospital, stops outraged.

MRS. MEADE What are you doing here? Haven't you been told twice already?

BELLE This time I'm conversing with Miz Wilkes.
(Mrs. Meade and Scarlett both gasp, but Belle turns back to Melanie)
You might as well take my money. It's good money, even if it is mine.
(hands the money wrapped in a handkerchief to Melanie)

MELANIE I'm sure you're very generous.

Uncle Peter and Scarlett are shocked. They look at one another in dismay.

BELLE No, I'm not. I'm a Confederate like everybody else, that's all.

MELANIE Of course, you are.

Involuntarily her hand goes out to touch Belle's arm. Belle is deeply moved, looks down at her arm, then up at Melanie.

BELLE There's some folks wouldn't feel that way. Maybe they're not as good Christians as you.
(a sharp look on this for Scarlett and Mrs. Meade)

She turns quickly and goes down the steps to the carriage from which she dismounted at the beginning of the scene. Mrs. Meade catches her breath, is about to explode, but Melanie has untied the handkerchief.

MELANIE Look, Mrs. Meade! It's a great deal of money! Ten. Twenty. Thirty. Fifty . . . And it isn't our paper money! It's gold!

Scarlett is suddenly aghast as over her shoulder we see a monogram on the handkerchief: "R.B."

SCARLETT Let me see that handkerchief!
(she takes it and looks in the corner)
"R.B."
(she looks up)

159 LARGE CLOSE UP—SCARLETT IN PROFILE IN F. G.

Belle driving off in Rhett's carriage in b.g.

SCARLETT And she's driving off in Rhett Butler's carriage! . . . Oh, if I just wasn't a lady, what wouldn't I tell that varmint!

She hurls the handkerchief to the ground as though it were a carrier of leprosy germs; and as the carriage bearing Belle disappears into the darkness, we

FADE OUT.

FADE IN:

TITLE: Panic hit the City with the first of Sherman's shells . . . Helpless and unarmed, the populace fled from the oncoming Juggernaut . . . And desperately the gallant remnants of an army marched out to face the foe . . .

160 LONG SHOT—ATLANTA STREET

Shells are bursting. Panicky crowds fleeing through the streets.

161 CLOSE SHOT—(LOW SET UP)

Artillery racing through scene, leaving a cloud of dust.

162 LONG SHOT—(SHOOTING FROM HIGH SET UP TOWARD HOSPITAL AND NATIONAL HOTEL)

The street filled with fleeing people, and foot soldiers are marching in opposite direction.

163 LONG SHOT—STREET (ANOTHER ANGLE)

CAMERA PANS with runaway wagon. A shell hits it.

164 LONG SHOT—LOWER END OF PEACHTREE STREET

CAMERA PANS with fire engine as it races through street.

165 LONG SHOT—STREET

Fleeing people afoot, carrying their belongings. Loaded wagons move down street in b.g., away from CAMERA. CAMERA DOLLIES IN AND OVER huge pile of debris as a shell bursts beyond it in the street.

166 INT. HOSPITAL IN CHURCH—CLOSE SHOT—STAINED GLASS WINDOW OF A RELIGIOUS TABLEAU—NIGHT—(JULY, 1864)

CONTINUED:

166 CONTINUED

A shell bursts outside, lighting up the sky. The reverberation shakes the window, cracks it, and a piece of glass with one of the religious figures on it falls out.

CAMERA PANS DOWN from the window, passing a minister who is reading over one of the beds.

MINISTER *(reading in f.g.)* The Lord is my Shepherd, I shall not want. He maketh me to lie down in green pastures. He leadeth me beside still waters. He restoreth my soul.
He leadeth me in the paths of righteousness for His Name's sake. Yea, though I walk through the valley of the shadow of death . . .

CAMERA IS NOW ON CLOSE SHOT of the bandaged soldier on the cot.

MINISTER'S VOICE I will fear no evil for Thou art with me; Thy rod and Thy staff, they comfort me.

167 PAN SHOT

—with Scarlett, Dr. Meade, and a Medical Corps Sergeant as they pass along the cots.

The sergeant is in full uniform with a bloodstained apron over him and his sleeves turned back from his wrists. Beds, almost touching each other, are crowded together—almost more than the church can hold. In them lie the wounded and dying, who scream out in terror, frightened by the continued explosions.

SCARLETT The Yankees! Oh, Dr. Meade! They're—they're getting closer!

DR. MEADE *(wearily, but very calm)* They'll never get into Atlanta. They'll never get through ol' Peg-Leg Hood.

CAMERA TRAVELS WITH DR. MEADE, SCARLETT, AND THE SERGEANT, as they walk through the wounded and dying men toward the nave of the church. Unkempt and staring men are tossing, moaning, and crying out. The place swarms with flies. Bandages and rags lie beside the beds. The room is lighted by smoking kerosene lamps. Only a few doctors and orderlies and women volunteer nurses are in attendance. Huge and grotesque shadows of the patients line the walls. As they pass, we pick up some of the background action and hear enroute the lines indicated below:

A man's voice is heard crying, ghastly, and ghostly:

SOLDIER *(crying out)* Gimme somethin' fo' the pain! Somethin' fo' the pain!

Dr. Meade calls back to the man, who is obviously in agony—his neck bandaged with bloodstained cloths as if he has been shot through the throat.

DR. MEADE Sorry, son. We haven't got anything to give you.

They continue on and pass a soldier with bandaged and bound arms, scratching his back against a pillar, like an animal.

SOLDIER These animules are driving me crazy.

A grave-faced, bearded man, reading quietly from a prayer book, is undisturbed by two battered veterans sitting up in the next beds playing seven up.

CARD PLAYERS What luck, you've got my jack!
Give me an ace, and I'll start another war!
I'll bid the Moon!

A young soldier dictating a letter to a woman who sits beside him writing on a block of paper with a lead pencil, her work lit by a kerosene lamp around which moths are fluttering. With one hand she brushes them away from the soldier. As Dr. Meade, Scarlett, and sergeant pass, we hear some of the soldier's words:

DYING SOLDIER —that I will never see you nor Pa again—

Scarlett, Dr. Meade, and the sergeant have reached the nave of the church. CAMERA STOPS BEHIND A FOREGROUND PIECE of a pulpit which hides the wounded man. We see only the heads and shoulders of Dr. Meade, Scarlett, and the sergeant as Dr. Meade bends over to make his examination.

DR. MEADE *(to the wounded man, looking up)* This leg's got to come off, soldier.

Scarlett, horrified, steps a little aside.

SOLDIER'S VOICE *(terrorized)* No . . . no . . . Lemme alone!

DR. MEADE I'm sorry, soldier.

CONTINUED:

167 CONTINUED

SERGEANT *(frightened)* We're all run out o' chloroform, Dr. Meade.

DR. MEADE Then we'll have to operate without it.

168 CLOSE UP—SCARLETT

Reacting in disgust and horror.

SOLDIER'S VOICE *(moaning)* No. No. Lemme alone. You can't do it! I won't let you do it to me!

169 DR. MEADE AND SERGEANT

DR. MEADE Tell Dr. Wilson to take this leg off immediately. It's gangrene.

SOLDIER'S VOICE No, no, don't.

DR. MEADE *(wearily passes his hand over his forehead)* I haven't seen my family in three days. I'm going home for half an hour.

As the sergeant steps forward to lift the soldier from the bed, Dr. Meade turns out of scene.

SERGEANT *(calls off)* Orderly! Give me a lift!

170 TRUCKING SHOT WITH DR. MEADE

—nearer the other end of the room, on his way out. His attention is attracted by the attitude of a patient in a bed. He steps over, lifts the eyelids of the unconscious man. He is dead.

DR. MEADE Nurse, you can free this bed.

He goes out.

171 BACK TO SCARLETT

As she hurries between cots, carrying a water bowl, she hears a voice.

FRANK KENNEDY'S VOICE Miss Scarlett!

She looks around and recognizes Frank Kennedy, a bandage around his face. We see clearly that his face is lined and his hair and beard, such as we see of it, have thin streaks of grey. The war has taken a terrible toll from him.

SCARLETT *(recognizing him)* Why—Frank Kennedy—!

FRANK KENNEDY Miss Suellen—is she well?

SCARLETT When did they bring you in, Frank? Are you all right? Are you bad hurt?

FRANK KENNEDY But Miss Suellen—is she—is she . . .

SCARLETT Oh, she's all right.

The sergeant comes into the scene.

SERGEANT *(to Scarlett)* Dr. Wilson needs you in the operating room, Mrs. Hamilton. He's going to take off that leg. Better hurry . . .

Scarlett turns away, calling back to Frank:

SCARLETT I'll be back.

She goes to the door outside the small adjacent room which is used as the operating room.

As she comes to the door she hears piercing cries from inside.

172 INT. OPERATING ROOM (FROM SCARLETT'S ANGLE)

The operation is in progress, but we see it only in tremendous shadows on the wall; the doctor with scalpel in hand and the screaming patient.

SOLDIER'S VOICE *(howling)* No! . . . No . . . Lemme alone! No! No . . . I can't stand it! No, no!

173 CLOSE SHOT—SCARLETT

She hesitates an instant, stands in the doorway looking. The agonized cries of the man sweep over her. She stands frozen with the horror of the picture.

MAN'S VOICE Don't cut. Don't cut. Don't! . . . Don't! . . . Please . . .

Scarlett turns and begins to run. Another explosion reverberates. The sergeant appears again, running after her:

DR. WILSON Where's the nurse?

SERGEANT Mrs. Hamilton! Dr. Wilson's waiting!

SCARLETT *(grimly—and with terror and disgust edging her voice)* Let him wait. I'm going home. I've done enough. I don't want any more men dying and screaming. I don't want any more.
(she runs out)

174 EXT. CHURCH HOSPITAL STEPS—NIGHT

As Scarlett comes out the door, a scene of violence strikes her.

175 EXT. STREET (FROM SCARLETT'S ANGLE)

The streets are blocked with carriages all moving in one direction. The carriages are full of women and children and darkies driving. Trunks piled in the carriages and belongings bundled inside sheets. Shells burst in the air in the distance. Another shell bursts on the ground in the street. It tears a great hole out of the street and crumples a lamppost. A horse stampedes down the street, berserk, dragging a riderless wagon behind it. The street becomes more crowded with old men on foot carrying trunks and staggering forward. There are children dragging barking dogs and clinging to their mothers' skirts. A city is evacuating. The street is filled with shouting, terrified people.

A fire engine goes clanging down the street, manned by men in red shirts.

Also moving in the opposite direction of the mob, pass bedraggled, weary files of Confederate soldiers forcing their way through the group toward the entrenchments and breastwork at the edge of the city. One huge man carries the rifles of three or four others who are too weary to bear their own weapons. Above the noise we hear women shrieking.

VOICES The Yankees!
The Yankees are coming!
The Yankees are coming!

176 BACK TO SCARLETT

She stands watching this panic for a moment. Then, CAMERA WITH HER, she runs quickly down the steps and in the direction opposite to the one taken by the sprawling, sweeping mass of humans fleeing the city.

Suddenly, above the din we hear the voices of darkies singing. They are singing a hymn, "Go Down Moses."

Scarlett keeps running. She stops. Out of a converging street she sees a troop of Negroes come marching. They are singing. Leading them are several white men in uniform. She stops and stares. The Negroes carry shovels and pickaxes on their shoulders. In the front rank of the Negroes is Big Sam and others she knows.

SCARLETT *(crying out)* Big Sam! Big Sam!

177 CLOSE SHOT—BIG SAM AND OTHERS IN THE LEAD

He stops as he sees Scarlett, turns to his companions.

BIG SAM Almighty Moses! It's Miss Scarlett!

SCARLETT *(calling again)* Big Sam! Big Sam!
(coming up to them and holding out her hand—Big Sam takes it)
Sam . . . 'Lige . . . 'Postle . . . Prophet.
(she shakes hands with the grinning blacks)
Oh, I'm so glad to see you. Tell me—about Tara—about my mother. She didn't write me.

SAM She's gone and got sick, Miss Scarlett.

SCARLETT Sick!

SAM Just a lil' bit sick, dat's all, Miss Scarlett. Your Pa—he jus' wild when dey wouldn't let him fight on account o' his broken knee—and he had fits when dey took all us feel' han's to dig ditches fo' de white sojers to hide in. But yo' ma says de Confedrutzy needs us. So we's goin' to dig—fo' the South.

SCARLETT *(agonized)* Sam, was there a doctor?

MOUNTED OFFICER *(riding in)* Sorry, ma'am, we've got to march.

SAM *(grinning)* Good-bye, Miss Scarlett. Don't worry—we'll stop dem Yankees.

They start off to catch up with the others.

BIG SAM Good-bye, Miss Scarlett.

SCARLETT Good-bye, Sam. Good-bye, boys.
(stops a minute, calls after them)
If any of you get sick or hurt, let me know.

BIG SAM AND OTHERS Good-bye, Miss Scarlett.

SCARLETT Good-bye.

She watches as the blacks march on. Shells burst in the air again. Scarlett stands a moment. She is stunned by the news from home and by the panic around her. Then she runs distractedly down the street.

178 RHETT IN HIS CARRIAGE

He is riding with the rout out of Atlanta. He passes Scarlett and sees her. He reins in his horses violently and starts turning them around. With

CONTINUED:

178 CONTINUED

difficulty he turns out of the dishevelled exodus parade. He starts back and overtakes Scarlett. He calls to her from the carriage:

RHETT Scarlett! Scarlett!
(Scarlett sees him. Runs to him with inarticulate cries of relief)
Whoa! Climb into this buggy! This is no day for walking. You'll get run over!
(without any ceremony and with only his left arm because his right is holding the restive horses, he drags her up onto the seat beside him.)

179 TWO SHOT IN CARRIAGE

SCARLETT *(barely able to stammer)* Oh, Rhett, Rhett. I've got to get out of here. Drive me to Aunt Pitty's, *please!*

RHETT Panic's a pretty sight, isn't it?

A shell explodes over a nearby street and a muffled roar goes up from the refugees fleeing. Scarlett is shaken out of her weariness. Rhett looks in the direction of the explosion and grins.

RHETT Whoa! Whoa! That's just another of General Sherman's calling cards. He'll be paying us a visit soon.

SCARLETT *(with renewed fright)* I've got to get out of here—I've got to get out before the Yankees come!

RHETT And leave your work at the hospital? Or have you had enough of death and lice and men chopped up?
(Scarlett glares at him)
Well, I suppose you weren't meant for sick men, Scarlett.

SCARLETT Don't talk to me like that, Rhett! I'm so scared! . . . I wish I'd get out of here!

RHETT Let's get out of here together. No use staying here and letting the South come down around your ears. There are too many nice places to go and visit . . . Mexico . . . London . . . Paris . . .
(he speaks slowly and makes each place sound like the most glamorous haven)

SCARLETT With you?

RHETT Yes, ma'am. With a man who understands you and admires you —for just what you are—
(not even deigning to look at her)

I figure we belong together—being the same sort.
(quietly but deliberately)
And I've been waiting for you to grow up, and get the sad-eyed Ashley Wilkes out of your heart. Well, I hear Mrs. Wilkes is going to have a baby in another month or so.
(with mock sympathy)
It's going to be hard—loving a man with a wife and a baby clinging to him.

Scarlett steals an angry look at him.

180 STREET—(FROM THEIR ANGLE)

A rush of traffic passes them, carriages loaded with trunks and Negroes whipping the horses.

181 TWO SHOT—RHETT AND SCARLETT IN CARRIAGE

He reins in the horses. They are near the front of Aunt Pittypat's house. Scarlett is in a rage, unable to answer or even look at him.

RHETT Whoa! Well, here we are. Are you going with me—or are you getting out?

SCARLETT *(turning to him, speaking viciously)* I hate and despise you, Rhett Butler! And I'll hate and despise you until I die!

She turns and leaps from the carriage. Her skirt catches on the wheel. Rhett leans over to release it.

RHETT *(looking at her—smiles)* Oh, no you won't, Scarlett. Not that long.

She runs off in a huff. Rhett looks after her a moment, laughs and drives off.

182 EXT. FRONT OF AUNT PITTYPAT'S HOUSE

As Scarlett runs in. A carriage stands at the curb. Uncle Peter is toting a trunk down the house steps. Prissy is beside him, helping balance the trunk on his back. Aunt Pittypat is also helping balance it by delicately holding one of its corners. Prissy spies Scarlett coming toward them. She rushes down the steps.

PRISSY *(excitedly)* Miss Scarlett . . . Miss Scarlett! Folkses is all goin' to Macon! And folkses is runnin' away and runnin' away!

CONTINUED:

182 CONTINUED

AUNT PITTYPAT *(coming down steps quickly)* I can't bear it! Those cannonballs right in my ears! I'll faint every time I hear one.
EXPLOSION

Aunt Pittypat closes her eyes and rocks—opens them and looks at Uncle Peter.

AUNT PITTYPAT Uncle Peter—look out for that trunk!

SCARLETT *(incredulously)* But, Aunt Pitty, you aren't leaving?

AUNT PITTYPAT I may be a coward, but—but—oh, dear, Yankees in Georgia! How did they ever get in?

SCARLETT *(with grim and sudden determination)* Oh, I'm going, too.
(screams)
Prissy, go pack my things! Get them, quick!
(she starts to run for the house)

PRISSY Yassum, we'se goin'—
(darts off)

SCARLETT Wait, Aunt Pitty, I won't take a minute.

AUNT PITTYPAT *(calling to Scarlett)* Oh, Scarlett, do you really think you ought to?

Dr. Meade appears in the scene, presumably coming from his house across the street.

DR. MEADE *(calling)* Scarlett! What is this?
(comes up to her)
You ain't planning on running away?

SCARLETT *(turning on him wildly, with mounting hysteria)* And don't you dare try to stop me. I'm never going back to that hospital! I've had enough of smelling death—and rot—and *death!* I'm going home—I want my mother! My mother needs me!

DR. MEADE *(sharply)* You've *got* to listen to me. You must stay here!

AUNT PITTYPAT Without a chaperone, Dr. Meade? It simply isn't done.

DR. MEADE Good Heavens, woman, this is a war—not a garden party.

AUNT PITTYPAT Oh.
(she exits scene)

DR. MEADE *(turns back to Scarlett)* Scarlett, you've got to stay. Melanie needs you.

SCARLETT *(wearily, her hysteria subsiding)* Oh, bother Melanie.

DR. MEADE She's ill already. She shouldn't even be having a baby—she may have a difficult time.

SCARLETT Well, can't we—can't we take her along?

DR. MEADE Would you want her to take that chance? Would you want her to be jounced over rough roads and have the baby ahead of time—in a buggy?

SCARLETT *(wildly)* It isn't my baby . . . You take care of her!

She runs toward the house. Dr. Meade starts after her.

183 TWO SHOT—DR. MEADE AND SCARLETT

Dr. Meade grabs Scarlett by the wrists, turns her around.

DR. MEADE Scarlett, we haven't enough doctors, much less nurses, to look after a sick woman. *You've* got to stay for Melanie.

SCARLETT What for! I don't know anything about babies being born.

PRISSY *(running into scene; jubilantly and idiotically)* Ah knows. Ah knows. Ah knows how to do it. Ah's done it lots and lots. Let me, Doctor. Let me—Ah can do everythin'.

DR. MEADE Good. Then I'll rely on you to help us.

PRISSY Yes, Doctor.
(she exits)

DR. MEADE *(turns back to Scarlett, speaking to her more tenderly and reasoningly)* Ashley's fighting in the field—fighting for the Cause. He may never come back; he may die, Scarlett . . . We owe him a well-born child.

Scarlett's expression has changed slowly at the mention of Ashley's name.

SCARLETT *(dully)* Ashley . . .

AUNT PITTYPAT'S VOICE If you're coming, Scarlett—hurry!

SCARLETT *(disregarding Pitty's call and talking almost to herself)* I promised Ashley . . . something . . .

CONTINUED:

183 CONTINUED

DR. MEADE Then you'll stay?
(Scarlett doesn't answer)
Good.
(turns, calls to Aunt Pitty as he starts to walk out of scene)
Go along, Miss Pittypat. Scarlett's staying.

Scarlett doesn't move, as Dr. Meade hurries out.

184 CLOSE SHOT—AUNT PITTYPAT IN CARRIAGE

AUNT PITTYPAT Go on, Uncle Peter. Oh, dear, I don't know what to do. It's like the end of the world.
(she starts weeping as the buggy leaves)
Uncle Peter, my smelling salts!

185 FULL SHOT—SCARLETT

Taken from the end of the path as she stands on the verandah (where we have last left her) watching the carriage leave.

She takes a few steps down into the path and stands in desperation and panic, looking around helplessly, not knowing what to do. Suddenly she remembers who is responsible for all her trouble. She turns her head slowly and looks up at the window of Melanie's room, hatred coming into her face.

SCARLETT *(hissing the words with hatred)* Melanie! . . . Melanie!
(she raises her fist in hatred; muttering slowly but speaking with increased violence, volume and anger as the speech reaches its climax)
It's all your fault! . . . I hate you! . . . I hate you and I hate your baby! If only I hadn't promised Ashley . . . If *only* I hadn't promised him . . .

After holding her look of hatred a moment, there is the sound of an explosion nearby. Scarlett reacts in terror and on her distorted, terrified face, we

FADE OUT.

FADE IN:

TITLE: SIEGE
The skies rained Death . . .

For thirty-five days a battered Atlanta hung grimly on, hoping for a miracle . . .

Then there fell a silence . . . more terrifying than the pounding of the cannon . . .

FADE OUT.

186 FADE IN:
EXTREME LONG SHOT—PEACHTREE STREET

From high angle, shooting down deserted Peachtree Street toward town.

In the distance the dust is being stirred up by a galloping horseman—a Confederate officer—WE HOLD ON HIM as he gallops toward the CAMERA—and as he reaches Aunt Pittypat's house in f.g., we hear Scarlett's voice screaming:

SCARLETT'S VOICE Stop! Stop!

Scarlett runs out of Pittypat's house toward the street.

187 MEDIUM LONG SHOT

As Scarlett runs screaming to the middle of the street.

SCARLETT *(screaming)* Stop! Please stop!

The horseman draws in his horse, so suddenly that the horse rears.

188 CLOSE TWO SHOT—SCARLETT AND RIDER

Scarlett looks up at him fearfully.

SCARLETT Is it true? Are the Yankees coming?

CAPTAIN I'm afraid so, ma'am. The army's pulling out.

SCARLETT *(terrified as the import of the news strikes her)* Pulling out of Atlanta?
(incredulously)
Leaving us to the Yankees?

CAPTAIN *(correcting her)* Not leaving, ma'am—*evacuating*. . . . We've got to, before Sherman cuts the McDonough Road to the South and catches the lot of us.

SCARLETT *(frantic)* Oh, it can't be true! It can't be true! What'll I do?

CAPTAIN Better refugee South—right quick, ma'am . . .
(he touches his kepi and spurs his horse)
If you'll excuse me, ma'am.

CONTINUED:

188 CONTINUED

He is off. Scarlett stands terrified for just a moment and then turns and runs frantically into the house, screaming.

SCARLETT *(screaming)* Prissy! Prissy!

CAMERA PANS WITH HER as she goes.

189 INT. AUNT PITTYPAT'S HOUSE—HALLWAY—SHOOTING OVER SCARLETT'S SHOULDER, and FOLLOWING HER IN —EARLY MORNING

Scarlett bursts into the hallway, calling frantically:

SCARLETT Prissy! Come here! Prissy!

Prissy ambles slowly out of a door into the hall.

SCARLETT Go pack my things, and Miss Melanie's, too. We're going to Tara right away. The Yankees are coming.
(she starts running up the stairs)

Prissy starts up the stairs after Scarlett.

MELANIE'S VOICE Scarlett! Scarlett!

190 SECOND-FLOOR HALLWAY—MELANIE'S OPEN BEDROOM DOOR IN F.G., HEAD OF STAIRS IN B.G.

As Scarlett reaches the head of the stairs. CAMERA SWINGS WITH SCARLETT as she goes through the open door into Melanie's bedroom, talking excitedly as she goes.

SCARLETT Oh, Melly, we're going to—
(she stops suddenly and looks at Melanie)
Melly!

On Melanie's face is a mixture of ecstasy and pain—her brow covered with perspiration. She looks at Scarlett sorrowfully a moment, then speaks:

MELANIE *(speaking with difficulty)* I'm sorry to be such a bother, Scarlett—

Scarlett is dismayed as she realizes all chance of their escape is cut off.

MELANIE'S VOICE —It began at daybreak.

SCARLETT *(horrified)* But—but the—the Yankees are coming!

CAMERA MOVES WITH SCARLETT as she moves in to Melanie.

MELANIE *(tears in her eyes—moves her head away slightly)* Poor Scarlett. You'd be at Tara now with your mother, wouldn't you, if it weren't for me?

Scarlett doesn't deny it, and by her attitude clearly affirms it. Melanie continues, turning her head back to Scarlett.

MELANIE Oh, Scarlett darling, you've been so good to me. No sister could have been sweeter.

Scarlett still doesn't speak; avoids Melanie's gaze.

MELANIE I've been lying here thinking . . . If I should die, will you take my baby?

SCARLETT *(annoyed)* Oh, fiddle-dee-dee, Melly. Aren't things bad enough without you talking about dying? I'll send for Dr. Meade right now.

MELANIE *(putting her hand out weakly in a gesture of protest)* Not yet, Scarlett. I couldn't let Dr. Meade sit here for hours—while—while—those—poor—wounded—boys . . .

Scarlett looks at Melanie—her eyes widening in panic.

SCARLETT *(under her breath)* Melly!
(then turns and calls frantically)
Prissy! Prissy!
(she starts to run for door)
Prissy!

191 INT. SECOND-FLOOR HALLWAY

SCARLETT *(runs from Melanie's room)* Come here quick!

CAMERA PANS with her as she goes to her bedroom door and opens it.

SCARLETT Prissy—

PRISSY Yas'm?

SCARLETT *(urgently)* Go get Dr. Meade—run quick!

PRISSY Yas'm.
(then her eyes widen in panic as she slowly realizes her midwife moment is at hand)
The baby!

SCARLETT Well, don't stand there like a scared goat—Run!

Prissy still stands paralyzed with fright.

SCARLETT Hurry! Hurry! I'll sell you South, I will. I swear I will! I'll sell you South!

Prissy hurries on down stairs.

DISSOLVE TO:

192 INT. MELANIE'S BEDROOM—CLOSE TWO SHOT—SCARLETT AND MELANIE—HOT NOON

Scarlett stands beside Melanie, holding her hand tightly and fanning her.

SCARLETT Where's that Prissy?
(CAMERA PANS WITH HER as she walks to the window)
Oh, this room's like an oven already and it isn't noon yet.
(she looks out the window, then turns back)
Oh, don't worry, Melly. Mother says it always seems like the doctor'll never come. If I don't take a strap to that Prissy . . .
(she sits wearily in a chair)
Oh, oh, Melly!
(she wrings a cloth out in water, keeping up a running flow of conversation to try to distract Melanie)
You know what I heard about Maybelle Merriwether? You remember that funny-looking beau of hers?
(crossing to Melanie with the wet cloth)
The one with a uniform like ladies' red flannel underdrawers?

MELANIE You don't have to keep on talking for my sake, Scarlett. I know how worried you are.

Scarlett looks up suddenly, hearing Prissy's voice from outside. She goes to the window and looks out.

193 EXT. STREET IN FRONT OF AUNT PITTYPAT'S HOUSE—HOT NOON—(FROM SCARLETT'S ANGLE)

Prissy is ambling along the street coming from the direction of the town, switching her skirts from side to side and looking over her shoulder to observe the effect.

194 INT. MELANIE'S ROOM

Scarlett, dismayed at having seen Prissy returning alone, without Dr. Meade, turns from the window, trying to cover up in front of Melanie.

SCARLETT Oh, Melly, I—I'll just go and fetch you some cooler water. *(picks up the water pitcher and leaves the room)*

195 INT. HALLWAY AND STAIRS

Prissy is mounting the stairs at a leisurely pace.

SCARLETT'S VOICE You're as slow as molasses in January.
(she enters scene)
Where's Dr. Meade?

PRISSY Ah ain' nebber seed him, Miss Scarlett.

SCARLETT What!

PRISSY No'm, he ain' at de horsepittle. A man, he tole me dat de doctah down at de car shed wid the wounded sojers.

SCARLETT Well, why didn't you go after him?

PRISSY Miss Scarlett—Ah wuz sceered ter go down dere ter de car shed —dey's folkses dyin' down dere an' Ah's sceered of daid folkses—

Scarlett glares at Prissy in a rage, controls herself, and makes a decision.

SCARLETT *(with fury in her tone)* Oh, you go sit by Miss Melly. And don't you be upsetting her or I'll whip the hide off you!

She is down the stairs almost on the words. CAMERA FOLLOWING HER. Scarlett snatches up her hat and is out the door.

196 MEDIUM CLOSE SHOT—PRISSY

Singing as she slowly mounts the stairs.

PRISSY "Jus' a few mo' days fer to tote de weary load—"

DISSOLVE TO:

197 EXT. STREET AT INTERSECTION PEACHTREE AND DECATUR—CAMERA TRUCKING WITH SCARLETT

The atmosphere of the whole is of terrific heat and sweat.

CAMERA IS SET UP to shoot over a pile of fallen timbers and other

CONTINUED:

197 CONTINUED

debris of the siege which blocks the left-hand side of the road. Scarlett comes toward CAMERA, sees the obstruction, climbs over it or goes around it.

198 EXT. PEACHTREE STREET BELOW DECATUR

The street is lined with horse- and mule-driven ambulances and men work quickly but silently, carrying the wounded on stretchers along the sidewalks and loading them into the lines of ambulances and carts. We see Scarlett coming down the street. As she nears the depot there is a growing sound of overwhelming pain, a composite tone of anguish; cries, moans, shrieks, and terrified curses.

199 EXT. PEACHTREE STREET—CLOSE MOVING SHOT—CAMERA SHOOTING TOWARD SCARLETT AS SHE WALKS—TRUCKING AHEAD OF HER

We see her puzzlement at the ever-increasing noise. Her steps become slower and slower and a worried frown creases her brow.

200 EXT. END OF PEACHTREE STREET

CAMERA SHOOTING toward rear of two ambulances parked almost wheel to wheel. Through this gap comes Scarlett into close f.g., and stops, aghast. The noise we have heard has reached its height. We FOLLOW her into:

201 PLAZA AND DEPOT—BIG PULL-BACK SHOT—(BOOM)

—in which the CAMERA, DRAWING FARTHER AND FARTHER BACK AND UPWARDS reveals the vast expanse of the railway yard close to the depot—completely covered with the bodies of wounded Confederates lying under the hot sun.

THE CAMERA STOPS on the Confederate flag, hanging limply from the top of the flagpole. Only a handful of male orderlies and women attendants move amongst the wounded, some of whom lie stiff and still—others writhing under the hot sun, moaning and crying out. Everywhere swarms of flies and thin puffs of dust blow over the men.

202 TRUCKING SHOT—CAMERA PULLING BACK BEFORE SCARLETT

Fighting her own desire to flee, to get away from this appalling scene, she forces herself to start through the rows of wounded to look for Dr.

Meade. The men are of all ages—some are boys not more than 15 or 16 years old. Others, old men in their 60s and 70s. Flies creep contentedly and undisturbed over bloodstained faces. Everywhere the men are crying for water in a steady, low moan of voices.

WOUNDED MEN *(as Scarlett passes)* Lady—water!
Please, lady, water!
Water!
Please . . .

Scarlett changes her course a little to reach an orderly who is binding a tourniquet about a soldier's arm.

SCARLETT Where's Dr. Meade?

WE CONTINUE TRUCKING AHEAD OF HER as she moves through the wounded toward the railway shed, looking around for some sign of Dr. Meade.

CAMERA MOVES to LONG SHOT of Scarlett in square.

SCARLETT Have you seen Dr. Meade?

STRETCHER-BEARER One side, lady, please.

The wounded on the ground clutch at Scarlett's passing skirts.

AD LIB VOICES Where's the doctor?
Water! Water!
Fetch me some water.
Water! Water!
Please . . .
Won't somebody fetch me a drink?
Help! Help! Can't you do something, lady?

SCARLETT *(as she moves through the square)* Dr. Meade! Have you seen Dr. Meade?

THE CAMERA STOPS on a torn Confederate flag flying above the vast field of wounded.

203 INT. RAILWAY SHED

Here, too, are wounded. Bright bars of sunlight come from a row of skylights overhead. Scarlett appears, stepping through wounded.

204 GROUP SHOT—DR. MEADE AND WOUNDED MAN

CONTINUED:

204 CONTINUED

Coat off, sleeves rolled to the elbow, his face dripping with perspiration, the doctor is working over the man's leg.

SCARLETT *(moving toward him)* Dr. Meade! At last!

DR. MEADE Oh, thank heaven you're here. I need every pair of hands.

She stares at him bewildered, dropping her skirts. They fall over the face of a wounded man who feebly tries to turn his head to escape their smothering folds.

DR. MEADE Well, come, child. Wake up! We've got work to do.

SCARLETT But Melly's havin' her baby. You've got to come with me.

DR. MEADE Are you crazy? I can't leave these men for a baby! They're dying—hundreds of them. Get some woman to help you.

SCARLETT But there isn't anybody. And oh, Dr. Meade, she might die.

DR. MEADE Die? Look at *them,* bleeding to death in front of my eyes! No chloroform—no bandages—nothing! Nothing to even ease their pain. Now run along and don't bother me.
(pats her on the shoulder)
Oh, don't worry, child. There's nothing to bringing a baby.
(he turns away, Scarlett immediately forgotten; to orderly)
Now bring the stretchers in here—
(to someone else)
Yeah, I'm coming.

Dr. Meade exits. Scarlett stands a moment, bewildered, not knowing who else to turn to; then her face sets with determination, and she exits back the way she came.

DISSOLVE TO:

205 INT. AUNT PITTYPAT'S HALLWAY AND STAIRS

Prissy comes down the stairs to meet Scarlett.

PRISSY Is de doctah come?

SCARLETT No. He can't come.

PRISSY *(terrified)* Oh, Miss Scarlett! Miss Melly bad off!

SCARLETT He can't come. There's nobody to come. Prissy, you've got to manage without the doctor. I'll help you.

Prissy's mouth falls open.

PRISSY Oh, lawsy, Miss Scarlett!

SCARLETT *(snaps)* Well, what is it?

PRISSY *(backing away)* Lawsy, we'se got ter have a doctah! Ah doan know nuthin' 'bout birthin' babies!

All the breath goes out of Scarlett's lungs in a gasp of horror. Prissy makes a lunge past her, but Scarlett grabs her.

SCARLETT *(with growing rage)* What do you mean?

PRISSY I don' know!

SCARLETT You told me you knew everything about it!

PRISSY Ah don' know huccome Ah tell sech a lie! Maw ain't never let me roun' when folkses wuz havin' dem.

Scarlett loses her temper completely and slaps the black face with all the force of her tired arm. Prissy screams, Scarlett stops, looks up the stairs, starts to drag Prissy across landing.

PRISSY *(crying)* Oh, Miss Scarlett!

SCARLETT *(with tremendous power—coldly clipping out quick orders like a general)* Stop it! Go light a fire in the stove and keep boiling water in the kettle. Get me a ball of twine—and all the clean towels you can find and—the scissors. Don't come telling me you can't find them.
(Scarlett pushes Prissy)
Go get them and get them quick!

Prissy now is really frightened, starts running down stairs.

PRISSY Yas'm.

MELANIE'S VOICE Scarlett! Scarlett!

SCARLETT *(without fear—with determination—almost with nobility—the great things in her character showing themselves at last)* Coming, Melly. Coming.

On the shot of Scarlett going determinedly up the stairs

DISSOLVE TO:

206 INT. MELANIE'S BEDROOM—MELANIE IN BED—SHADOW EFFECT

Scarlett comes into scene to her.

MELANIE Oh, Scarlett, you'd better go before the Yankees get here.

SCARLETT I'm not afraid. You know I won't leave you.

MELANIE It's no use. I'm going to die.

SCARLETT *(firmly and authoritatively)* Don't be a goose. Hold on to me! Hold on to me!

Throughout scene Scarlett's voice and attitude are those of such confidence and assurance as to try to dismiss Melanie's fears.

207 CLOSE SHOT—MELANIE—SHADOW EFFECT

MELANIE Talk to me, Scarlett! Please! Talk to me! Keep on talking to me!

208 ANOTHER SHADOW EFFECT—MELANIE AND SCARLETT —(PRISSY IN B.G.)

SCARLETT Don't try to be brave, Melly. Yell all you want to. There's nobody to hear.

209 BIG HEAD CLOSE UP—PRISSY

PRISSY Maw says effen you put a knife under de bed it cut de pain in two.

DISSOLVE TO:

210 EXT. RED HORSE SALOON—DECATUR STREET—NIGHT

Prissy is peering in through the swinging doors, calling:

PRISSY Capt'n Butler! Capt'n Butler!

BARTENDER *(turns and peers over swinging door at her)* Who do you want?

PRISSY *(quaking)* Capt'n Butler.

BARTENDER He's upstairs. Belle Watling's giving a party.
(he turns away)

PRISSY Yassuh. Thank you.

Prissy, nervous, not knowing what to do, makes up her mind, retreats a few steps, looks up at the lighted windows above the saloon and calls:

PRISSY Capt'n Butler! Oh, Capt'n Butler!

The window opens, and Belle sticks out her handsome and gaudily bedizened head.

BELLE What's all the rumpus about?

Prissy stands speechless and awed at the sight of this famed heroine. She finally finds her tongue.

PRISSY Ah's got a message for Capt'n Butler, Miz' Watling.

Rhett appears in the window beside Belle—three other buxom ladies in flamboyant evening dress behind him.

PRISSY Capt'n Butler, you come out hyah in de street ter me!

RHETT What is it, Prissy?

PRISSY Miss Scarlett, she done sent me fer you! Miss Melly . . .

He remembers.

PRISSY She done have her baby today!
(proudly)
A fine baby boy an' Miss Scarlett an' me, we brung it!

RHETT *(astounded)* Do you mean to tell me that Scarlett—

PRISSY *(with lowered eyes and swinging on her toes modestly)* Well, it was mostly me, Capt'n Butler, only Miss Scarlett she helped me a little. An' Ah don' expec' no doctah could have done no better! Only Miss Melly, she feelin' kind o' po'rly now it's all over!

RHETT Yes, I can believe that!

The girls in the window laugh.

PRISSY An' de Yankees is comin' an' Miss Scarlett, she said—

There is the crash of an explosion from outside the city.

PRISSY *(trembling with fright)* Oh, Capt'n Butler, de Yankees is hyah! . . . Please come an' bring yo' cah'rige fo' us right away!

CONTINUED:

210 CONTINUED

RHETT I'm sorry, Prissy—but the army took my horse and carriage. You better come upstairs and I'll see what I can do.

PRISSY Oh, no, Capt'n Butler! Mah Maw'd wear me out wid a corn stalk effen Ah was to go into Mrs. Watlin's.

RHETT *(laughs and turns back into the room)* Any of you beauties know where I can steal a horse—for a good cause?

DISSOLVE TO:

211 EXT. AUNT PITTYPAT'S—NIGHT

ANGLE shooting down street toward town. Before we see anything we hear the clop-clop-clop of the horse. Then out of the darkness appears a sad-looking horse and cart, Rhett driving it. Prissy sits in the seat with Rhett. The effect is almost that of a delivery wagon casually drawing up to a suburban home on a summer's night.

RHETT Whoa, Marse Robert!

212 HORSE AND WAGON—WIDER ANGLE—SHOOTING TOWARD TOWN

Another distant explosion and sparks shoot high into the sky above the housetops in b.g. Prissy crawls out of the back of the cart.

SCARLETT'S VOICE Rhett? Is that you, Rhett?

PRISSY We'se here, Miss Scarlett! We'se here!

Scarlett runs into scene to meet Rhett. Scarlett's face is drawn, her hair unkempt.

The scene throughout is punctuated by sounds of exploding ammunition, in sharp contrast to Rhett's easy and casual attitude.

SCARLETT Oh, Rhett, I knew you'd come!

She pushes Prissy toward the house. Prissy runs on inside.

RHETT Good evening. Nice weather we're having. Prissy tells me you're planning on taking a trip.

SCARLETT If you make any jokes now, I'll kill you!

RHETT *(mockingly)* Don't tell me you're frightened!

SCARLETT I'm scared to death. If you had the sense of a goat, you'd be scared, too.

Rhett meanwhile has tied the horse to the hitching post in front of the house. There is a terrific explosion and Scarlett turns in terror.

SCARLETT *(terrified)* Oh, the Yankees!

RHETT *(laughing)* No, no. Not yet! That's what's left of our army, blowing up the ammunition so the Yankees won't get it.

SCARLETT *(terrified)* Oh, we've got to get out of here!

She grabs Rhett by the arm and almost pulls him to the house.

RHETT At your service, Madam. Just where were you figuring on going?

SCARLETT Home—to Tara!

They stop in doorway.

RHETT Tara? Don't you know that they've been fighting all day around Tara? Do you think you can parade right through the Yankee army with a sick woman, a baby, and a simple-minded darky?
(satirically, with a new suspicion)
Or do you intend leaving them behind?

SCARLETT They're going with me, and I'm going home! And you can't stop me!

RHETT You little fool—don't you know it's dangerous jouncing Mrs. Wilkes over miles of open country?

SCARLETT I want my mother! I want to go home to Tara!

RHETT Tara's probably been burned to the ground. The woods are full of stragglers from both armies. The least they'll do is take the horse away from you. And even though it isn't much of an animal, I did have a lot of trouble stealing it.

SCARLETT *(hysterically)* I'm going home if I have to walk every step of the way! I'll kill you if you try to stop me! I will! I will! I will! I will!

She bursts into hysterical tears and starts beating Rhett's chest with her fists. Rhett for the first time reveals his true feelings. Soothingly and comfortingly he puts his arms around Scarlett.

RHETT Sh! Sh! Sh! All right. All right. Now you shall go home. I guess

CONTINUED:

212 CONTINUED

anybody who did what you've done today can take care of Sherman. Stop crying—
(as she quiets, he takes out his handkerchief)
Now blow your nose like a good little girl.

He helps her blow her nose. They go out of scene into the house.

213 INT. LIVING ROOM—AUNT PITTYPAT'S HOUSE

Scarlett's open trunk stands in the middle of the room; and Prissy, dashing about in a frenzy of fear and ineptitude, is carrying some pieces of china across the room to the trunk. Forgetting it is china, she dumps it into the trunk and it crashes.

SCARLETT'S VOICE *(calling)* Prissy! Prissy! What are you doing?

PRISSY I'se packin', Miss Scarlett.

SCARLETT'S VOICE Well, stop it—and come get the baby.

PRISSY Yas'm.

She drops what she has in her hands into the trunk and slams trunk lid, then picks up shawl, and runs toward CAMERA.

214 INT. MELANIE'S BEDROOM—MELANIE IN BED—NIGHT

Above the bed is a photograph of Ashley in uniform, Charles Hamilton's sword on the wall beside it. Melanie lies quietly, her face deathly white, her eyes sunken and black circled but serene . . . one arm about the bundled infant beside her.

Rhett and Scarlett enter, followed after an appreciable moment by Prissy.

SCARLETT Melly—Melly—

RHETT Mrs. Wilkes, we're taking you to Tara.

MELANIE *(faint-voiced, tries to smile weakly)* Tara—no—

Scarlett enters to the bed.

SCARLETT It's the only way, Melly.

MELANIE No—no—

SCARLETT Sherman will burn the house over our heads if we stay. It's all right, Melly. It's all right.

Scarlett picks up the baby, Melanie's eyes following her nervously.

215 CLOSE UP—BABY—(IN SCARLETT'S ARMS)

MELANIE'S VOICE *(wanly)* My baby! My poor baby!

216 CLOSE UP—SCARLETT

As she looks at Ashley's baby in her arms. She closes her eyes as if to choke off her thoughts.

217 BACK TO SCENE

RHETT *(to Melanie)* Have you the strength to put your arms around my neck?

MELANIE I think so.
(she puts her arms about his neck but they fall back limply)
Oh.

Rhett bends over and picks her up, mattress and all. Melanie makes a feeble gesture toward the wall.

MELANIE Oh . . . Oh . . . Ashley—Charles—

Rhett looks at her as though she is delirious, not knowing what she means, but Scarlett interrupts impatiently:

RHETT What is it? What does she want?

SCARLETT Ashley's picture—Charles' sword— She wants us to bring them.

RHETT Get them.

He goes out of scene toward the door. Prissy follows, carrying the baby. Scarlett removes Ashley's picture and Charles' sword from the wall above the bed. She picks up the lamp and follows the others.

218 DOWNSTAIRS HALLWAY

The little procession comes down the stairs, with Scarlett holding the lamp in the lead.

219 EXT. FRONT OF MISS PITTYPAT'S HOUSE—AT FRONT DOOR—MEDIUM SHOT—NIGHT

Scarlett comes out the door, stops short, gazing off down Peachtree

CONTINUED:

219 CONTINUED

Street. Behind her is Rhett, with Melanie in his arms. Prissy, carrying the baby, is at his heels.

SCARLETT *(alarmed)* What—what's that?

220 FULL SHOT—PEACHTREE STREET AND THE CITY IN THE DISTANCE—FROM THEIR POINT OF VIEW—HOLDING SCARLETT AND RHETT (MELANIE IN HIS ARMS) IN F.G.—*(COSGROVE SPLIT SCREEN)*

The glow of fire above the trees of the distant town is seen for the first time.

RHETT Our gallant lads must have set fire to the warehouses near the depot. There's enough ammunition in the boxcars down there to *blow* us to Tara.

221 GROUP SHOT—ON THE VERANDAH OF MISS PITTYPAT'S HOUSE

Scarlett's face is white, anxious.

RHETT We'll have to hurry if we're going to get across the tracks.

SCARLETT *(with panic)* You're not going *that* way!

RHETT We have to. The McDonough Road's the only one the Yankees haven't cut yet.

He goes down the steps out of scene. HOLD CAMERA to see the others following.

222 SHOOTING ACROSS REAR OF WAGON TOWARD MISS PITTYPAT'S HOUSE—MEDIUM SHOT

Rhett is already installing Melanie and the mattress in the back of the wagon. Prissy enters with the baby, followed by Scarlett. Rhett quickly takes the baby from Prissy, placing it beside Melanie. He boosts Prissy up and fits the tailboard into place.

223 PEACHTREE STREET—LONG SHOT—HORSE AND WAGON IN F.G., FACING CAMERA—INCREASED FIRE EFFECT IN SKY—(COSGROVE SPLIT SCREEN)

Rhett and Scarlett approach the head of the wagon. She is still carrying the lamp. Rhett takes it from her, puts it down on the mounting block, and, lifting her in his arms, deposits her on the wagon seat. He climbs up beside her and picks up the reins.

SCARLETT Oh, wait! I forgot to lock the front door.
(Rhett laughs)
Well, what're you laughing at?

RHETT At you, locking the Yankees out.

He whacks the reins on the horse's back, turns the wagon around, and starts off down the street. The wagon disappears into the deep shadows of the overhanging trees. In the foreground the oil lamp, still burning, sheds its little circle of yellow light on the street.

224 PEACHTREE STREET

Toward CAMERA comes the horse at a lope, the wagon swaying behind it as it bumps over the ruts. The horse and the wagon and the people in it are only dim figures in the semi-darkness under the trees, the only moving objects to be discerned on the street. There are a number of distant detonations as the wagon passes CAMERA which PANS with it, revealing once again at the far end of the street the fire glow and smoke rising above the distant rooftops.

225 TREE SHADOWED PORTION OF PEACHTREE STREET—CHURCH IN F.G.—LONG SHOT

Showing the wagon coming out of the darkness of the sheltering trees into the relatively open space in front of the church. The wagon makes a half-turn, heading into the business section of Peachtree Street. The baby wails. Prissy cries out as she is bruised against the side of the wagon. From the front seat Scarlett reaches back to impose silence on Prissy by pinching. The detonations continue.

226 BUSINESS SECTION OF PEACHTREE STREET—LONG SHOT—SHOOTING AWAY FROM FIRE ACROSS INTERSECTING STREET TOWARD APPROACHING WAGON IN B.G.

As the wagon approaches the intersection, it is forced to halt by a detachment of weary, slipshod Confederate troops who appear in f.g., crossing Peachtree Street and heading down the intersecting thoroughfare. An officer counts: "One—Two—Three—Four" in a pathetic effort to count the step and keep up the morale of his men.

227 *TWO SHOT—(TRANSPARENCY)*—RHETT AND SCARLETT ON WAGON

Impatiently, they watch the troops pass.

SCARLETT Oh, dear! I wish they'd hurry!

RHETT *(smiles grimly)* I wouldn't be in such a hurry to see them go if I were you, my dear. With them goes the last semblance of law and order.

228 *BAKERY SHOP WINDOW*

One pane of glass has already been broken. Outside the window, a Decatur Street tough flings a huge missile, smashing the rest of the window so that it seems to splinter directly past the CAMERA.

229 *TWO SHOT—RHETT AND SCARLETT*

RHETT The scavengers aren't wasting any time. We'd better get out of here fast.
(points off straight ahead)
Look!

230 *PEACHTREE STREET—AT FIVE POINTS—SILHOUETTE SHOT OF LOOTERS AGAINST BACKGROUND OF FIRE—NIGHT*

This SHOT should be designed to give a Dante's Inferno effect, with riotous figures of men and women silhouetted against the flames. Some of them are drunk, others laden with loot. More and more figures join the others. There are sounds of breaking glass, splintering wood, women's cries, the yelling of men.

231 *MEDIUM CLOSE SHOT—RHETT AND SCARLETT—(PROCESS B.G.)*

Rhett swings the whip, wagon starts to move.

232 *CAMERA IS SHOOTING UP PEACHTREE STREET AWAY FROM FIRE—LONG SHOT—HORSE AND WAGON*

In f.g. is the intersection of Marietta Street. The wagon is coming toward CAMERA. Four toughs appear, from behind CAMERA. One of them sees the horse, points.

FIRST TOUGH There's a horse!

SECOND TOUGH Git him!

They start forward.

233 HIGH ANGLE—FOLLOW SHOT OF WAGON—(CAMERA TRUCKING)—SHOOTING ACROSS SCARLETT'S AND RHETT'S BACKS

The fire at the end of the street is no longer in view because this is a HIGH, SHARPLY ANGLED SHOT. The toughs run into scene, obviously intending to stop the wagon.

FIRST TOUGH *(yelling)* Give us that horse!

234 CLOSE UP—SCARLETT—TERRIFIED

235 CLOSE SHOT—TOUGH HANGING ON TO HORSE

Rhett jumps on horse's back, pulls his arm back.

236 CLOSE SHOT—RHETT

On horse's back. Tough's head in f.g. Rhett brings his fist down and knocks Tough out of scene. Starts back to wagon seat.

237 LONG SHOT—GROUP OF TOUGHS—(RUNNING TO F.G.)

238 LONG SHOT—STREET—HITCHING POST IN F.G. (Low Set Up)

Rhett's wagon turns at intersection, rides out of scene.

239 CLOSE UP—GROUP OF TOUGHS

TOUGH Down the alley. Cut 'em off!

240 LONG SHOT—ENTRANCE TO ALLEY

Wagon appears, rides down alley. CAMERA PULLS BACK. Toughs run in, stop wagon. Horse rears.

241 MEDIUM CLOSE SHOT—RHETT AND SCARLETT—(PROCESS B.G.)

Rhett pulls reins, reaches out of scene to hit Tough. Gets back on seat. Hits at another tough, who jumps into scene, knocks him out. He whips the horse and the wagon starts out.

242 LOW ANGLE SHOT—TOUGHS

CONTINUED:

242 CONTINUED
They leap at the horse.

TOUGH Get out of that wagon!
Come on, get out of there!
Get out of that wagon!

Rhett fights them off. Scarlett and Prissy scream.

TOUGH Give us that horse!

Rhett knocks the last Tough off the wagon, whips the horse, and the wagon drives off. The horse and wagon go out of scene PAST CAMERA.

243 REAR VIEW OF WAGON—SHOOTING DOWN ALLEY TOWARD FLAMES IN B.G.

The wagon bounces about from side to side dangerously, as it rocks down alley away from CAMERA. A burning building is at the far end of the alley.

244 CLOSE SHOT—MELANIE

Lying faceup on the mattress, one limp arm about the bundled baby. They are being roughly tossed about. Melanie is biting her lip to keep from crying out.

245 HORSE AND WAGON IN A BRIGHT GLARE OF FLAMES

The horse abruptly stops without being pulled in and rears back. Scarlett cries out.

*246 TWO SHOT—(TRANSPARENCY)—*RHETT AND SCARLETT

She is clinging to him desperately. Even he looks alarmed. Behind them, Prissy's frightened face appears from the back of the wagon. She screams.

247 BURNING BUILDING AND BOXCAR—FROM THEIR ANGLE

Only a few feet beyond the boxcar is a flaming building. Sparks, embers, and bits of burning wood are showering the boxcar. Carry over this SOUND of Prissy's scream.

248 CLOSE THREE SHOT—SCARLETT, RHETT, PRISSY

Prissy screams. Scarlett is terrified.

PRISSY Oh, Miss Scarlett! Miss Scarlett!

Clark Gable
as Rhett Butler

Vivien Leigh as
Scarlett O'Hara

A studio publicity shot of Scarlett and Rhett in a romantic moment

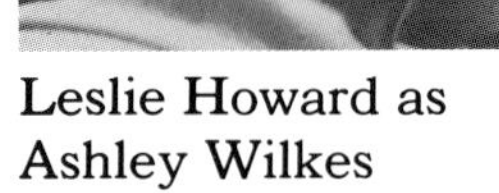

Leslie Howard as
Ashley Wilkes

Olivia de Havilland as
Melanie Hamilton

Thomas Mitchell as
Gerald O'Hara

Barbara O'Neil as Ellen O'Hara

Hattie McDaniel as Mammy

Butterfly McQueen as Prissy

Ona Munson as Belle Watling

Ann Rutherford and Evelyn Keyes as Scarlett's sisters, Carreen and Suellen

Fred Crane and George Reeves as the Tarletons, Brent and Stuart. (Note: Mr. Reeves was wrongly credited on the screen as Brent Tarleton.)

Laura Hope Crews as Aunt Pittypat

Harry Davenport as
Dr. Meade

Carroll Nye as
Frank Kennedy

The family at evening prayer. Kneeling on the floor, Gerald, Ellen, Carreen, and Suellen pray dutifully, and behind them the servants, led by Pork and Mammy (center), bow their heads in devotion. Scarlett, however, is thinking about Ashley.

Scarlett and Ashley on the staircase at Twelve Oaks, where the gentry of the country have gathered for a barbecue

Scarlett, having learned from the Tarletons that Ashley is to marry his cousin Melanie, runs away down Tara's long drive. On the porch, the boys stare after her in surprise.

Scarlett, still in widow's weeds, scandalizes Atlanta society by accepting a dance with Captain Butler.

Christmas dinner at Aunt Pittypat's house. In the center of the photo is Uncle Peter, played to perfection by Eddie Anderson.

Scarlett searches for Dr. Meade among thousands of wounded and dying soldiers at the train station.

The famous scene where Prissy confesses that she knows "nothing 'bout birthing babies"

Fleeing from the advancing Yankees, Rhett carries Melanie down the stairs of Aunt Pitty's house as Scarlett holds a lamp to light the way.

The spectacular fire scene. The figures in the foreground are not Gable and Leigh, but doubles.

In the stolen wagon on the outskirts of Atlanta, Prissy tells Rhett that Melanie has fainted.

Scarlett and Gerald at war-ravaged Tara. With the death of his wife, Gerald's mind has gone, too; he thinks she's still alive.

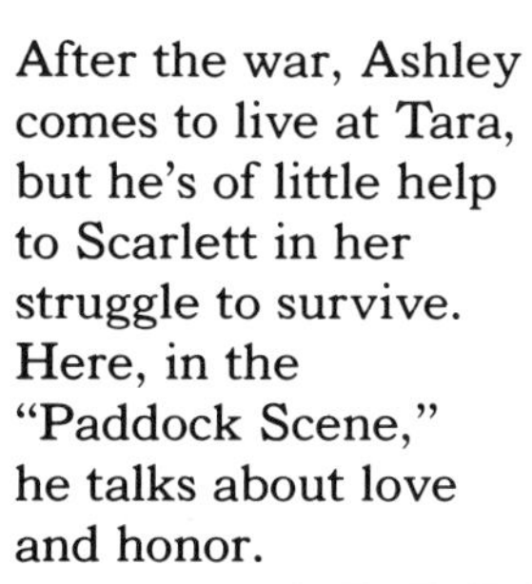

After the war, Ashley comes to live at Tara, but he's of little help to Scarlett in her struggle to survive. Here, in the "Paddock Scene," he talks about love and honor.

The climax of the film: Rhett tells Scarlett he's leaving her for good.

SCARLETT Hush up! Hush up!

PRISSY Oh, Miss Scarlett! Oh!

RHETT They haven't left much for the Yankees to take, have they?

SCARLETT Rhett, how are we going to get through?

RHETT We'll have to make a dash for it before the fire reaches that ammunition!

On hearing this line, Prissy hurls herself to the floor of the wagon, screaming with terror. Rhett decides what to do—looks around frantically, then decides on his course, which is to the left, veers horse around, strikes him with whip, and exits left.

249 HORSE AND WAGON—BOXCAR AND BURNING BUILDING IN VIEW

Rhett lashes at the animal, pulling him around to make a half-turn away from the burning building and the boxcar and across the open freight yards. The panic-stricken horse finally starts forward. The wagon goes out of view. CAMERA LEFT.

250 CLOSE SHOT—HORSE

As it rears, frightened, after it stops.

251 TWO SHOT—SCARLETT AND RHETT

Rhett looks around, sees boxcars with flames getting nearer the boxes of explosives, whips horse.

RHETT Come on.

252 LONG SHOT—WAGON AT RAILROAD TRACK

Burning buildings in b.g. Rhett gets out of wagon, goes to horse's head, starts to pull horse's bridle.

253 MEDIUM CLOSE SHOT—RHETT AT HORSE'S HEAD

RHETT
(pulling at horse)
Come on! Come on! Throw me your shawl.
(he reaches out of scene)

254 MEDIUM CLOSE SHOT—SCARLETT

Prissy in back of wagon. Scarlett throws the shawl.

255 MEDIUM CLOSE SHOT—RHETT AT HORSE'S HEAD

He catches the shawl, ties it around the horse's head.

RHETT Sorry, but you'll like it better if you don't see anything.

256 LONG SHOT—WAGON AT R.R. TRACKS—(BURNING BUILDINGS IN B.G.)

Rhett finishes tying shawl over the horse's head.

257 MEDIUM CLOSE SHOT—EXPLOSIVES IN BOXCAR

The fire is nearer.

258 LONG SHOT—WAGON AT TRACKS

The fire is in the background.

RHETT Come on, come on!

He pulls the horse, turns the horse, and then leads him away from CAMERA.

259 LONG SHOT—EXPLOSIVES IN BOXCAR

The fire is nearer.

260 LONG SHOT

Slowly, pulling the reluctant horse, Rhett heads away from CAMERA toward the spot still clear of flame. A moment after they have disappeared through the opening, the flames reach their climax, the boxcars start to blow up, the largest building at the left end of the screen collapses, and the screen becomes a mass of flames.

DISSOLVE TO:

261 EXT. ROAD ON EDGE OF TOWN—LONG SHOT—HORSE AND CART AND TROOPS—HOT, DUSTY NIGHT

The foreground sky is red, trailing off into darkness.

The horse and wagon are careening down the road away from the CAMERA, toward the rear of retreating troops headed in the same direction.

The soldiers in this scene are walking tiredly, dispiritedly, heads down, too weary to hurry, too weary to care, dragging their rifles. Many are barefooted, some in dirty bandages, so silent that they might all be ghosts.

Rhett is forced to slow up.

262 *REVERSE ANGLE—TROOPS AND WAGON*

Burning buildings in the not too distant background. Along the road past CAMERA go the disorganized, retreating Confederates, their figures highlighted by the flames. For the most part they are foot soldiers, but amongst them are mounted officers in the last stage of fatigue.

263 *AT THE SIDE OF THE ROAD*

A Confederate horseman enters scene, the horse stopping of its own volition. The rider, an old man with white hair and in ragged uniform, is slouched in his saddle as if asleep. Slowly, limply, he slides from the saddle to the ground. A couple of foot soldiers enter scene to him.

264 *TWO SHOT—RHETT AND SCARLETT ON THE WAGON—HIGH ANGLE FROM SIDE OF THE ROAD—RETREATING TROOPS IN B.G.*

The dispirited shadows of Hood's army continue to shuffle past silently.

RHETT *(softly)* Take a good look, my dear. It's a historic moment. You can tell your grandchildren how you watched the Old South disappear one night.

Rhett and Scarlett look around.

265 *GROUP SHOT—RETREATING CONFEDERATES ON THE ROAD—HORSE AND CART IN B.G.*

A young soldier, sixteen years old at the most, dragging his rifle, which is almost as tall as he is, and stumbling along like a sleepwalker, stops, wavers, and falls. Without a word, two men fall out of the last rank and walk back to him. One, a tall, spare man with a long black beard, silently hands his own rifle and the boy's to the other. Then, stooping, he jerks the boy to his shoulders. He starts off slowly after the retreating column, his shoulders bowed under the weight.

266 *TWO SHOT—RHETT AND SCARLETT ON THE SEAT*

RHETT *(his eyes still on the passing soldiers)* They were going to lick the Yankees in a month . . . the poor, gallant fools . . .

SCARLETT *(bitterly)* They make me sick—all of them. Getting us all into this with their swaggering and boasting.

CONTINUED:

266 CONTINUED

RHETT *(with a sad smile, sits still, the reins in his hands, a curious, moody look on his swarthy face)* That's the way I felt once—about their swaggering and boasting.

SCARLETT Oh, Rhett, I'm so glad you aren't with the army!

He turns to give her a contemptuous look.

SCARLETT *(not noticing his look)* You can be proud now—proud that you've been smarter than all of them . . .

RHETT *(moodily)* I'm not so proud . . .

He brings the whip down on the horse's back and they drive out of scene.

267 MEDIUM LONG SHOT—RHETT AND SCARLETT ON THE CART—BURNING BUILDING IN B.G.

The wagon goes down the road, the red glow from the fire lighting the scene.

DISSOLVE TO:

*268 EXT. M*cDONOUGH ROAD—AT A FORK IN THE ROAD—NIGHT

CAMERA SHOOTING DIAGONALLY across the road, beyond which are the fields and scattered trees of the open countryside. In the b.g., a faint red glow in the sky. The horse and cart appears and pulls up to a stop.

269 TWO SHOT—RHETT AND SCARLETT ON CART

SCARLETT Why did you stop?

RHETT *(indicating fork in road)* This is the turn to Tara . . . let the horse breathe a bit.
(he turns to back of wagon)
Mrs. Wilkes—

PRISSY Miss Melly done fainted way back, Captain Butler.

RHETT Well, she's probably better off. She couldn't stand the pain if she were conscious. Scarlett, are you still determined to do this crazy thing?

SCARLETT Oh, yes, yes!
(eagerly)
I know we can get through, Rhett. I'm sure we can.

RHETT Not *we,* my dear—*you.* I'm leaving you here.

SCARLETT *(aghast)* You're what?

Rhett laughs, hands the reins to her, calmly jumps clear of the wagon wheel down to the ground.

SCARLETT *(terrified)* Rhett! Where are you going?

270 CLOSE TWO SHOT—RHETT AND SCARLETT

RHETT *(smilingly after a second)* I'm going, my dear, to join the army.

SCARLETT *(relieved)* Oh, you're joking! I could kill you for scaring me so!

RHETT I'm very serious, Scarlett. I'm going to join up with our brave lads in grey.

SCARLETT *(incredulous)* But they're running away!

RHETT Oh, no. They'll turn and make a last stand—if I know anything about them. And when they do, I'll be with them. I'm a little late but "better late than"—

SCARLETT *(interrupting, looking at him with horror)* Rhett, you *must* be joking!

RHETT Selfish to the end, aren't you? Thinking only of your own precious hide with never a thought for the noble Cause.

SCARLETT *(wailing)* Rhett! How could you do this to me? And why should you go now that—after it's all over—and I need you! Why? Why?

RHETT Why?
(with a trace of contempt for his own patriotism)
Maybe it's because I've always had a weakness for lost causes . . . once they're really lost . . .
(with a little laugh—introspectively)
Or, maybe—maybe I'm ashamed of myself. Who knows?

SCARLETT You should *die* of shame to leave me here alone and helpless!

RHETT You, helpless! Heaven help the Yankees if they capture you. . . . Now climb down here, I want to say good-bye.

CONTINUED:

270 CONTINUED

SCARLETT No!

RHETT Climb down!
(he lifts her down)

SCARLETT Oh, Rhett! Please, don't go! You can't leave me! Please! I'll never forgive you!

RHETT I'm not asking you to forgive me. I'll never understand or forgive myself. And if a bullet gets me, so help me, I'll laugh at myself for being an idiot.
(drawing her closer)
But there's one thing I do know. And that is that I love you, Scarlett. In spite of you and me and the whole silly world going to pieces around us—I love you. Because we're alike. Bad lots, both of us . . . selfish and shrewd, but able to look things in the eyes and call them by their right names.

SCARLETT Don't hold me like that!
(her head is down, she tries to push him away)

RHETT Scarlett, look at me! I love you more than I've ever loved any woman. And I've waited longer for you than I've ever waited for any woman.

SCARLETT Let me alone!

RHETT Here's a soldier of the South who loves you, Scarlett—wants to feel your arms around him—wants to carry the memory of your kisses into battle with him.
(he grasps her more firmly but finds no response in her eyes)
Never mind about loving me. You're a woman sending a soldier to his death—with a beautiful memory . . . Scarlett, kiss me . . . kiss me once.

SCARLETT *(wrenches free)* You low-down, cowardly, nasty thing, you!

She draws back her arm and slaps him with all the force she has left. He steps back, his hand going to his face. Scarlett breaks with exhaustion, worry, and half-hysteria.

SCARLETT *(sobbing)* They were right! . . . Everybody was right! . . . You—you aren't a gentleman! . . .

RHETT *(his mood is gone; he speaks quietly and with a little smile)* A minor point—at such a moment . . .
(he hands her his dueling pistol)
Here. If anyone lays a hand on this nag, shoot him—but don't make a mistake and shoot the nag.

Scarlett looks at him for a second in doubt. Then the shrewd, practical Scarlett seizes the gun.

SCARLETT *(waving the gun)* Oh, go on! I want you to go! I hope a cannonball lands slap on you!
(she starts to cry)
I hope you're blown into a million pieces! I—

Rhett laughs. He is amused, half bitter.

RHETT Never mind the rest. I follow your general idea. And when I'm dead on the altar of my country, I hope your conscience hurts you.
(doffs his hat)
Good-bye, Scarlett.
(he turns and disappears into the darkness)

Scarlett stands watching his figure retreating into the darkness. As his figure disappears, the sound of his footsteps is still heard for a moment or two. Scarlett turns, her shoulders drooping, back to the wagon, her knees shaking. She walks a few steps farther toward the horse.

Sobbing, she buries her face against the neck of the horse, clinging to it. She is alone with the wagon and its helpless load on the road. The horse's head droops a little lower, and Scarlett's stormy sobs gradually die away into strangled gasps of utter weariness. With a long, shaken breath, she lifts her head and draws the back of her hand across her eyes, wiping the tears away like a tired child. Then, in a characteristic little way, she lifts her chin with determination. But as she takes hold of the horse's bit, her whole form is sagging from emotional let-down; and when she speaks, her voice is dull in contrast with her tempestuous words to Rhett a moment ago.

SCARLETT *(dully)* Come on, you. We're going home . . .

Pulling at the bit, she starts leading the horse off. As the old nag stumbles abjectly forward, drawing the wagon with its pitiful load, we hear the baby's pitiful wail, and

DISSOLVE TO:

*271 LONG SHOT—SKY—(COSGROVE)—*DAWN—RAIN

A bolt of lightning flashes through the rain in the sky.

*272 EXT. AT BRIDGE AND SWAMP—(GREENISH RAIN EFFECT)—*CLOSE UP—SCARLETT

The rain falling on her terrified face. We hear the rumble of horses' hooves and artillery wheels passing over the wooden bridge above her.

CAMERA (ON BOOM) PULLS BACK until we see that the wagon with Prissy, Melanie, and the baby is in a swamp under a bridge. Scarlett stands at the horse's bridle, knee-deep in the green slime of the swamp. The wagon is tilted at a precarious angle, having been pulled down a slippery embankment to comparative safety under the bridge. Prissy is cowering in the front seat.

In continuous movement, CAMERA NOW TILTS UPWARD until it includes the lower portion of artillery wheels passing overhead on the wooden bridge.

273 CLOSE UP—PRISSY

Whimpering and nearly overcome with terror.

274 CLOSE SHOT—MELANIE AND BABY

Melanie holds her hand over the baby's face to protect it from the rain, which falls through the cracks in the floor of the bridge.

275 LONGER ANGLE (continuation of above boom shot)

The last of the artillery passes over the bridge. Scarlett wipes her hand over her face in relief and starts tugging at the horse to start it out of the swamp.

276 MEDIUM CLOSE SHOT—UNDER BRIDGE—SCARLETT

Shadow effect of passing artillery over head of Scarlett.

Prissy comes into scene behind her.

PRISSY Oh, Miss Scarlett, I'm so scared—so scared, Miss Scarlett! Miss Scarlett!
(she cries)

DISSOLVE TO:

277 VULTURES IN A HOT NOON SKY

278 LONG SHOT—BATTLEFIELD—(COSGROVE)—HOT NOON

The wagon jolting away from CAMERA over an endless battlefield strewn with dead soldiers in blue and grey. Prissy still in the seat beside Scarlett; the nag so worn out, he can hardly stumble forward.

279 CLOSE UP—MELANIE

Her eyes flutter. She speaks with an effort:

MELANIE Oh . . . Oh, my poor baby! Oh . . .
(she puts her hand over the baby's face to shade it from the sun)

280 CLOSE TWO SHOT—SCARLETT AND PRISSY

Both near exhaustion.

SCARLETT *(turns back to Melanie)* Don't worry, Melly. Mother will take care of him when we get home.

PRISSY Miss Scarlett, ah's powerful hungry. We'se got ter have somethin' ter eat.

SCARLETT *(shortly)* Oh, hush up. We're nearly at Twelve Oaks—We'll—we'll stop there.
(to the horse)
Go on!

281 CLOSE UP—HORSE'S HEAD

Foam covers his mouth as he strains forward.

282 CLOSE SHOT—WAGON WHEELS AND HORSE'S FEET—(SHOOTING DOWN)

Passing over dead bodies.

283 LONG SHOT—(continuation of 1st Cosgrove)

The wagon going away from CAMERA, the endless stretch of corpse-covered ground ahead of them.

DISSOLVE TO:

284 EXT. TWELVE OAKS—DUSK

Open on a sign on the broken gate post at the front entrance of Twelve Oaks:

CONTINUED:

284 CONTINUED

TWELVE OAKS
JOHN WILKES, Owner
Anyone disturbing the peace of this plantation will be prosecuted.

Part of the sign has been broken off or burned, so that some of the words are unfinished.

DISSOLVE TO:

285 INT. RUINED TWELVE OAKS

Scarlett is entering in the ruined hall, looking around her aghast.

286 CLOSE UP—SCARLETT

She is looking upward. CAMERA MOVES in closer to the heartbroken tears in her eyes.

287 PAN SHOT OF RUINS—(FROM SCARLETT'S VIEWPOINT)

CAMERA MOVES up the ruins of the once beautiful staircase, to reveal the gaping holes in the ceiling—and the sky.

288 CLOSE UP—MELANIE—IN WAGON

With difficulty she raises herself to look over the side in the direction of the house. Her eyes fill with horror as she sees:

289 EXT. RUINED TWELVE OAKS—JOHN WILKES' GRAVE

(From Melanie's angle in cart) It is against a broken wall, surrounded by a few burned boards, and on it is the roughest kind of board tombstone, on which has been scratched in charcoal: JOHN WILKES, 1864.

290 CLOSE UP—MELANIE

Her face disappears as she drops back onto the floor of the wagon, overcome with sadness.

291 INT. RUINED HALL—CLOSE UP—SCARLETT

Looking up staircase, heartbroken.

SCARLETT *(her head lowering in sorrow)* Oh, Ashley, Ashley! I'm glad you're not here to see this.
(muttering vehemently)
The Yankees! The dirty Yankees!

She hears the moo of a cow and looks off in the direction from which it comes, startled.

292 RUINED SECTION OF HALL

After holding the scene a moment, a cow walks out from behind the broken wall into the hall.

293 CLOSE UP—SCARLETT

SCARLETT *(screaming violently)* Prissy! Prissy! Come tie up this cow!

294 CLOSE UP—PRISSY—ON WAGON SEAT

PRISSY *(whining)* We don' need no cow, Miss Scarlett. We'll be home soon, and Ah's skeered o' cows!

295 CLOSE UP—SCARLETT

SCARLETT Tear up your petticoat and tie her on to the back of the wagon! We need milk for the baby and—we don't *know* what we'll find when we get home.

As she says this last line, Scarlett's face takes on an expression of dread as she realizes she's given voice to her fears.

DISSOLVE TO:

296 LONG SHOT—ENTRANCE GATE AT TARA—NIGHT

Scarlett drives the horse and wagon in through the gate, Prissy seated beside her. Hold the scene sufficiently long to allow the entire procession to pass through the gates, including the cow tied to the back of the wagon with strips of Prissy's apron. An owl hoots eerily in the dark trees. The horse comes to a stop all by itself as Scarlett leans from side to side on the seat, peering up the driveway.

297 CLOSE TWO SHOT—PRISSY AND SCARLETT

SCARLETT *(turning back to Melanie)* Melly! Melly! We're home! We're at Tara!

MELANIE'S VOICE *(very weak)* Oh, Scarlett! Thank goodness!

Scarlett rises to her feet and lashes at the horse. He doesn't move.

CONTINUED:

297 CONTINUED

SCARLETT *(striking at him vehemently and clucking)* Hurry! Move, you brute!

The horse's legs buckle and he goes down. A shiver passes over him and his muscles relax.

PRISSY *(terrified)* Miss Scarlett! He's daid!

Scarlett leaps down from the wagon paying no attention to the horse and, talking as she does, runs toward the CAMERA at right angles to the wagon, through the gate, and up the driveway. Her hand to her head, she peers ahead as she runs.

SCARLETT I can't see the house! Is it there? I can't see the house!
(with rising terror)
Have they burned it?
(she stops)

298 CLOSE UP—SCARLETT

As she searches the darkness (looking straight into CAMERA) her face is gradually and slightly lighted by the moon.

299 SHOT OF THE SKY

Clouds moving and baring the moon.

300 CLOSE UP—SCARLETT—(HER FACE LIGHTED BY THE MOON)

The anxiety on her face changes to joy as she sees the house. Her face lighted by the changing light of the moon across which the clouds are still moving.

SCARLETT *(her voice raised in a wild cry)* It's all right! It's all right! They haven't burned it! It's still there!

301 LONG SHOT—TARA—(FROM SCARLETT'S ANGLE)

As the clouds uncover the moon and the house is plainly revealed in the moonlight.

302 MEDIUM LONG SHOT—TARA

Scarlett runs across the lawn toward the house, screaming:

SCARLETT Mother! Mother!

She runs slightly left to right to match the angle of her run in succeeding scene.

303 EXT. TARA—FRONT OF HOUSE—NIGHT

Out of the darkness, Scarlett comes running toward the verandah steps. She is almost staggering with weariness, and her breath is coming in spent, sobbing gasps. She runs up those familiar steps, she goes to the front door and starts to open it. It is locked. She knocks; and when there is no answering sound or movement, she knocks again—more loudly and more loudly in a gathering crescendo of hysteria until finally she is hammering frantically on the door with both fists, screaming:

SCARLETT Mother! I'm home. Mother, let me in! It's me—Scarlett!

The door opens slowly, silently, and Gerald is there—in the dark hallway. Scarlett, with both quivering hands upraised where she has been pounding at the door, stares for a second at his terribly changed face and then throws herself forward, clinging to him. Slowly, with a curious effect of dazed fumbling, his arms go about her.

SCARLETT *(AS CAMERA MOVES CLOSER)* Oh—oh, Pa! I'm home . . . I'm home . . .

Gerald, holding her in his arms, stares at her dazedly, blinking heavily once or twice. He begins to tremble— "as if he had been awakened from a nightmare into a half-sense of reality. The eyes that looked into hers had . . . a fear-stunned look. He was only a little old man and broken."

GERALD Katie—Katie Scarlett—Oh, darlin'!

304 INT. HALLWAY

Mammy appears behind Gerald in the hallway. Scarlett turns to her and is engulfed in her arms.

SCARLETT Mammy! Mammy! I'm home! I'm home!

MAMMY Honey—honey chile—

Clinging, Scarlett rests her head wearily on Mammy's bosom.

SCARLETT *(with a long sigh)* Oh, Mammy, I'm so—so—Where's Mother?
(looking up suddenly into Mammy's face)

CONTINUED:

304 CONTINUED

MAMMY *(after an instant's pause, obviously avoiding a direct reply)* Why . . . Miss Suellen and Miss Carreen—dey was sick wid de typhoid. Dey had it bad but dey's doin' all right now . . . jus' weak lak li'l kittens . . .

SCARLETT *(impatiently)* But . . . but . . . where's *Mother?*

MAMMY *(again hesitates; avoids Scarlett's eyes)* Well, Miss Ellen . . . she went down to nuss dat Emmy Slattery, dat white trash . . . an' she tuk down wid it, too. An' las' night she—

CAMERA MOVES CLOSER TO SCARLETT'S FACE. Drawing back in Mammy's arms, Scarlett stares at her for a long moment—blankly at first, then her eyes begin to dance with anguish and her lips part, as little by little is mirrored on her face the dawning of full realization. Until finally her face is frozen in a mask of horror. With that perfectly immobile face, she "swallows and swallows but a sudden dryness seems to have stuck the sides of her throat together," and when she speaks at last it is in a ghastly, harsh, whispering travesty of her voice.

SCARLETT *(the word long and drawn-out, almost with a curious effect of wonder)* Mother! . . .

Slowly she pulls back from Mammy; breaks the clinging hold of her arms. She starts running, staggering a little on her feet, calling:

SCARLETT Mother!
(she turns to look into Ellen's office, still calling:)
Mother!
(she runs out of the office, turns, and runs toward the parlor, still calling:)
Mother!

Until she stops before the open door of the parlor from which candlelight comes.

305 CLOSE SHOT—SCARLETT—OUTSIDE LIGHTED DOORWAY

As she goes in, her face a mask.

306 INT. PARLOR—FROM SCARLETT'S VIEWPOINT—HOLDING HER IN F.G.

On a table, with candles at her head and feet, Mrs. O'Hara's body lies, covered with a sheet except for her face.

307 PARLOR—REVERSE ANGLE—MRS. O'HARA'S BODY IN F.G.

Scarlett enters slowly, like a sleepwalker, her eyes fixed on the figure of her mother. In this trancelike state, she moves into a CLOSE UP, staring at her mother's face. Scarlett screams, strangled, prolonged and piercing. She throws herself down on her knees beside the table at her mother's feet, buries her head on the bier, sobs.

SLOW FADE OUT.

308 FADE IN:
INT. HALLWAY AT TARA—DAWN
(SHOOTING AT THE CLOSED DOOR OF THE LIVING ROOM)

Mammy and Pork are wearily and anxiously watching the closed door. Slowly it opens and beyond the body of Mrs. O'Hara may be seen a window, grey with the early-morning light. The dish of grease, which has served as a candle, has burned out but is still sending up a thin spiral of smoke in the dawn.

Scarlett comes out of the parlor. She is beyond grief. Her face, tear-stained and agonizingly tired, shows what she has been through during the entire night. No tears are left. She is drained of emotion. As she marches slowly into the hall, the CAMERA RETREATS IN FRONT OF HER.

Pork and Mammy glance at each other. Mammy tentatively extends an arm as though to touch Scarlett, and then withdraws it.

MAMMY *(seeking to control the emotion in her voice)* Miss Scarlett, honey—

PORK *(same)* If dey's anything Ah can do, Miss Scarlett—

Scarlett starts slowly down the hall. Pork picks up a primitive candle like the one over Ellen's body, and he and Mammy anxiously follow Scarlett, CAMERA TRUCKING WITH THEM.

SCARLETT What did you do with Miss Melly?

MAMMY Don' you worry yo' pretty haid 'bout Miss Melly, chile. Ah done slapped her in bed a'ready, 'long wid de baby.

CONTINUED:

308 CONTINUED

SCARLETT *(nods, then says)* Better put that cow I brought into the barn, Pork.

PORK Dere ain' no barn no mo', Miss Scarlett. De Yankees done buhned it fo' fiahwood.

MAMMY Dey used de house fo' dey haidqua'ters, Miss Scarlett.

PORK Dey camped all aroun' de place.

SCARLETT Yankees . . . in Tara!

MAMMY Yassum—and dey stole mos' everything dey didn' burn . . . all de cloe's and all de rugs . . .
(heartbroken)
an' even Miss Ellen's rosaries!

SCARLETT I'm starving, Pork. Get me something to eat.

MAMMY Dere ain' nothin' to eat, honey. Dey tuck it all.

SCARLETT *(incredulous)* All the chickens—everything?

PORK Dey tuck dem de fust thing. And whut dey didn't eat dey cah'ied off 'cross dey saddles.

SCARLETT *(wild)* Don't tell me any more about what *"they"* did!

MAMMY *(suddenly remembering)* Der's some radishes and turnips in the garden. We been eatin' dem de las' few days.

Scarlett suddenly sees her father through the open door to Ellen's study.

309 INT. STUDY

Gerald sits, a broken and distracted figure, neither awake nor asleep, neither alive nor dead. He is a weird sight, sitting in the half-darkness—the dawn, which is creeping in through the window, just lighting his face. As we get close to him we realize he is shuffling papers, obviously only going through the motions of examining them. Scarlett goes to him and strokes his head silently. Suddenly she sees something next to him. It is a bottle of locally made corn whiskey, and next to it a gourd.

SCARLETT What's this, Pa? Whiskey?
(she pours whiskey into gourd and drinks)

GERALD *(even his voice is vague)* Yes, daughter.

Scarlett takes another drink.

GERALD Here, Katie Scarlett! That's enough. You're not knowing spirits. You'll make yourself tipsy.

SCARLETT *(bitterly)* I hope it makes me *drunk.* I'd like to be drunk. *(she finishes her drink, sees Gerald's puzzled, hurt face and rises, approaches Gerald and pats him on the knee)*
Oh, Pa.
(she sits down and as she does so, sees papers in his hands)
What are those papers?

GERALD Oh . . .
(looks at them as if seeing them for first time)
Bonds—they're all we've saved—all we have left—bonds.

SCARLETT *(hopefully)* What kind of bonds, Pa?

GERALD *(shuffling them)* Why, Confederate bonds, of course, daughter.

SCARLETT *(sharply)* Confederate bonds! What good are they to anybody?

GERALD *(with a flash of his old peremptory manner)* I'll not have you talkin' like that, Katie Scarlett!

SCARLETT *(dismayed)* Oh, Pa, what are we going to do with no money —nothing to eat.

GERALD *(confused and hurt, like a small boy)* We must ask your mother.
(as though he's made a discovery)
That's it! . . . We must ask Mrs. O'Hara.

SCARLETT *(startled)* Ask . . . Mother?

A look of horror comes over her face as she realizes for the first time that her father's mind is gone. Gerald looks up at her with a gentle smile and pats her hand.

GERALD Yes—Mrs. O'Hara will know what's to be done. Now don't be botherin' me. Go out for a ride. I'm busy.

SCARLETT *(in a hushed voice)* *(her arms going around the seated figure and standing behind him where he cannot see her trembling lips)* Oh, Pa

CONTINUED:

309 CONTINUED

. . . don't worry about anything. Katie Scarlett's home. You needn't worry.

She turns her head sharply, bites her lip, and with supreme effort controls her tears. She leaves Gerald and walks into the hall.

310 INT. HALLWAY—DAWN (SLIGHTLY LIGHTER THAN BEFORE)

Scarlett comes out of Ellen's office, dazed by this fresh shock. Mammy enters to her as she closes the door.

MAMMY *(plaintively)* Miss Scarlett, whut we goin' to do wid nothin' to feed dose sick fo'ks an' dat chile?

SCARLETT *(dully)* I don't know, Mammy—I don't know.

CAMERA TRUCKS AFTER SCARLETT as she walks away. She continues down the hall toward the covered passage leading to the yard. Mammy waddles after her.

MAMMY We ain't got nothin' but radishes in the garden.

As Scarlett approaches the stairs, CAMERA STILL WITH HER, Prissy hurries down from the floor above.

PRISSY *(wailing)* Miss Scarlett, Miss Carreen and Miss Suellen, dey's fussin' to be sponged off.

SCARLETT *(despairingly)* Where are the other servants, Mammy?

MAMMY Miss Scarlett, dere's only jus' Pork and me left. De others went off to de war or runned away.

Scarlett wordlessly turns away from the stairs toward the door leading to the covered porch, CAMERA STILL FOLLOWING HER. Prissy's wailing voice follows her:

PRISSY'S VOICE Ah cain't take care of dat baby an' sick fo'ks, too. Ah's only got two han's.

Scarlett passes into the covered way, where Pork is lying in wait for her near the door.

PORK *(in complaining voice)* Who's gwine milk dat cow, Miss Scarlett? We'se house workers.
Scarlett walks past, ignoring him.

311 INT. COVERED WAY

Scarlett walks down the covered way and stands looking out onto the grounds.

312 EXT. GROUNDS OF TARA—(FROM SCARLETT'S VIEW-POINT OR OVER HER SHOULDER)—EARLY MORNING

"Deep ruts and furrows were cut into the road where horses had dragged heavy guns along it and the red gullies on either side were deeply gashed by the wheels. The cotton was mangled and trampled where cavalry and infantry, forced off the narrow road, had marched through the green bushes, grinding them into the earth. Here and there in road and fields lay buckles and bits of harness leather, canteens flattened by hooves and caisson wheels, buttons, blue caps, worn socks, bits of bloody rags, all the litter left by a marching army."

313 CLOSE SHOT—SCARLETT (IN COVERED WAY)

In reaction to the desolation, she is nearing the end of her rope. She exits from the covered way and starts across the grounds.

314 LONG SHOT—DESOLATE FIELDS

As Scarlett walks away from the CAMERA toward the vegetable garden, which is on a knoll to the right, passing the well, the ruined orchard and the cottonfield with only a few miserable patches of white remaining. In the b.g., we see charred slave quarters and barn, the paddock, the scorched trees, the skeleton of the cotton press, and the ruins of the split-rail fence which had been around the kitchen garden.

315 CLOSE SHOT—VEGETABLE GARDEN—RUINED OUT-HOUSES IN B.G.

The soft earth, scarred with hoofprints and heavy wheels—the vegetables mashed into the soil.

Scarlett wearily comes into the garden and looks down at the earth. As she stoops to pick some radishes from a short row, CAMERA PANS DOWN WITH HER.

She kneels and eats several as fast as she can get them into her mouth, not bothering to remove the dirt. Suddenly she gets ill at her stomach—and slowly, miserably, she retches as she falls face forward on the ground and sobs.

CONTINUED:

315 CONTINUED

CAMERA HOLDS on the portrait of the defeated, prostrate, and sobbing figure. This is the lowest moment in Scarlett O'Hara's life—and we should feel that she is completely defeated.

After we have held this portrait, the sobs slowly stop—and CAMERA MOVES DOWN to Scarlett's head. Her head moves somewhat so that we see her face—and we see her expression change slowly into bitter determination. Ever so slowly, and with grim determination, she pulls herself up on her hands, and as CAMERA STARTS TO DRAW BACK she rises first to one knee—and finally straight up.

This is the crucial moment of Scarlett O'Hara's life. And it is the most magnificent moment of her life. Out of this complete defeat a new and mature Scarlett O'Hara is born. She stands there, fist clenched, her dress soiled, face smudged with dirt, and speaks slowly with grim determination—measuring each phrase carefully. Before speaking she raises her clenched fist and looks up, delivering her speech to the sky:

SCARLETT As God is my witness . . . As God is my witness . . . They're not going to lick me! . . . I'm going to live through this and when it's over I'll never be hungry again . . . No, nor any of my folks! . . . if I have to lie—steal—cheat—or *kill!* As God is my witness, I'll never be hungry again!

She stands, her fist still clenched, as CAMERA DRAWS BACK on the determined figure outlined against the devastation of the plantation.

CAMERA PULLS BACK FARTHER AND FARTHER—revealing Scarlett standing near an enormous ruined oak, backgrounded only by the sky.

THE CAMERA FINALLY PULLS BACK TO AN EXTREME LONG SHOT

A puff of early-morning wind stirs the trees and bushes—like a harbinger of a new day.

FADE OUT.

FADE IN:

TITLE: And the Wind swept through Georgia . . .

SHERMAN!

To split the Confederacy, to leave it crippled and forever humbled, the Great Invader marched . . . leaving behind him a path of destruction sixty miles wide, from Atlanta to the sea . . .

Tara had survived . . . to face the hell and famine of defeat . . .

DISSOLVE TO:

316 EXT. TARA CREEK BOTTOM COTTON PATCH—LATE AFTERNOON, NOVEMBER, 1864—LONG SHOT

The stalks and leaves of the cotton are withered. Only scattered blooms still cling to the plants, many having already fallen to the ground: for this is autumn. Scattered over the field are all that are left of the people of Tara: The Shot is framed on the side with the foreground figure of Gerald (in profile) sitting aimlessly playing with a blade of grass or something of the sort. The next nearest the CAMERA are Mammy and Prissy; then a little farther away Suellen and Carreen; and Scarlett, the farthest away, pulling desperately at a well rope and swinging the bucket clear of the well brim. Next to her on the ground are two pails. (Pork is not in the field as the scene opens, as he is off scene milking the cow.)

317 CLOSE SHOT—SUELLEN AND CARREEN

In ragged, soiled dresses, they are picking cotton in sullen silence. Both girls look weary and ill. They have both only recently gotten over sickness and have been driven to extremely hard work by Scarlett.

SUELLEN *(straightening up)* Oh, my back's near broken . . .
(with a sob)
Look at my hands!
(holds them out)
Mother said you could always tell a lady by her hands.

Her hands are scratched and grubby.

CARREEN *(sweetly)* I guess things like hands and ladies don't matter so much any more . . . You rest, Sue. You're not well yet and I can pick cotton for both of us.

SUELLEN Scarlett's *hateful*—making us work in the fields like—
(she starts to sob)

SCARLETT'S VOICE Too bad about that!

CONTINUED:

317 CONTINUED

Both sisters turn startled and frightened as Scarlett enters to them. She is carrying two large buckets of water, which she deposits on the ground.

SCARLETT Now get back to work! I can't do *everything* at Tara all by myself.

SUELLEN What do I care about Tara! I hate Tara!

Scarlett looks at her for a moment in rage, then slaps her as hard as she can so that Suellen almost collapses with sobbing.

SCARLETT Don't you ever dare to say you hate Tara again! That's the same as hating Pa and Ma!
(she picks up water buckets and walks out of scene)

318 LONG SHOT—FIELD

As Scarlett crosses, walking toward Pork, who is approaching with a milk pail—Mammy a little behind him. Prissy can be seen working in the distance in the b.g.

319 INT. COVERED WAY

—as Scarlett enters wearily. Gerald is there. He looks up as Scarlett comes in and sets down the buckets.

GERALD Katie Scarlett, there's something I must speak to you about.

SCARLETT *(wearily)* Yes, Pa. What is it?

GERALD I've been talking to Prissy and Mammy, and I don't like the way you're treating them. You must be firm with inferiors but you must be gentle with them—especially darkies.

SCARLETT *(tired but patient)* Yes, Pa, I know, but I'm not asking them to do anything I'm not doing myself.

GERALD Nevertheless, Katie Scarlett, I don't like it . . . I shall speak to Mrs. O'Hara about it.

Scarlett is about to reply, but controls herself—impatiently and wearily leaves him and walks through the door into the hall.

320 INT. HALL

—as Scarlett enters.

Melanie has just come down the stairs. She is barefoot and wears a loose and worn-out robe over her nightgown. She is obviously weak, for she is bracing herself against the wall for support. Scarlett stops short.

SCARLETT *(sharply)* What are you doing out of bed, Melly?

MELANIE Scarlett, darling, I must talk to you. You're all working so hard . . . I can't lie in bed doing nothing . . .

SCARLETT *(roughly)* Go on back upstairs. You're as weak as a newborn colt.

MELANIE Please, Scarlett, let me—

SCARLETT Stop being noble, Melanie Wilkes. I've got enough on my hands without you making yourself sick so you'll *never* be any use.

MELANIE *(hurt but contrite)* Oh, I—I didn't think of it that way.

She goes back up the steps, Scarlett watching for a moment. Suddenly she hears the sound of horses' hooves outside. She listens a moment, then looks off through the window in the hall beside the front door.

321 EXT. FRONT OF TARA (FROM SCARLETT'S VIEWPOINT THROUGH THE WINDOW, OR WITH SCARLETT IN F.G. LOOKING OUT)

Leisurely riding up the driveway toward the front door is a Yankee cavalryman. He dismounts, tosses the bridle reins over the hitching post, takes his pistol from its holster, and, glancing to right and left, starts toward the front door of the house.

322 CLOSE SHOT—SCARLETT

She stands frozen with fear for just a second, then quickly exits, CAMERA PANNING WITH HER, as she runs out and to the stairs.

323 CLOSE SHOT (LOW CAMERA SET UP)—FRONT DOOR

—as it opens and the Yankee's legs walk into the house.

324 CLOSE SHOT—BUREAU DRAWER

Scarlett's hands quickly open the drawer and take a pistol from it—the one Rhett had given her on McDonough Road.

325 CLOSE SHOT—LEGS OF YANKEE CAVALRYMAN

—turning into Ellen's study.

326 CLOSE SHOT—SCARLETT ON UPPER STAIRS

Pistol in hand, she leans down and takes off her improvised and worn shoes.

327 CLOSE SHOT—YANKEE'S ARMS

—as he finds Ellen's sewing box and his hands open it.

328 CLOSE SHOT—SCARLETT ON STAIR

She is halfway down the last flight of stairs, close to the wall and nervous. The sound of the footsteps below stop.

MAN'S VOICE Who's there?

Scarlett stands still, her heart pounding. She drops her arm to her side and hides the pistol, which she holds slightly behind her.

MAN'S VOICE Halt or I'll shoot.

329 CLOSE SHOT—YANKEE CAVALRYMAN (FROM SCARLETT'S ANGLE)

He is in the hall, exiting from Ellen's study. He looks up at Scarlett. In one hand he holds his pistol and in the other he holds Ellen's sewing box, which we have seen the night of Scarlett's arrival home.

YANKEE Y'all alone, little lady?

He grins and puts his pistol back in its holster.

330 CLOSE SHOT—SCARLETT

Her hands clutching the pistol, she stares down at him silently.

331 LONGER SHOT

Scarlett glaring down furiously at the Yankee—the Yankee grinning up at her.

YANKEE Y'ain't very friendly, are you?
(he opens the sewing box and holds up the earbobs)
Y'got anything else besides these earbobs?

SCARLETT *(with hatred and fury)* You Yankees have been here before.

YANKEE *(looks around the hall, laughs)* Regular little spitfire, ain't you?

He suddenly notices that Scarlett is holding something behind her skirts.

YANKEE What've you got hidden in your hand?

He starts up the steps toward her, eyeing her mockingly. Scarlett stands without moving to stop him, letting him approach until he has nearly reached her.

332 VERY LARGE CLOSE UP—YANKEE'S FACE

Eyeing Scarlett, his face comes closer and closer to the CAMERA, until Scarlett's hand comes into the scene, pointing the pistol directly at his head. His eyes widen in horror, which we hold for a second as he looks at the muzzle. Then the pistol fires straight into his face.

333 BACK TO SCENE

The body rolls backward down the stairs and lands faceup on the floor below. The face is terribly marked with powder smoke and burns—and blood streams from the pit where the nose had been. In the f.g., a thin wisp of smoke from the pistol which Scarlett still holds in her hand.

Scarlett gazes down, her hatred giving way to horror at the realization of what she has done. She hears footsteps from the upper flight of stairs and turns to see Melanie on the landing, clad only in her nightgown. She is holding out Charles' naked saber.

Melanie stops and looks down at the scene below.

334 HIGH ANGLE SHOT FROM LANDING (OVER MELANIE'S SHOULDER)

—at Scarlett on the stairs beneath her; and at the body of the marauder beneath Scarlett in turn, lying on the hall floor.

335 CLOSE UP—MELANIE

Standing with the sword in her hand. "There was a glow of grim pride in her usually gentle face, approbation and a fierce joy in her smile . . ."

336 BACK TO SCENE

Scarlett looks up at Melanie, frightened. The sound of feet running outside, and Suellen's voice:

SUELLEN'S VOICE Scarlett! Scarlett!

CARREEN'S VOICE *(frightened)* Scarlett! What happened? What happened?

Melanie thinks quickly, turns to the window, and throws it open.

337 EXT. (OVER MELANIE'S SHOULDER THROUGH THE WINDOW)

Suellen and Carreen, Gerald with them, are running toward the house.

MELANIE *(with teasing gaiety)* Don't be scared, chickens. Your big sister was trying to clean a revolver and it went off and nearly scared her to death.
(she laughs)

338 SUELLEN, CARREEN, AND GERALD—OUTSIDE

CARREEN Oh, thank goodness.

SUELLEN *(crossly)* Haven't we got enough to frighten us?

GERALD *(reprovingly)* Tell Katie Scarlett she must be more careful.

They turn and exit.

339 BACK TO SCENE

SCARLETT *(admiringly)* What a cool liar you are, Melly.

Melanie runs down the few steps to Scarlett.

MELANIE We must get him out of here, Scarlett, and bury him. If the Yankees find him here—they'll—
(she steadies herself on Scarlett's arm)

SCARLETT I didn't see anyone else. I think he must be a deserter.

MELANIE But even so we've got to hide him. They might hear about it and they'd—they'd come and get you.

Scarlett looks at her, then goes down the stair.

340 LOWER HALL AND STAIRS

The dead Yankee lies sprawled across the foreground. Scarlett comes down toward him from the stair, fascinated but revolted.

SCARLETT I could bury him in the arbor, where the ground is soft, but—
(then, up to Melanie)
—but how will I get him out of here?

MELANIE We'll both take a leg and drag him.
(she starts down)

SCARLETT You couldn't drag a cat!

Melanie smiles and advances to Scarlett.

MELANIE *(as she joins Scarlett, again clutching her for support)* Scarlett, do you think it would be dishonest if we went through his haversack?

SCARLETT I'm ashamed I didn't think of that myself.
(drops to her knees)
You take his haversack. I'll search his pockets.

Stooping over the dead man with distaste, she unbuttons the remaining buttons of his jacket and systematically begins rifling his pockets. Melanie starts for the haversack, but is weak and sits abruptly on the floor, leaning back against the wall.

MELANIE *(shakily)* You look—I'm feeling a little weak.

SCARLETT *(pulling out a bulging wallet wrapped about with a rag—in a whisper)* Melly, I think it's full of money!
(she tears off the rag and with trembling hands opens the leather folds)
Oh, Melly, look—look!

Melanie looks and her eyes dilate. Jumbled together are a mass of bills, United States greenbacks mingling with Confederate money and, glinting from between them, a few gold pieces.

SCARLETT Ten . . . Twenty . . . Thirty . . . Forty . . .

MELANIE *(as Scarlett starts fingering bills)* Don't stop to count it now. We haven't time—

SCARLETT Do you realize this means we'll have something to eat?

MELANIE Look in his other pockets! Hurry! Hurry!
(her gentle eyes hard)
Darling, we've got to get him out of here.

SCARLETT *(hands wallet to Melanie)* Here—

Scarlett bends over, catches the dead man by his boots, and tugs. He is heavier than she realized, and she feels suddenly weak. Turning so that she backs the corpse, she catches a heavy boot under each arm and throws her weight forward. The body moves, and she jerks again. Tugging and straining, perspiration dripping from her forehead, she starts to

CONTINUED:

340 CONTINUED

drag him down the hall toward the front door, a red stain following her path.

SCARLETT *(gasping)* If he bleeds across the yard, we can't hide it. Give me your nightgown, Melly. I'll wad it around his head.
(Melanie's white face goes crimson)
Oh, don't be silly. I won't look at you. If I had a petticoat or pantalettes, I'd use them.

CAMERA PANS with Scarlett as she turns back to the dead soldier.

341 CLOSE SHOT—MELANIE

Terribly embarrassed, she is crouching against the wall. As the CAMERA MOVES UP to a CLOSE UP OF ONLY HER FACE AND SHOULDERS, she reaches down out of scene and pulls the ragged garment over her head—and, painfully embarrassed and shielding her naked shoulders as best she can with one arm, silently tosses it to Scarlett.

342 CLOSE SHOT—SCARLETT

She catches the gown, throws a quick disgusted glance at Melanie, and starts wrapping it around the man's head, muttering disgustedly.

SCARLETT Thank Heavens I'm not that modest!
(calls over her shoulder to Melanie)
Now go back to bed. You'll be dead if you don't. I'll clean up the mess after I've buried him.
(she wraps his head in the nightgown)

343 CLOSE UP—MELANIE

Still with one arm across her naked shoulder, she looks down at the pool of blood with a sick face.

MELANIE *(in a sick whisper)* No, I—I'll clean it up.

344 CLOSE SHOT—SCARLETT

She finishes wrapping the man's head and stands up.

SCARLETT *(looking down at him)* Well, I guess I've done murder.
(she draws the back of her hand across her eyes, throws out her chin)
Oh, I won't think about that now. I'll think about that tomorrow.

As she lifts up the soldier's legs and starts to drag him out, we

FADE OUT.

345 *FADE IN:*
EXTREME LONG SHOT—TARA—MAY, 1865—DAY (COSGROVE)

Gerald is galloping like the wind toward Tara, approaching the fence.

QUICK DISSOLVE TO:

346 *INT. HALL—TARA*
VERY LOW CAMERA SET UP, wide-angle lens shooting the entire length of the hall.

The door flies open and Gerald bursts in, making a great clutter of noise. Melanie, Scarlett, Suellen, and Carreen pour into the hall from all directions—Carreen and Suellen together.

CAMERA MOVES UP TO CLOSE SHOT OF GERALD, as fast as the CAMERA can move. As the CAMERA reaches his mad face:

GERALD Katie Scarlett! Katie Scarlett! It's over! It's over! It's all over! The war! Lee surrendered!

On the word "surrendered" swing the CAMERA to a TWO SHOT OF CARREEN AND SUELLEN—larger than waist size.

almost simultaneously

SUELLEN
It's not possible!

CARREEN
Oh, why did we ever fight!

SWING CAMERA, as fast as it can move, to a LARGE CLOSE UP OF MELANIE.

MELANIE *(ecstatic)* Ashley will be coming home!

SWING CAMERA RAPIDLY TO AN EXTREMELY LARGE CLOSE UP OF SCARLETT: just barely taking her face within the CAMERA line:

SCARLETT Yes, Ashley will be coming home. We'll plant more cotton. Cotton ought to go sky high next year. . . .

DISSOLVE TO:

347 LONG SHOT—ROAD—IN FRONT OF TARA—SEPTEMBER, 1865—DAY

On the road is a weary procession of Confederate soldiers returning from the war, stretching back and dotting the road in small groups as far as we can see. Most are walking, barefoot. All are in ragged uniforms, about one-fourth of which wear blue coats which have been taken from Yankee prisoners or from the dead. At least half the men seen are wounded—some with a missing leg, some with a missing arm, some with bandages, etc. It is a pitiful portrait of the lame, the halt, and the blind that now constitutes the largest part of what is left of Southern manhood. Some are on horses in even more wretched condition than their riders.

Over this the title:

TITLE: Home from their lost adventure came the tattered cavaliers . . .

Grimly they came hobbling back to the desolation that had once been a land of grace and plenty . . .

And with them came another Invader . . . more cruel and vicious than any they had fought . . . the carpetbagger . . .

As the TITLE FADES OFF, we hear a male voice singing "Marching Through Georgia," and a buggy appears in the b.g., coming toward CAMERA. In it are Jonas Wilkerson, the ex-overseer of Tara, and beside him sits a flashily dressed, free-issue Negro, who is doing the singing. The horse, at a gallop, bears down upon some of the returning foot soldiers, forcing them off the road. As the buggy comes abreast of the CAMERA, it almost strikes one man, who has put up his arm and is standing in front of the buggy to stop it. He is supporting another soldier, who is obviously very weak and wounded. Wilkerson pulls up sharply, having almost hit the man.

WILKERSON *(standing up, in a rage)* Get out of the road, Rebel! Get out of the way.

SOLDIER Have you room in your carriage for a dying man?

WILKERSON I got no room for any Southern scum, alive or dead! Get out of the way!

He half raises his whip threateningly. The soldier just looks at him. For a moment the two men's eyes are locked, then Wilkerson's eyes waver and glance away.

SOLDIER *(quietly)* I reckon he'd rather try and walk it, at that.

WILKERSON *(violently—whips his horse)* Gid-ap!
(yells at soldiers)
Jump, you grey-backed beggars!

NEGRO Hunh . . . Ack' as tho day won de war!

The horse starts through and the stragglers scamper away. Wilkerson spits on them as his buggy breaks through their ranks and passes on.

348 EXT. TARA—DAY—SEPTEMBER, 1865
MEDIUM SHOT shooting at SCUPPERNONG ARBOR, which is in back of the smokehouse at the side of Tara . . .

In the f.g. on the lawn are three men wrapped in blankets—one lying peacefully stretched out, and two sitting playing cards. None of them speaks.

THE CAMERA STARTS TO MOVE UP TO A CLOSE SHOT AT THE ARBOR, where, behind a screen of bushes and blankets draped over the structure, are the heads and shoulders of three scarecrow soldiers. One is Frank Kennedy. The other two men have been stripped and one is trimming his whiskers with a pair of shears. Sound of splashing from behind the bushes.

Frank Kennedy seems reluctant. Mammy stands determined on the lawn, a pitchfork in her hands.

MAMMY Now you come on. Gimme dem pants, Mr. Kennedy. Come on.

He throws his uniform trousers over the hedge. Mammy spears them on her pitchfork.

MAMMY Now you scrub yo'seff wid dat strong lye soap befo' Ah comes an' scrubs you mah'seff! Ah's gwine to put dese britches in de boilin' pot!

She walks a few steps to the boiling pot and drops the trousers in, throws the pitchfork on the ground, and starts toward the covered way, muttering to herself:

MAMMY *(muttering)* The whole Confed'rut army got de same troubles —crawlin' cloe's an' dysent'ry!

349 NEAR THE END OF THE COVERED WAY

As Mammy enters scene she meets Suellen, who has just come out.

SUELLEN *(sputters)* I think it's humiliating the way you're treating Mr. Kennedy!

MAMMY You'd be a sight mo' humiliated effen Mr. Kennedy's lice gits on you!

Suellen is indignant. FOLLOW MAMMY as she leaves her and passes the COVERED WAY on her way to the smokehouse. On the steps and the porch are seven to ten gaunt Confederate soldiers hungrily devouring food. A couple of the men are crippled, and the others in various states of disrepair. Their clothing, recently boiled by Mammy, is clean but ragged and unpressed. A table bearing food is set up on the porch at which Prissy is cutting a watermelon. Pork is busying himself in the b.g., seeing that the men are fed. As Mammy approaches and turns to go toward the smokehouse, CAMERA SWINGS IN THE OPPOSITE DIRECTION to the steps of the covered way. Melanie is sitting on the steps folding a pile of mended garments, her work basket beside her feet. A tired and foot-sore Confederate in washed and dried clothes is also sitting on the steps, eating. Little Beau is toddling about on uncertain legs, sometimes falling forward, catching himself with both hands, and then straightening up again to toddle about the soldier. Gurgling with delight, making little inarticulate noises, he is trying to play with the soldier; pestering him, flirting with him, plucking grass with his baby fists and throwing the grass at the soldier, etc. Melanie looks up and sees what the baby is doing.

MELANIE Oh, come on, Beau. Leave this gentleman alone, because he's tired and hungry.

THE SOLDIER I don't mind, ma'am, it's good to see a youngster again. Nice little fellow. Another two years of war and we could have had him with us in Cobb's legion.

MELANIE *(eagerly)* Were you in Cobb's Legion?

SOLDIER Yes, ma'am.

MELANIE Why then you must know my husband, Major Wilkes!

SOLDIER Oh yes, ma'am . . . he was captured at Spottsylvania, I think.

MELANIE *(horrified)* Captured!
(then suddenly relieved)
Oh, thank heaven, then he isn't—
(she stops herself)
Oh, my poor Ashley, in a Yankee prison!

SCARLETT'S VOICE Melanie!

Melanie turns to see Scarlett motion to her. Scarlett stands just outside the door to the house. Melanie goes to her. As she leaves, Melanie glances back doubtfully at little Beau, whom she is leaving behind. The soldier pats the child's shoulder with his free hand.

MELANIE Yes, Scarlett. I—come along, Beau.

SOLDIER I'll watch out for him, ma'am. We're good friends.

MELANIE Oh, thank you.

She rises and goes up the steps toward Scarlett.

350 TWO SHOT—SCARLETT AND MELANIE

Melanie enters scene, Scarlett talking as she does:

SCARLETT *(scolding, in a low voice)* Here I slave day and night just so we can have enough food to keep body and soul together . . . And you give it all away to these starving scarecrows. I'd as soon have a plague of locusts around the place!

MELANIE Oh, don't scold me, Scarlett, please. I've just heard that Ashley was taken prisoner.

SCARLETT Ashley a prisoner!

MELANIE Yes . . . and maybe if he's alive . . . and well . . . he's on some Northern road right now . . . and maybe some Northern woman is giving him a share of her dinner and helping my beloved to come back home to me.

Scarlett, ashamed and abashed, lowers her eyes, touches Melanie on the arm.

SCARLETT *(quietly)* I hope so, Melly.

CAMERA PANS WITH SCARLETT as she turns from Melanie to go into the house, moody, her thoughts on Ashley.

CONTINUED:

350 CONTINUED

KENNEDY'S VOICE Miss Scarlett!

Scarlett stops and turns back. Kennedy approaches her from direction of the covered way, embarrassed and breathless. He is wrapped in pinned-up blankets and quilts.

351 INT. TARA HALL

Through the open door, as Scarlett and Kennedy enter, a few men seen in the b.g. on the steps of the covered way.

During the following dialogue CAMERA TRUCKS WITH SCARLETT AND KENNEDY as they turn and walk toward the front door, Frank having difficulty with his blankets and quilts.

KENNEDY Miss Scarlett, I wanted to take up something with your Pa, but he doesn't seem to . . .

SCARLETT *(interrupting impatiently)* Perhaps I can help you. I'm the head of the house now.

KENNEDY Well, I—I—
(he claws at his beard)
Miss Scarlett, I was aiming to ask him for Suellen.

SCARLETT *(simulating amazement)* Do you mean to tell me, Frank Kennedy, you haven't asked for her after all these years that she's been *counting* on you?

KENNEDY *(grins in embarrassment and hems and haws, moving from one foot to the other)* Well, the truth is . . . I'm so much older than she is —and—Well, now I haven't a cent to my name.

SCARLETT *(encouragingly)* Who *has,* nowadays?

KENNEDY *(with simple dignity)* Miss Scarlett, if true love carries any weight with you, you can be sure your sister will be rich in that . . . I'll go out somewhere and get myself a little business. And as soon as I get on my feet again—we can—

SCARLETT *(kindly)* All right, Frank. I'm sure I can speak for Pa. You go ask her now.

KENNEDY Oh, thank you, thank you, Miss Scarlett!

By now they are at the front door. Frank Kennedy opens it in frantic excitement and runs out onto the verandah.

352 EXT. VERANDAH

As Kennedy bursts out the door and starts across, he almost knocks over Melanie and Mammy, who have come up onto the verandah from the grounds.

KENNEDY Excuse me, Mrs. Wilkes, excuse me!

He flutters off, as Scarlett comes out from the hall. Melanie and Mammy look after Kennedy, astonished.

MELANIE *(she turns to Scarlett)* Scarlett, what seems to be the trouble with Mr. Kennedy?

SCARLETT More trouble than he guesses. He's finally asked for Suellen's hand.

MELANIE Oh, I'm so glad.

SCARLETT It's a pity he can't marry her now. At least be one less mouth to feed . . .

She looks at Melanie, who is looking down the driveway, and follows Melanie's gaze.

353 DRIVEWAY (FROM POINT OF VIEW OF SCARLETT AND MELANIE)

Up the driveway, under the trees in the distance, a solitary soldier is walking from the road toward the house.

354 BACK TO SCENE

SCARLETT *(grumblingly)* Oh, another one! I hope this one isn't hungry.

MAMMY He'll be hongry.

MELANIE *(turns to go back across the porch)* I'll tell Prissy to get an extra plate.

She stops suddenly, her hand goes to her throat, clutching it as though it is torn with pain. Scarlett comes to her, catching her arm. After only a second Melanie throws the hand off her arm and flies down the steps.

MELANIE Ashley!

355 LONG SHOT—DRIVEWAY (FROM SCARLETT'S VIEW-POINT)

CONTINUED:

355 CONTINUED
Across the lawn, her skirts streaming behind her, her arms outstretched, Melanie flies closer to the approaching figure.

MELANIE Ashley!

We cannot identify the soldier in this long angle, but we see that his face is covered with a dirty blond beard. He is wearing a ragged mixture of blue and grey uniforms.

MELANIE Ashley!

ASHLEY Darling!

With incoherent cries Melanie throws herself into his arms.

356 CLOSE UP—SCARLETT

She is in ecstasy and starts to run down the steps, only to be grabbed by Mammy's black hand, which comes into the scene.

MAMMY'S VOICE Miss Scarlett!

357 CLOSE TWO SHOT—MAMMY AND SCARLETT

Scarlett turns frantically to see why she has been stopped.

MAMMY *(quietly)* Don't spoil it, Miss Scarlett.

SCARLETT *(frantically)* Turn me loose, you fool! Turn me loose! It's Ashley!

Mammy does not relax her grip. She looks Scarlett straight in the eye, and after a moment, speaks:

MAMMY *(still quietly and calmly)* He's *her* husban', ain' he? *(Scarlett looks at Mammy, after a moment lowers her eyes and relaxes)*

FADE OUT.

358 FADE IN:
EXT. TARA—NEAR NEW AND IMPROVISED LEAN-TO—OPEN ON CLOSE UP—BIG IRON KETTLE OVER A FIRE—DAY—NOVEMBER, 1865

Scarlett's hand holds a paddle and is stirring the dark brown mess of cooking soft-soap. CAMERA PULLS BACK and we see Scarlett's face over the kettle, filled with disgust at her task. Pork comes into scene, stands before her.

PORK Miss Scarlett, ma'am . . .

SCARLETT *(without looking up, with irritation)* High time you got back! Did you get the horse shod?

PORK Yas'm—he shod all right.
(clearing his throat)
Miss Scarlett, ma'am—

Scarlett looks down at her own improvised shoes, which are reinforced with pieces of carpet.

SCARLETT Fine thing—when horses can get shoes and humans can't.
(hands the paddle to Pork and steps back)
Here . . . Stir this soap.

PORK *(taking the paddle)* Yas'm.
(starting once more to say something)
Miss Scarlett, ma'am . . . Ah gotter know how much money hav' you got lef'. In gol'?

SCARLETT *(surprised)* Ten dollars. Why?

PORK *(shakes his head mournfully)* Dat won' be ernuff.

SCARLETT *(annoyed)* What in Heaven's name are you talking about?

PORK Well, Miss Scarlett, Ah seed dat no-'count white trash Wilkerson dat useter be Marse Gerald's overseer here. He's a reg'lah Yankee now an' he was makin' a brag dat his carpetbagger frien's done run de taxes way up sky-high on Tara.

SCARLETT How much more have we got to pay?

PORK Ah heerd de tax man say t'ree hun'red dollahs.

SCARLETT *(gasps)* Three hundred! Might just as well be three million! But we've got to raise it, that's all!

PORK Yas'm . . . How?

SCARLETT
(she thinks a second, then:)
I'll go ask Mr. Ashley.

PORK He ain' got no t'ree hun'red dollahs, Miss Scarlett.

CONTINUED:

358 CONTINUED

SCARLETT *(irritated by his evident enjoyment)* I can ask him if I want to, can't I?

Scarlett picks up a shawl which has been hanging nearby, puts it around her, and hurries off out of scene. Pork remains gazing woefully after her, takes off his hat, and scratches his woolly head.

PORK Askin' ain' gittin'.

359 LONG SHOT

—as Scarlett hurries across the rear grounds to Ashley, who is fixing the paddock fence.

360 EXT. PADDOCK FENCE—DAY

Scarlett comes over the hill, stops, and looks tragically and with affection at the picture of Ashley, who is inadequately and weakly attempting to split rails. She comes to him.

SCARLETT Ashley!

He has stopped work as she approaches him. He laughs.

ASHLEY They say Abe Lincoln got his start splitting rails. Just think what heights I may climb to once I get the knack.

SCARLETT Ashley, the Yankees want three hundred dollars more in taxes!
(as she takes a step closer to him)
What shall we do? Ashley, what's to become of us?

ASHLEY *(his smile has faded)* What do you think becomes of people when their civilization breaks up? Those who have brains and courage come through all right. Those who haven't are winnowed out.

SCARLETT *(angry)* For heaven's sake, Ashley Wilkes, don't stand there talking nonsense at me when it's *us* who are being winnowed out!

ASHLEY You're right, Scarlett. Here I am talking tommyrot about civilization when your Tara's in danger . . . You've come to me for help, and I've no help to give you . . .
(he speaks as a defeated man, his eyes eluding hers, without fear or apology, but simply as one overwhelmed by disaster)
Scarlett, I—I'm a coward.

SCARLETT You, Ashley? A coward? What are you afraid of?

ASHLEY Oh, mostly of life becoming too real for me, I suppose. Not that I mind splitting rails.
(his eyes stray off as to some remote star now extinguished)
But I do mind very much losing the beauty of that—that life I loved. If the war hadn't come I'd have spent my life happily buried at Twelve Oaks. But the war *did* come . . . I saw my boyhood friends blown to bits. I saw men crumple up in agony when I shot them . . . And now I find myself in a world which to me is worse than death . . . a world in which there's no place for me!
(looks at Scarlett with admiration)
Oh, I can never make *you* understand because you don't know the meaning of fear. You never mind facing realities and you never want to escape from them as I do.

SCARLETT *(leaping at the word)* *Escape?*
(she turns a quick, guilty look at the house, then)
Oh, Ashley, you're *wrong!* I do want to escape, too! I'm so very tired of it all. I've struggled for food and for money. I've weeded and hoed and picked cotton until I can't stand it another minute! I tell you, Ashley, the South is dead! It's dead! The Yankees and the carpetbaggers have got it and there's nothing left for us!

Ashley, who has been looking at her in disbelief, now peers at her sharply —as she lays her hand, feverish and urgent, on his arm.

SCARLETT Oh, Ashley, let's run away! We could go to Mexico. They want officers in the Mexican army—and we could be so happy there. Ashley, I'd work for you! I'd do anything for you! You know you don't love Melanie. You told me you loved me that day at Twelve Oaks. And, anyway—Melanie can't—Dr. Meade told me she couldn't ever have any more children. And I could give you—

Ashley is startled. His eyes fall.

ASHLEY Oh, can't we ever forget that day at Twelve Oaks?

SCARLETT Do you think *I* could forget it! Have you forgotten it? Could you honestly say you don't love me?

Ashley draws a deep breath, then:

ASHLEY No. I don't love you.

SCARLETT It's a lie!

ASHLEY *(his voice deadly quiet)* Well, even if it is a lie, do you think I could go off and leave Melanie and the baby? Break Melanie's heart? Scarlett, are you mad? You couldn't leave your father and the girls . . .

SCARLETT I could leave them! I'm sick of them—I'm tired of them!

ASHLEY Yes, you're sick and tired. That's why you're talking this way. You've carried the load for all of us. From now on I'm going to be more help to you, I promise!

SCARLETT There's only one way you can help me. Take me away! There's nothing to keep us here!

ASHLEY Nothing. Nothing—except honor.

She looks at him, defeated and baffled, turns away, drops her head in her hands, and starts to cry. It is the first time Ashley has seen any weakness in her. He goes to her swiftly and takes her in his arms, cradling her comfortingly, pressing her head to his heart, whispering:

ASHLEY Oh, dear! Dear! My brave dear. Darling! Oh, no! Don't cry! You mustn't! No, don't cry!
(she continues to cry)
Don't! Don't! No, don't!

SCARLETT You do love me! You do love me! Say it—

ASHLEY Don't! Don't!

SCARLETT Say it! You love me! Say it!

Suddenly he shakes her, shakes her until her hair tumbles down about her shoulders.

ASHLEY We won't do this, I tell you we won't do it!
(and he fairly throws her clear of him)
It won't happen again! I'll take Melanie and the baby and go!

SCARLETT *(oblivious to what he is saying and laughing triumphantly)* You love me! Say it! Say it! You love me! You love me! You love me! Say it! Say it!

ASHLEY All right, I'll say it! I love your courage and stubbornness! I love them so much that a moment ago I could have forgotten the best wife a man ever had! But, Scarlett, I'm not going to forget her!

SCARLETT *(as it sinks in)* Then there's nothing left for me. Nothing to fight for. Nothing to live for.

ASHLEY Yes, there is something. Something you love better than me, though you may not know it.
(he stoops quickly, scrapes up a handful of moist earth, and presses it into the palm of her hand)
Tara!

She is looking at her handful of earth. Then her head comes up.

SCARLETT Yes—I still have this . . .
(she starts out, stops, and turns)
You needn't go. I won't have you all starve simply because I threw myself at your head. It won't happen again.

She walks away from him toward the covered way.

361 LONG SHOT

Scarlett approaching the covered way. In the distance in the b.g., the figure of Ashley. Seated near, in the covered way, is Gerald. On the other side of the covered way a carriage is driving up.

362 CLOSE SIDE ANGLE—SCARLETT

Walking, depressed, still clutching the earth that Ashley had pressed into her hand. Over the Shot the sound of carriage wheels. At first Scarlett isn't aware of the sound, then hears it, stops, and looks up startled.

363 LONG SHOT—THROUGH COVERED WAY—(FROM SCARLETT'S ANGLE)

The carriage rolling up the driveway. It is obviously very new and freshly painted—shining with varnish and new harness. In it are Jonas Wilkerson, flashily dressed, and Emmy Slattery, also showily dressed; but the ANGLE is not sufficiently close for the occupants to be recognizable in this Shot.

364 INT. COVERED WAY

Gerald seated on the steps, distracted, counting out Confederate bonds. Scarlett enters to him. She walks out toward the front lawn.

365 LONG SHOT—EXT. LAWN AND DRIVEWAY—IN FRONT OF COVERED WAY

The carriage slows down and stops at the front door of the house. We see that it is Emmy Slattery and Jonas Wilkerson. Emmy starts to climb out

CONTINUED:

365 CONTINUED

of the carriage as Scarlett comes out onto the lawn from the covered way and hurries up the side steps to the verandah.

366 CLOSE SHOT—SCARLETT ON THE VERANDAH

She realizes who her visitors are, gasps in amazement.

SCARLETT *(almost to herself)* Why, it's Emmy Slattery!

367 CLOSE SHOT—EMMY SLATTERY AND WILKERSON

—starting toward the steps, Emmy tossing her head.

EMMY *(with an ingratiating smile)* Yes'm, it's me.

SCARLETT'S VOICE *(furiously)* Stop!

Emmy and Wilkerson stop, startled. Emmy cowering on the first step, and Wilkerson just behind her. Scarlet runs into scene and stands above them, towering over them in rage.

WILKERSON You haven't forgotten your old overseer, have you?
(puts an arm around Emmy)
Well . . . Emmy's Mrs. Wilkerson now.

SCARLETT *(in fury)* Get off those steps, you trashy wench! Get off this land!

Emmy's jaw drops further and she glances around at Wilkerson, who is trying to be dignified but who is very angry.

WILKERSON You can't speak that way to my wife.

SCARLETT Wife!
(laughs contemptuously)
High time you made her your wife! Who baptized your other brats after you killed my mother?

She glares at Emmy in a rage.

EMMY Oh!
(she retreats hastily down the step and Wilkerson stops her flight toward the carriage with a rough grip on her arm)

WILKERSON *(snarling)* We came out here to pay a call—a friendly call—and talk a little business with old friends . . .

SCARLETT *(beside herself; her voice like a whip)* Friends? When were we ever friends with the like of you?

Emmy breaks her husband's grip and runs in fright from the terrifying Scarlett, scrambling into the carriage.

WILKERSON *(his fury equal to Scarlett's)* Still high-and-mighty, ain't you? Well, I know all about you. I know your father's turned idiot—
(his voice raised in anger)
You can't pay your taxes and I come out here to offer to buy the place from you—to make you a right good offer. Emmy had a hankering to live here . . .

SCARLETT *(shouting)* Get off this place, you dirty Yankee.

368 CLOSE SHOT—GERALD IN COVERED WAY

He is listening to the argument—a mad gleam in his eye.

WILKERSON'S VOICE You bog-trotting, high-flying Irish will find out who's running things around here when you get sold out for taxes!

369 BACK TO SCARLETT AND WILKERSON

WILKERSON *(continues)* I'll buy this place, lock, stock, and barrel—and I'll live in it. But I'll wait for the Sheriff's sale!

Scarlett raises her fist in fury, is suddenly aware of the damp clay still in her hand—and flings it into Wilkerson's face.

SCARLETT That's all of Tara you'll ever get!

WILKERSON *(wiping his face)* You'll be sorry for that.

He turns and starts for the carriage, Scarlett looking after him furiously.

370 CLOSE SHOT—GERALD

The mad gleam in his eye has turned to rage. He exits in the direction of the lean-to.

371 MEDIUM SHOT

Wilkerson in the carriage, taking up the reins—Emmy beside him, whimpering.

WILKERSON *(calling back in rage)* We'll be back!

372 EXT. LEAN-TO

CONTINUED:

372 CONTINUED

Gerald has already untied the Yankee Cavalryman's horse from the rail. He swings himself on the unsaddled horse, shouting:

GERALD I'll show you who the owner of Tara is!
(he wheels and charges past with a terrific bull-like roar)

373 MEDIUM SHOT—CARRIAGE

Driving out—Wilkerson turning back and shaking his fist and Emmy laughing beside him.

374 LONG SHOT

The carriage rolling down the driveway, toward the entrance gate. Gerald comes around the corner of the house at a gallop. Suellen and Carreen run out of the house, attracted by the commotion. Scarlett looks up, starts running after her father in panic.

SCARLETT Pa! Come back!

375 MEDIUM SHOT—CARRIAGE

Nearer the entrance gate. Wilkerson whips his horse to get away from the madman who is after him.

376 MEDIUM SHOT—GERALD ON HORSE

Furiously cutting across the lawn in front of the house, heading for a jump over the fence to cut off the carriage. Scarlett still running and screaming after him.

SCARLETT Pa, come back! Pa!

377 CLOSE SHOT—SCARLETT

She halts, gazing off at the chase in fright.

378 MEDIUM SHOT—CARRIAGE

Just turning through the gate.

379 ROADSIDE FENCE

Gerald coming toward Camera at full gallop. As the horse starts to jump.

380 CLOSE UP—GERALD

His fist raised, roaring and bellowing.

GERALD Yankee coward!

381 ROADSIDE FENCE—LOW CAMERA SET UP SHOOTING UP AT HORSE

The horse jumps, clears the fence, but stumbles against the ditch on the other side, throwing its rider.

382 CLOSE SHOT—SUELLEN AND CARREEN

—standing side by side on the lawn—Suellen with her mouth agape, her hand raised in terror. Carreen closing her eyes and shielding her face with her hand.

383 CLOSE UP—SCARLETT

—letting out a terrific scream.

384 CLOSE SHOT—GERALD'S BODY

—lying motionless where he has fallen. Scarlett's scream continues over the Shot.

The horse's head appears in the scene, nuzzling the still body, then whinnies mournfully.

DISSOLVE TO:

385 GERALD'S AND ELLEN'S GRAVES

The wind is blowing the leaves across the headstones.

DISSOLVE TO:

386 INT. TARA HALL—CLOSE SHOT—GERALD'S WATCH—DAY

PORK *(o.s.)* Lawsy, Miss Scarlett! Dat's Mist' Gerald's watch!

CAMERA BACKS AWAY to show Scarlett holding her father's watch out to Pork, who bends over it, breathless.

SCARLETT You take it. It's for you. Pa'd want you to have it.

PORK You ain't got no bizness partin' from dis watch now, Miss Scarlett! You need all yo' valables ter sell fer dat tax money!

SCARLETT Do you think I'd sell Pa's watch?
(she puts it into his hand)
And don't cry. I can stand everybody's tears but yours.
(she goes into the parlor, dragging her feet, moodily)

387 INT. PARLOR

SCARLETT *(she enters to Mammy)* Oh, Mammy! Mammy!
(she goes to the window and stands looking out)

MAMMY *(she goes to her, lays a consoling hand upon her shoulder)* You been brave so long, Miss Scarlett. You jes' gotter go on bein' brave. Think 'bout yo' Pa like he useter be.

SCARLETT I can't think about Pa. I can't think of anything but that three hundred dollars!
(she moves away from the window and, wretchedly, across the room.)

MAMMY *(mumbling)* Ain' no good thinkin' 'bout dat, Miss Scarlett. Ain' *no*body got dat much money . . . Nobody but Yankees and Scallawags got dat much money now.

Scarlett stops still in her tracks. She frowns. Then, low, but quite matter-of-fact:

SCARLETT Rhett.

MAMMY Who dat? A Yankee?

Scarlett goes to the mirror, stares at herself. She runs her hands over her thin figure, pinches her cheeks.

SCARLETT Oh, Mammy, I'm so thin and so pale. I haven't any clothes!

Suddenly she straightens up as she catches a glimpse of the green portieres hanging at the windows. She swings around abruptly and with sudden, brisk decision, walks to them.

SCARLETT *(fingering the material and looking up)* Scoot up to the attic, Mammy, and get down Ma's old box of dress patterns.

MAMMY Whut you up ter wid Miss Ellen's po'teers?

SCARLETT You're going to make me a new dress.

MAMMY Not outta Miss Ellen's po'teers! Not while Ah got bref in mah body!

SCARLETT *(still staring at the portieres)* Great balls of fire! They're *my* portieres now!
(she jerks down the portieres, pole and all; drapes the material over her shoulder; turns back to Mammy)

I'm going to Atlanta for that three hundred dollars, and I've got to go looking like a queen.

MAMMY Who gwine to 'Lanta wid you?

SCARLETT *(sharply)* I'm going alone.

MAMMY Dat's whut you thinks. Ah's gwine to 'Lanta wid you—wid you and dat new dress.

SCARLETT *(with fake sweetness)* Now, Mammy darling . . .

MAMMY No use tryin' to sweet-talk me, Miss Scarlett. Ah know'd you since Ah put de fus' pair of diapers on you. Ah said Ah's gwine to 'Lanta wid you and gwine Ah is.

FADE OUT.

388 FADE IN:
INT. MAIN ROOM OF THE OLD FIRE HOUSE—CLOSE SHOT—FIRE ENGINE—DAY

A Yankee Corporal of the Guard enters. PAN WITH HIM as he passes the fire engine, upon which are hanging a couple of U.S.A. tunics and Rhett's hat. Voices off scene:

MAJOR *(showing his cards and almost arrogantly)* Kings and treys.

RHETT'S VOICE *(over shot)* Oh, too good for me!
(he throws in his cards, facedown on the table; buttering the major)
You know it's a pity we couldn't have fought the *war* out in a poker game. You'd have done better than General Grant, with far less effort.

The major laughingly rakes in the chips, very pleased with himself. The corporal of the guard enters during this action.

MAJOR *(looks up sharply)* What is it, Corporal?

CORPORAL Sir, there's a lady to see Captain Butler. Says she's his sister.

MAJOR Another sister?
(good-naturedly)
This is a jail, not a harem, Captain Butler!

The two captains laugh. One winks to the other.

CORPORAL No, Major. She ain't one of those. This one's got her mammy with her.

CONTINUED:

388 CONTINUED

RHETT She has? I'd like to see this one, Major, without her mammy. Let's see, my losses for the afternoon come to what? Three hundred and forty?
(bends over to scribble his IOU)
My debts do mount up, don't they, Major?

MAJOR All right, Corporal! Show Captain Butler's—sister to his cell.

RHETT Thank you, Major.
(he rises)
Excuse me, gentlemen!

He walks out of scene in direction taken by the corporal of the guard.

MAJOR *(to the two captains)* It's hard to be strict with a man who loses money so pleasantly.
(he looks at the IOU)

They all laugh.

389 OUTSIDE DOOR TO RHETT'S CELL

Rhett enters scene, greets Scarlett, who is being ushered in from the other direction by the corporal of the guard.

SCARLETT Rhett!

RHETT Scarlett!
(he takes her in his arms)
My dear little sister!
(he kisses her delicately on the brow—turns to the corporal, who is looking on enviously)
It's all right, Corporal. My sister has brought me no files or saws.

The corporal gives him a look, annoyed at his dismissal and because he can't be a witness to this scene. He exits. Rhett ushers Scarlett into his cell.

390 INT. RHETT'S CELL

The cell is a converted horse stall, the adjoining stall being occupied by a horse. Rhett and Scarlett are just entering. He closes the door behind them. Scarlett gives a suspicious little look at the door being closed.

RHETT Can I really kiss you now?

SCARLETT *(a sidelong glance from her. Then, too demurely)* On the forehead, like a good brother.

RHETT *(drops his hands)* No, thanks. I'll wait and hope for better things.

SCARLETT Oh, Rhett! I was so distressed when I heard you were in jail. I simply couldn't *sleep* for thinking . . . It's not true they're going to hang you?

RHETT Would you be sorry?

SCARLETT *(as though she couldn't stand the thought)* Oh, Rhett!

RHETT *(laughing)* Well, don't worry—yet. The Yankees have trumped up some charges against me but what they're really after is my money. They seem to think I made off with the Confederate treasury.

SCARLETT *(almost betraying herself)* Well—well, did you?

RHETT What a leading question! But let's not talk about sordid things like money! . . . How good of you to come and see me! And how pretty you look.

SCARLETT Oh, Rhett, how you do run on—teasing a country girl like me!

RHETT Thank heaven you're not in rags. I'm tired of seeing women in rags. Turn around.

She turns around slyly and flirtatiously.

RHETT *(his eyes take her in greedily)* You look good enough to eat. Prosperous, too.

SCARLETT
(her manner in answer is falsely too light)
Thank you, I've been doing very well. Everybody's doing well at Tara . . . Only I got so bored, I just thought I'd treat myself to a visit to town.

RHETT You're a heartless creature, but that's part of your charm. You know you've got more charm than the law allows.
(he has seated her on the couch and has drawn up a stool beside her)

SCARLETT Now, I didn't come here to talk silliness about me, Rhett. I came because I was so *miserable* at the thought of you in trouble. Oh, I

CONTINUED:

390 CONTINUED

know I was mad at you the night you left me on the road to Tara, and I still haven't forgiven you . . .

RHETT *(with mock concern)* Oh, Scarlett, don't say that!

SCARLETT Well, I must admit I might not be alive now, only for you.
(she gently squeezes his arm)
But when I think of myself with everything I could possibly hope for, and not a care in the world, and you here in this horrid jail . . .
(she tries lightening matters with a little joke, indicating Rhett's next-door neighbor)
And not even a human jail, Rhett, a horse jail!
(then the tears come quite convincingly)
Listen to me trying to make jokes, when I really want to cry. In a minute I *shall* cry!

He stares at her incredulously.

RHETT Scarlett, can it be possible . . . !

SCARLETT *(sniffing)* Can what be possible, Rhett?

RHETT That you've grown a woman's heart? A real woman's heart?

SCARLETT *(eagerly, leaning provocatively toward him)* I have, Rhett. I know I have.

RHETT Well, it's worth being in jail just to hear you say that. It's well worth it . . .

Impulsively, really moved, he has seized her hands, leans over and kisses them. He feels her hands, then turns the palms upwards, looks down at them. Unaware of what he is thinking, she closes her eyes and lifts her face to his, obviously waiting for him to kiss her. But his tone changes.

RHETT *(with quiet sarcasm)* You can drop the moonlight and magnolia, Scarlett.
(her eyes open in surprise)
So things have been going well at Tara, have they?

She nods, mutters a frightened "Ye-es."

RHETT *(with violence)* What have you been doing with your hands?

Then she tries to wrench them away, but he holds them hard, running his thumbs across the calluses.

SCARLETT *(hastily, panicky)* Just because I went riding last week, without my gloves . . .

RHETT *(angrily)* These don't belong to a lady! You've been working with them like a field hand! Why did you lie to me, and what are you *really* up to?

SCARLETT Now, Rhett . . .

RHETT *(disgusted with himself)* Another minute and I'd almost have believed that you cared for me—
(he drops her hands as though they were two hot potatoes, and steps back from her)

SCARLETT But I do care . . .

RHETT *(savagely)* Suppose we get down to the truth. You want something from me! And you want it badly enough to put on quite a show in your velvets! What is it? Money?

Then the mask comes off. She faces him, hesitates a second, then blurts it out:

SCARLETT I want three hundred dollars to pay the taxes on Tara. Oh, Rhett, I did lie to you when I said everything was all right. Things are just as bad as they possibly could be! And you've got millions, Rhett.
(her emotion is genuine now and needs no playacting)

RHETT *(with cryptic dryness)* What collateral are you offering?

SCARLETT *(thinks, then touching her earbobs)* My earbobs.

RHETT *(quickly)* Not interested.

SCARLETT *(fast)* A mortgage on Tara.

RHETT *(equally fast)* What would I do with a farm?

SCARLETT *(pleading; rapidly)* You wouldn't lose. I'd pay you back out of next year's cotton—

RHETT Not good enough. Have you nothing better?

SCARLETT *(a deep breath; then:)* You once said you loved me . . . If you still love me, Rhett—

RHETT You haven't forgotten I'm not a marrying man.

CONTINUED:

390 CONTINUED

SCARLETT No. I haven't forgotten.

RHETT *(contemptuously)* You're not worth three hundred dollars, Scarlett.
(bitterly)
You'll never mean anything but misery to any man.

SCARLETT *(she breaks out)* Go on! Insult me! I don't care what you say! Only give me the money! I won't let Tara go! I can't let it go while there is a breath left in my body! Oh, Rhett, won't you please give me the money!

RHETT *(stopping her, his poise and humor gradually returning)* I couldn't give you the money if I wanted to. My funds are in Liverpool, not Atlanta. If I tried drawing a draft, the Yankees'd be on me like a duck on a June bug . . .
(looks at her and smiles)
So you see, my dear, you've abased yourself to no purpose.

Her face goes ugly, and she swings at him with an incoherent cry. Rhett is beside her quick as a flash. He controls her body with one arm around both of hers, and claps his hand tightly over her mouth. She struggles against him, tries to scratch his face and bite his hand.

RHETT *(as to a bad child)* Here! Here! Stop it! Do you want the Yankees to see you like this?

He takes his hand from her mouth, and her struggling ends as quickly as it began. She is out of breath, his arm is still around her.

SCARLETT *(very cold)* Take your hands off me, you skunk!

Rhett releases her. Scarlett arranges her clothing and starts out, talking as she goes.

SCARLETT You knew what I was going to say before I started. You knew you wouldn't lend me the money and yet—and yet you let me go on.

RHETT *(talking to her as she goes)* I enjoyed hearing what you had to say . . . Cheer up. You can come to my hanging. And I'll remember you in my will.

SCARLETT *(at the door)* I'll come to your hanging—the only thing I'm afraid of is that they may not hang you in time to pay the taxes on Tara.

He looks at her in admiration as she goes out.

391 EXT. PEACHTREE STREET—IN FRONT OF FIRE HOUSE

Shooting toward the door. Scarlett emerges, her eyes flashing, her lips compressed. Just as she is about to step over the threshold, a voice offscreen stops her.

BELLE WATLING'S VOICE Tell him "Belle Watling."

Scarlett is startled. CAMERA PULLS BACK QUICKLY, pauses first on Mammy, waiting outside the door for Scarlett. Mammy stares wide-eyed and openmouthed at Belle. Then CAMERA reveals Belle in her elaborate carriage. She is talking to the corporal.

CORPORAL Where you been lately? Thought you deserted Captain Butler.

BELLE *(extends her hand)* Oh, I keep myself occupied . . . Help me out.

The corporal obeys. Belle sees and recognizes Scarlett. Their eyes meet. Scarlett draws a deep breath, pulls her skirts away from any contact with Belle's skirts. Belle understands, smiles. She goes into the jail. Scarlett stands frozen. Mammy goes to her.

MAMMY Who dat? Ah ain' never seed hair dat color before in mah life. Does you know a dyed-hair woman?

SCARLETT I wish I knew that one. She'd get my money for me.

392 PEACHTREE STREET—TRUCKING SHOT—SCARLETT AND MAMMY

The bustle is far greater than during the war. Rebuilding activity; drays of lumber being unloaded in front of ruined buildings. Buildings plastered with signs indicating Yankee occupation: "Jonathan Cushing, M.D."; "Hezekiah Green, Insurance"; "de Caleb Adams, Attorney at Law." All these combine to make the b.g., a dramatization of the new Atlanta.

MAMMY No matter whut dey done to you in dat jail—

CONTINUED:

92 CONTINUED

(she is following Scarlett. The crowd on the sidewalk: Yankee men and women and free issue Negroes turn to stare; but Scarlett hurries on) Dey din' do no mo'n you deserve for visitin' white trash in a jail!

Scarlett has hurried on, unheeding. As Scarlett and Mammy walk down the crowded Atlanta street, they are jostled by carpetbaggers and free Negroes on the sidewalks.

AD LIBS Fresh and green right off the farm . . .
Say, what you doin' tonight, sissy?
That's one of them Georgia peaches . . .
Nothin' like that in Ohio . . .

Scarlett disregards these remarks and continues walking as though nothing had been said. Standing on a soapbox at the edge of the sidewalk next to the street is a carpetbagger. He is speaking to a group which is crowded about him.

ORATOR Do you know what we're going to do?

AD LIB What?

ORATOR We're goin' to give every last one of you forty acres and a mule.

NEGRO An' a mule?

ORATOR Forty acres and a mule . . .

NEGRO Gee-ee!

ORATOR . . . Because we're your friends and you're going to become voters—and you're going to vote like your friends do.

AD LIB *(to Scarlett)* What's your hurry, sister?

MAMMY Whut's come over dis hyah town?

SCARLETT The Yankees have come over it! Same as they've come over all of us.

MAMMY Out of our way, trash! Get out of the way here! Get away! Go on!

Then, from off-screen, a voice calls. The voice of Frank Kennedy.

FRANK'S VOICE Surely it can't be Miss Scarlett!

Scarlett turns, astonished. Frank Kennedy is standing in front of his store.

FRANK *(warmly)* And Mammy!

MAMMY It sure is good to see home fo'ks.

FRANK I didn't know you were in Atlanta!

SCARLETT I didn't know you were.

FRANK Didn't Miss Suellen tell you about my store?

SCARLETT Did she? I don't remember. Have you a store?
(his gesture points it out. It is a proud gesture. But her interest is not yet engaged)
This?

FRANK Won't you come in and look around a bit?

They go in. Mammy stays outside, looking eagerly in at the window.

393 INT. FRANK KENNEDY'S STORE

A general merchandise store, stacked and untidy. A lady customer is doing business with a clerk. Scarlett and Frank enter. Scarlett stops on the threshold. Looks about her, bewildered.

FRANK I don't suppose it looks like much to a lady. But I can't help being proud of it.

Scarlett looks at him with new respect.

SCARLETT You're not making money?

FRANK I can't complain. In fact, I'm mighty encouraged. Folks tell me I'm just a born merchant. It won't be long now before Miss Suellen and I can marry.

A new idea begins forming in her mind.

SCARLETT Are you doing as well as all that?

FRANK Yes, I am, Miss Scarlett. I'm no millionaire yet, but I've cleared a thousand dollars already.

But Scarlett's interest is now very much alive. Her eyes are snapping up every detail of the store. She discovers the lumberyard outside the window.

CONTINUED:

393 CONTINUED

SCARLETT Lumber, too!

FRANK Well, that's only a sideline.

SCARLETT A sideline, Frank? With all the good Georgia pine around Atlanta, and all this building going on?

FRANK *(he laughs coyly)* I've got to be thinking about buying a home!

SCARLETT What do you want a home for?

FRANK For Miss Suellen and me to set up housekeeping.

SCARLETT Here in Atlanta?
(this is a setback)
You'd want to bring her to Atlanta, wouldn't you? There wouldn't be much help in that for Tara!

FRANK I don't rightly know what you mean, Miss Scarlett.

SCARLETT I don't mean a thing.
(but she becomes more than usually feminine)
Frank, how would you like to drive me out to my Aunt Pitty's?

FRANK Nothing would give me more pleasure, Miss Scarlett.

They go out together.

DISSOLVE TO:

394 EXT. THE STORE

Scarlett and Frank emerge from the store. Frank goes at once to the hitching post to remove the nose-bag from his horse's head. Mammy climbs up in the backseat.

SCARLETT *(to Frank)* I think you'd better stay for supper tonight, too. I'm sure Aunt Pitty would be agreeable, and I know I'd like a good long visit with you!

FRANK You act on me just like a tonic, Miss Scarlett! And will you tell me all the news? All the news of Miss Suellen?

He is helping her into the buggy. Scarlett looks down at him, then turns guiltily away. Is evidently upset. Frank is frightened.

FRANK What's the matter, Miss Scarlett? Miss Suellen's not ill, is she?

Mammy turns in surprise.

SCARLETT Oh, no! No! Oh, I thought surely she'd written you! Oh, I guess she was too ashamed to write you! She should be ashamed! Oh, to have such a mean sister!

Frank is now beside himself with terror. He hurries around the buggy, climbs up beside her, picks up the reins, but before he starts the horse:

FRANK You must tell me, Miss Scarlett! Don't leave me on tenterhooks!

SCARLETT Well, she's going to marry one of the county boys next month! She just got tired of waiting, was afraid she'd be an old maid. Oh, I'm sorry to be the one to tell you!
(with an intimate gesture)
Oh, it's cold and I left my muff at home. Would you—would you mind if I put my hand in your pocket?

Frank is stunned. Mammy's eyes are very large, indeed, as the buggy drives out of the scene.

DISSOLVE TO:

395 INSERT: BANK DRAUGHT

—for $300.00 made to the order of the Tax Collector of Clayton County. Scarlett's hand is just finishing writing her signature: Scarlett O'Hara Kennedy.

DISSOLVE TO:

396 INT. HALL—TARA—DAY—WINTER, 1865–1866

Suellen and Melanie have just come out of Ellen's study and are crossing the hall. Suellen is sobbing and Melanie is trying to comfort her.

SUELLEN *(sobbing)* But, Melanie, you don't realize what she's done. She's gone and married my Mr. Kennedy! He was my beau and she's gone and married him!

MELANIE *(her arm around Suellen, comfortingly)* She did it to save Tara. You must understand that, Suellen.

SUELLEN I hate Tara! And I hate Scarlett! She's the only thing I hate worse than Tara.

During the last speech CAMERA HAS STARTED TO MOVE PAST THEM into ELLEN'S STUDY, where we find Ashley and Scarlett facing each other.

CONTINUED:

396 CONTINUED

ASHLEY It's all my fault. I should have committed highway robbery to get that tax money for you!

SCARLETT I couldn't let you do anything like that! And anyway, it's done now.

ASHLEY *(bitterly)* Yes, it's done now.
(he strolls to window, talking as he goes, his back to Scarlett)
You wouldn't have let *me* do anything dishonorable. But you'd sell yourself in marriage to a man you didn't love . . . Well, at least you won't have to worry about my helplessness anymore.

SCARLETT *(suddenly)* What do you mean?

ASHLEY I'm going to New York. I've arranged to get a position in a bank there.

SCARLETT *(panicky)* But you *can't* do that!
(she desperately reaches for an idea)
I—I counted on you to help me start a lumber business—Ashley. . . .
I *counted* on you!

ASHLEY *(still looking out the window; his shoulders present a picture of defeat)* Scarlett, I'd be no good to you. I don't know anything about the lumber business.

SCARLETT *(frantic)* You know as much as you do about banking.
(gets sudden idea)
And, I'd give you half the business.

ASHLEY *(embarrassed at being unable to say "yes," and pleadingly in the hope he can make her somehow understand)* That's generous of you, Scarlett. But it isn't that—if I go to Atlanta and take help from you again, I bury forever any hope of standing alone.

SCARLETT Oh, is that all? Well, you could gradually buy the business and then it would be your own.

ASHLEY No, Scarlett.
(he walks to the door)

SCARLETT *(starts crying)* Ashley! Ashley!

Ashley slowly goes to her. Melanie enters, now with little Beau clinging to her skirts. Scarlett quickly throws herself down on the sofa and bursts into wild crying.

MELANIE *(sitting next to her)* Scarlett, Scarlett! What is it?

SCARLETT *(blubbering)* Ashley's so mean and hateful!
(she burrows her head into Melanie's shoulder)

MELANIE What have you done?

ASHLEY She—she wanted me to go to Atlanta—

SCARLETT To help me start my lumber business. And he won't lift a finger to help me. He doesn't care if I starve.

Ashley closes his eyes in pain.

MELANIE How can you refuse her, Ashley, after all she's done for us? How *unchivalrous* of you!

Scarlett peeps out slyly to see the effect on Ashley of her performance and of Melanie's arguments.

ASHLEY Melanie . . .
(he throws out his hands helplessly)

MELANIE *(vigorously)* Think, Ashley, think!
(then, pleadingly)
If it hadn't been for Scarlett I'd have died in Atlanta—and maybe we wouldn't have little Beau.
(she strokes the child's head)
And when I think of her picking cotton and plowing just to keep food in our mouths, I could just—
(she looks at Scarlett, kisses her hair in fierce loyalty)
Oh, my darling!

Ashley, who has been taking this attack with his back to us, turns slowly. He looks, then speaks with resignation.

ASHLEY *(quietly)* All right, Melanie . . . I'll go to Atlanta . . . I can't fight you both.

He turns, walks out of room. In his eyes (and also in his posture) we see the same look we have seen when he spoke about being lost forever if he went to Atlanta. This is Ashley's final defeat. All hope of his ever being a man able to face the new world is gone.

FADE OUT.

397 FADE IN:

CONTINUED:

397 CONTINUED
EXT. LUMBER MILL—NIGHT—SUMMER

Open on CLOSE SHOT idle buzz saw lighted only by a couple of oil lanterns which have been set on the ground. PAN CAMERA OVER to BOARD FENCE, on which we see the shadows of a file of convict laborers, as we hear their chains on the sound track.

CAMERA MOVES BACK to reveal the convicts—a line of miserable white men silently trudging through the yard, starved, bent, and weary. They are of all ages, but one thing they have in common: all are emaciated. Many of the men glisten with perspiration; they are unkempt and to varying degrees, unshaven.

A man stands over them, a tough, evil-looking little Irishman—Johnny Gallegher.

GALLEGHER Halt!

The men stop in front of Scarlett, who is standing at the side of the building, in a doorway leading into the mill office. Her figure is silhouetted against the light behind her. She stands like a general, feet spread, her hands behind her, looking down at the line of men, hard and businesslike. Behind her stand a terrified Frank Kennedy and a horrified Ashley. In the course of the scene Ashley dejectedly leaves and goes back into the office. Gallegher approaches Scarlett.

GALLEGHER Here's your mill hands, Mrs. Kennedy. The pick of all the best jails in Georgia.

SCARLETT *(hard and cold)* Humph! They look pretty thin and weak to me, Gallegher.

GALLEGHER They're the best you can lease, ma'am. And if you'll just give Johnny Gallegher a free hand, you'll get what you want out of 'em.

SCARLETT All right, you're the foreman. All I ask is that you keep the mill running and deliver my lumber when I want it.

GALLEGHER Johnny Gallegher's your man, Miss—but remember, no questions and no interference.

SCARLETT That's a bargain. Start in the morning, Gallegher.
(she turns back into the mill office)

398 INT. MILL OFFICE

As Scarlett walks into the office we see that Ashley has gone over to a corner, immersed in his thoughts and in horror at what he has just seen.

GALLEGHER'S VOICE *(from outside)* Hey, you there on the end! Get a move on!

We hear the clank of chains as the men start away. Frank timidly approaches Scarlett.

FRANK But, Scarlett, this isn't right and you know it! It's bad enough for a woman to be in business at all, but—

SCARLETT *(interrupting sharply)* What are you complaining about? You never would have owned a mill if I hadn't taken things over.

FRANK But I didn't want a mill in the first place! And we couldn't have bought it if you hadn't pressed all our friends for the money they owed me.
(looks over at Ashley)
Isn't that right, Ashley?

Ashley doesn't answer. Only lowers his head and covers his eyes with his hands.

SCARLETT *(to Frank)* What are you running—a charitable institution? Now go back to the store, Frank—and then go home and take your medicine. You're not looking very well.
(she gives Frank a little kiss on the ear or nose)

FRANK But, Sugar, don't you think you'd better come home with me?

SCARLETT *(disgusted and in a temper)* Great balls of fire! Don't bother me anymore! And don't call me "Sugar"!

FRANK All right, all right.

He withdraws, picks up his hat, calls to Ashley:

FRANK Good night, Ashley . . .

Ashley doesn't reply. Frank exits, shaking his head.

FRANK *(on his way out)* My, my! She can get mad quicker than any woman I ever saw!

399 TWO SHOT—ASHLEY AND SCARLETT

ASHLEY *(looks up as Scarlett walks toward him)* Scarlett, I don't like to

CONTINUED:

399 CONTINUED
interfere, but I do wish you'd let me hire free darkies instead of using convicts. I believe we could do better.

SCARLETT Why, their pay would break us! Convicts are dirt cheap. If we just give Gallegher a free hand with them—

ASHLEY *(bitterly)* A free hand! You know what that means? He'll starve them and whip them— Didn't you see them? Some of them are sick, underfed—

SCARLETT *(impatiently)* Oh, Ashley, how you do run on! If I let you alone you'd be giving them chicken three times a day and tucking them to sleep with eiderdown quilts.

ASHLEY Scarlett, I will not make money from the enforced labor and misery of others.

SCARLETT But you weren't so particular about owning slaves!

ASHLEY That was different. We didn't treat them that way. Besides, I'd have freed them all when Father died if the war hadn't already freed them.

Scarlett goes to him with some gentleness and some patience. After all, it is *Ashley.*

SCARLETT I'm sorry, Ashley. But have you forgotten so soon what it was like without money? . . . I found out that money is the most important thing in the world and I don't intend ever to be without it again! I'm going to have money enough so the Yankees can *never* take Tara away from me! And I'm going to make it the only way I know how!

ASHLEY But we're not the only Southerners who've suffered, Scarlett. Look at all our friends. They're keeping their honor, and their kindness, too.

SCARLETT Yes, and they're starving. I've got no use for fools who won't help themselves. Oh, I know what they're saying about me, and I don't care! I'm going to make friends with the Yankee carpetbaggers, and I'm going to beat them at their own game—and you're going to beat them with me!

DISSOLVE TO:

400 EXT. KENNEDY STORE—DAY—SUMMER

CAMERA IS SHOOTING UP at two workmen hanging a large, new sign over the storefront, which has been enlarged to twice its original size. The sign reads:

WILKES and KENNEDY
Contractors, High Grade Lumber, Builders' Supplies

See us for furniture

SCARLETT'S VOICE That's it! Move it a little over to that side.

CAMERA MOVES BACK AND DOWN to reveal Scarlett standing on the street directing the hanging of the sign. We note that the store has been enlarged and is very prosperous: customers are seen going in and coming out of the store.

A flashily dressed Yankee approaches Scarlett.

YANKEE 'Afternoon, Mrs. Kennedy.

SCARLETT Good afternoon.

YANKEE Business is certainly growing, ain't it?

SCARLETT *(turning on her sweetest smile)* It certainly is . . .

DISSOLVE TO:

401 CLOSE TWO SHOT—MELANIE AND SCARLETT

MELANIE But, Scarlett, you're doing business with the same people who robbed us and tortured us and left us to starve!

SCARLETT All that's past, Melly—and I intend to make the best of things, even if they are Yankee things.

DISSOLVE TO:

402 CLOSE TWO SHOT—MRS. MEADE AND MRS. MERRIWETHER

MRS. MEADE And did you know, Dolly Merriwether, that Dr. Meade actually saw her peddling lumber to those Yankees *herself!*

MRS. MERRIWETHER And that isn't all!

DISSOLVE TO:

403 CLOSE TWO SHOT—AUNT PITTYPAT AND INDIA

CONTINUED:

403 CONTINUED

INDIA *(with ill-concealed rage)* I think it's shocking what she's doing to my brother Ashley!

AUNT PITTYPAT *(tearfully)* And she's even taken to driving her own buggy! Oh!

DISSOLVE TO:

404 EXT. KENNEDY STORE—DAY

Rhett stands at the curb with his back to Frank Kennedy's old buggy, which now bears the sign: "Wilkes and Kennedy." He is elegantly outfitted and smoking a cigar, and smiling as he watches Scarlett who, unaware of his presence, is coming toward him. As she gets nearer, Rhett steps forward:

RHETT *(stepping forward)* My dear Mrs. Kennedy. My very dear Mrs. Kennedy!

SCARLETT I don't see how you have the *gall* to face me!

RHETT When I think that you could have had my millions if you'd just waited a little while!
(shakes his head and clucks in mock regret)
Ah, how fickle is woman!

Scarlett, in her indignation, speaks rapidly, like a businesswoman. Rhett takes his time about his questions and behaves as though they were something of the greatest importance.

SCARLETT What is it you want? I've important things to do.

RHETT Would you mind satisfying my curiosity on a point which has bothered me for some time?

SCARLETT Well, what is it? Be quick.

RHETT Tell me, Scarlett, do you never shrink from marrying men you don't love?

SCARLETT *(in a rage)* How did you ever get out of jail! Why didn't they hang you?

RHETT *(coolly)* Oh, that! Not much trouble. There's nothing much that money won't buy.
(motions to the sign with his head)
I observe it's even bought you the honorable Mr. Wilkes.

Scarlett closes her lips tightly and narrows her eyes, but controls herself and speaks coolly:

SCARLETT So you still hate Ashley Wilkes! . . . Do you know, I believe you're jealous of him!

RHETT *(throws back his head and laughs)* You still think you're the belle of the county, don't you? You'll always think you're the cutest little trick in shoe leather and that every man you meet is dying of love for you.

SCARLETT *(brushing by him, advancing with contempt)* Let me by.

She climbs into her buggy. Rhett elaborately helps her in, talking as he does:

RHETT Don't get angry, Scarlett . . . Tell me, where are you going?

SCARLETT I'm going out to the mill, if it's any of your business.

RHETT Through Shantytown? Alone? . . . Haven't you been told it's *dangerous* for you to drive alone through all that riffraff?

SCARLETT *(takes a pistol from under the cushion of the buggy, shows it to him)* Don't worry about me. I can shoot straight if I don't have to shoot too far.

She cracks the whip on the horse and drives off, leaving Rhett standing looking after her admiringly, shaking his head.

RHETT What a woman!

DISSOLVE TO:

405 EXTREME LONG SHOT—SHANTYTOWN—DUSK

406 EXT. SECTION OF SHANTYTOWN—FULL SHOT—DUSK

In b.g., amongst the trees, are dirty tents and lean-tos, and around a number of open fires degenerate-looking whites and blacks are discovered, some lounging, others munching hungrily.

In the f.g., is the silhouetted form of a powerfully built Negro lying with his back to CAMERA, his shoulder and head pillowed against a log, his slouch hat pulled over his eyes as he sleeps. This is Big Sam, but his features are not recognizable at this time. Just beyond Big Sam another big black is seen adding sticks to a fire, under a whiskey still, while an

CONTINUED:

406 CONTINUED

evil-looking white man tips an old five-gallon oil can and discovers that they are out of water. Picking up a stick close by, he passes it through the handle of the bucket and nudges the colored man by the fire. The black man takes one end of the stick while the white grips the other. Both exit with the bucket. CAMERA PANS IN OPPOSITE DIRECTION, so that we see the road through the trees on the edge of the settlement, and see a buggy in the far distance as it comes along the road.

407 EXT. WOODS ROAD—CLOSE SHOT—DUSK

Scarlett, seen driving along in a buggy, is nearing the vicinity of Shantytown. She glances ahead and casually around as if in fear of passing through this section alone. She clucks to the horse and loosens the reins, urging the horse into a trot. A carriage robe is over her lap.

408 EXT. SMALL STREAM—MEDIUM SHOT—DUSK

The two men, carrying the can on a stick, are just starting to fill the can with water. The black man is filling the bucket as the white man stands, attracted by something o.s. He taps the black man on the shoulder, calling his attention to the off-scene buggy approaching. They both start up the bank.

409 EXT. BRIDGE

Scarlett slows the horse down slightly as she goes to cross a small, crudely built bridge. As the wheels of the buggy start over the bridge, Scarlett is startled by the sudden appearance of the two men who are coming up the bank toward the opposite end of the bridge. Scarlett clucks to her horse, and, at the same time, reaches for her whip. As the horse lunges, the white man springs onto the road with a leap, grabbing the horse's reins and pulling him to a sudden stop. The rear end of the buggy has just cleared the bridge.

SCARLETT *(thoroughly frightened)* What do you want?

WHITE MAN *(leering at Scarlett)* Can you give me a quarter?

SCARLETT Let go of my horse!

She furiously lashes at her horse and at the man. The white man grips the reins firmly in both hands, with jaw set, as he holds the horse, turning to the Negro.

WHITE MAN Hold this horse!

As the Negro holds the horse, which lunges and rears, the white man crosses and grapples with Scarlett, who now turns the whip on him. He grabs her whip hand and is attempting to pull her from the buggy. Scarlett fights like a wildcat, grabs gun, and starts to level it, but the white man grips her wrist.

410 CLOSE ON GUN

As the white man's hand twists the gun from Scarlett's hand, the gun falls to the floor of the buggy.

411 CLOSE SHOT—BIG SAM

Still in silhouette, his features unrecognizable, Big Sam rouses lazily from his slumbering position, starts to stretch and yawn. His hat comes off. The faint off-scene noises of Scarlett's voice are heard:

SCARLETT'S VOICE Help! Help! Help!

The huge black man is attracted by the faint off-scene calls. As he leaps to his feet, his hat falls to the ground and for the first time we see his face. He starts out of the scene toward the sound of the voice.

412 LONG SHOT

As Big Sam runs toward the road.

413 SCARLETT AND WHITE MAN

Still in desperate struggle, in silhouette. The excited horse starts backing toward the bridge. One of the rear wheels drops off the side of the bridge and is on the verge of tipping over. Scarlett, dropping to the floor of the buggy, is fighting like a wildcat. The buggy is now tipping at an angle. Scarlett has fallen to the floor of the buggy and is hanging to it desperately and bracing herself against the white man's pull, who stands on the bridge and tries to drag her from the buggy.

414 EXT. THE BRIDGE—MEDIUM CLOSE SHOT—DUSK

LOW SET UP WITH CAMERA ANGLING UP over the rear wheels while the rig tips at an angle with one wheel off the bridge and the other one moving back and forth; with each backward move it gets closer and closer to the edge. It is just on the verge of going off as the full figure of Big Sam appears from thicket in background—he rushes toward the bridge and buggy—then for a later cut the legs of Big Sam are seen rushing to the rear of the buggy. He braces himself as he grips bed of

CONTINUED:

414 CONTINUED

buggy with hands, strains—and both wheels are lifted and swung onto the floor of the bridge.

415 EXT. OF BRIDGE—CLOSE SHOT—DUSK

Shooting over Scarlett's back and into the face of the white man. The rig is now in a more level position. The white man is about to drag Scarlett from the rig as a big hand enters the scene and grips the white man's throat and a huge, black fist cracks against the white man's chin, causing him to snap back and go out of scene. As the white man's face disappears, Big Sam swings into the scene with his back to the CAMERA. He glances down at his fallen opponent, then turns, and goes toward Scarlett. The sight of her face causes Big Sam to stop and stare, as if almost unable to believe his eyes.

BIG SAM Miss Scarlett!

At this moment the other black crashes into the scene from behind, locks both arms around Big Sam's throat, and, taking him off-balance, drags him back out of scene.

416 CLOSE SHOT—SCARLETT

Scarlett comes slowly out of her daze, glances around, frightened, and sees the two men off-scene fighting—but does not recognize Big Sam.

417 BIG SAM AND NEGRO—(AS SEEN FROM SCARLETT'S ANGLE)

They are in a desperate struggle close to the edge of the bridge. Finally, Big Sam lands a terrific blow on his opponent's jaw, and the man goes down. Big Sam bends to pick up his body.

418 SCARLETT

—still not recognizing Big Sam, grips one rein, and frantically starts the horse.

419 BIG SAM AND NEGRO

Big Sam throws his opponent's body over into the stream and turns hurriedly to go after Scarlett.

420 LONG SHOT

Big Sam chasing after Scarlett's buggy.

BIG SAM *(calling as he runs)* Miss Scarlett! Miss Scarlett. . . . Wait! . . . It's Sam! Big Sam from Tara! Wait, Miss Scarlett!

421 MEDIUM CLOSE SHOT—SCARLETT IN BUGGY

Riding furiously.

BIG SAM'S VOICE Wait!

422 EXT. WOODS—LONG SHOT—BIG SAM RUNNING CAMERA PANS with him.

BIG SAM Miss Scarlett! Miss Scarlett!

423 CLOSE SHOT—SCARLETT

She looks back over her shoulder and finally recognizes Sam.

BIG SAM'S VOICE It's Sam!

SCARLETT *(incredulously)* Sam! Big Sam!

She pulls at the reins and the buggy stops. Big Sam runs in, panting.

SCARLETT *(hysterical)* Sam, Sam!

BIG SAM Is yo' hu't, Miss Scarlett? Did dey hu't yo'?

Scarlett starts to cry.

BIG SAM Don' yo' cry, Miss Scarlett. Big Sam'll git yo' out o' this in a jiffy.

He gets into buggy, and takes the reins.

BIG SAM Hawse—Make tracks!

424 LONG SHOT—BUGGY

Riding swiftly through woods.

FADE OUT.

425 FADE IN:
INT. AUNT PITTYPAT'S PARLOR—NIGHT

Open on CLOSE SHOT SCARLETT, dressed as she was when we last saw her near Shantytown, her dress torn and her hair awry. She is frightened and is biting her nails nervously and watching Big Sam and Kennedy out of the corner of her eye. CAMERA PANS OVER TOWARD BIG SAM AND KENNEDY, on the way passing Mammy and Pittypat,

CONTINUED:

425 CONTINUED

who are also listening. Mammy is sitting gloomily following the activity with wary eyes and occasionally stealing glances out of the corner of her eyes at Scarlett. Pittypat sits tearfully sniffing at her smelling salts.

FRANK'S VOICE *(as Camera moves)* You're a good boy, Sam, and I won't forget what you've done . . .

CAMERA HAS NOW REACHED BIG SAM AND FRANK, who stand nearer the doorway. Big Sam is frightened, but Frank is curiously and unprecedentedly calm. He is wearing a light overcoat, ready to go out.

FRANK *(handing him some money)* You get to Tara just as quick as you can—and stay there!

BIG SAM Ah sho' will. Ah's had ernuff o' dem carpetbaggers. Thank you, Mistuh Frank . . .
(turns to Scarlett)
Good-bye, Miss Scarlett.
(he exits as we hear Scarlett's voice)

SCARLETT'S VOICE Good-bye, Sam, and thank you.

We hear the front door close behind Sam as the CAMERA MOVES WITH FRANK OVER TO SCARLETT. Frank, for the first time in their married life, is not the henpecked husband. He is kindly and sweet but speaks with authority:

FRANK Scarlett, change your dress and go over to Miss Melly's for the evening. I've got to go to a political meeting.

SCARLETT *(in a rage)* Political meeting! How can you go to a political meeting after what I've been through this afternoon?
(she bursts into tears of rage)

FRANK *(leans over and kisses her on the cheek)* Now, Sugar, you're more scared than hurt.

CAMERA MOVES IN TO A CLOSE UP OF SCARLETT, looking from right to left at Mammy and Pittypat, complainingly, feeling very much the martyr at the lack of attention.

SCARLETT Nobody cares about me! You all act as though it was nothing at all!

CAMERA MOVES BACK to Frank, who calmly puts on his hat, and as he is deliberately putting his pistol in his pocket, we

DISSOLVE TO:

426–450 INT. MELANIE'S HOUSE—THE PARLOR—NIGHT

Melanie, Mrs. Meade, India Wilkes, and Scarlett sit around the table sewing. Mammy sits by the door apart. Tension.

We hold this scene through a period of silence broken only by the ticking of a clock. Scarlett looks up and around the room; her nerves strained to the breaking point—and finally she can stand it no longer.

SCARLETT The men talk, talk, talk about protecting our women! Then after what happened to me this afternoon, Frank has to go to a political meeting!

She looks around the room, but there is no reaction from anyone except from India, who sits coldly staring at her with hatred in her eyes.

SCARLETT *(looks at India, her eyes snapping)* And if it won't pain you too much, India Wilkes, I'd be much obliged if you'd tell me why you're staring at me? Has my face gone green or something?

INDIA *(venomously)* It won't pain me! What happened this afternoon is just what you deserved! If there was any justice, you'd have gotten worse!

MELANIE *(impatiently)* Oh, India! Hush!

SCARLETT Let her talk, Melanie! She's always hated me! Ever since I took your brother, Charles, away from her! But she was too much of a hypocrite to admit it! If she thought anyone would take after her, she'd walk the streets naked!

India has hated too long to speak quickly. When she does speak, her words are filled with venom.

INDIA I do hate you! You've done all you could to lower the prestige of decent people! And now you've endangered the lives of our men because they've got to . . .

MELANIE *(fortissimo)* India!

Now India stops.

MRS. MEADE I don't think we'd better say any more, or one of us will be saying too much.

CONTINUED:

426–450 CONTINUED

Now Scarlett rises and looks about her.

SCARLETT What's going on around here I don't know about?

But Mammy is on her feet.

MAMMY Shh!

The women all turn to her. She indicates the door and they all turn, frightened, as we hear the sound of footsteps.

MAMMY Somebody comin' up de walk. Somebody dat ain' Mist' Ashley!

MELANIE *(she rises calmly)* Will you hand me the pistol, please, Mrs. Meade?
(and, as Mrs. Meade obeys)
Whoever it is, we know nothing.

Scarlett is now completely bewildered. Off-screen is a knock on the door. Mammy goes to the door and opens it quickly. Rhett enters. He does not trouble to remove his hat, but speaks directly to Melanie.

RHETT Where have they gone? Mrs. Wilkes, you've got to tell me! It's life or death!

INDIA Don't tell him anything! He's a Yankee spy!

RHETT Quickly, please! There may still be time!

MELANIE How did you know?

RHETT I've been playing poker with two Yankee captains! The Yankees knew there'd be trouble tonight. They've sent their Cavalry out to be ready for it! Your husband and his friends are walking into a trap!

INDIA Don't tell him! He's trying to trap you!

Melanie pays no attention. She is looking Rhett steadily in the eye and he is returning her gaze. After a moment, she speaks:

MELANIE *(very steadily)* Out Decatur Road. The old Sullivan plantation. The house is burned. They're meeting in the cellar.

RHETT I'll do what I can.
(he goes)

SCARLETT What's all this about? If you don't tell me, I'll go crazy!

MELANIE We thought it best not to tell you, Scarlett. Ashley and Frank and the others have gone to clean out those woods where you were attacked. It's what a great many of our Southern gentlemen have had to do lately for our protection.

India concentrates her hatred in a low hiss.

INDIA And if they're captured, they'll be hanged, Scarlett. And it will be your fault!

MELANIE *(with quiet but cold authority)* Another word and you go out of this house, India. Scarlett did what she thought she had to do. And our men are doing what they think they have to do.

SCARLETT *(she is dazed)* Frank! . . . And Ashley! . . . It isn't possible . . .
(she sinks dazed into a chair)

A horse neighs off-screen and the sound of a Cavalry detachment is heard from the street.

MAMMY Dar's hawses, Miss Melly. Hyah dey come.

Melanie sits in her chair and resumes her sewing.

MELANIE Your sewing, your sewing!

The women all follow suit. There is a knock on the door. Melanie's eye imposes discipline, then:

MELANIE Open the door, Mammy.

The door opened, a Captain and two other federal soldiers enter.

CAPTAIN Good evening, Mrs. Kennedy. Which of the ladies is Mrs. Wilkes?

MELANIE *(with great dignity)* I am Mrs. Wilkes.

CAPTAIN *(looks around the room quickly as though searching for male occupancy)* I should like to speak to Mr. Wilkes, if you please.

MELANIE He's not here.

CAPTAIN Are you sure?

MAMMY Don' you doubt Miss Melly's word!

CAPTAIN I meant no disrespect, Mrs. Wilkes. Give me your word, and I won't search the house.

CONTINUED:

426–450 CONTINUED

MELANIE Search if you like. But Mr. Wilkes is at a political meeting at Mr. Kennedy's store.

CAPTAIN *(grimly)* He's not at the store. There's no meeting tonight! No *political* meeting! We'll wait outside till he and his friends return.

He bows stiffly and goes out. Then his voice is heard off-screen.

CAPTAIN'S VOICE Sergeant, surround the house. Put a man at each door and window. Keep back out of sight among the bushes.

Silence, then:

MELANIE Keep on with your sewing, ladies, and I'll read aloud.
(she opens a book)
"The Personal History and Experience of David Copperfield. Chapter One. I Am Born."

She looks up, annoyed, at a cough from Scarlett, then doggedly continues:

MELANIE "To begin my life with the beginning of my life, I record that I was born—"

DISSOLVE TO:

451 CLOSE SHOT—CLOCK ON WALL

Pendulum swinging.

DISSOLVE TO:

452–458 INT. MELANIE'S PARLOR—GROUP AS BEFORE

MELANIE *(reading)* "Chapter Nine. I Have a Memorable Birthday."
(she takes a drink)
"I pass over all that happened at school, until the anniversary of my birthday came round in March. Except that Steerforth was more to be admired than ever, I remember nothing. He was going away at the end of the half-year, if not sooner, and was more spirited and independent than before in my eyes, and therefore more engaging than before; but beyond this I remember nothing."

Over above sound track we have the following cuts:

INDIA'S FACE, terrified.

MRS. MEADE'S FACE, terrified.

SCARLETT'S FACE, terrified.

(Each Close Up is larger than the others—Scarlett's Close Up being only her eyes.)

HANDS SEWING.

FEET TAPPING NERVOUSLY.

THE PENDULUM OF THE CLOCK SWINGING.

459 BACK TO GROUP

From off-screen comes the sound of drunken singing, distant at first, then drawing nearer—the voices of Rhett, Dr. Meade, and Ashley. The women are petrified.

460 CLOSE UP—INDIA

Her eyes wide.

MELANIE'S VOICE "The great—"

461 CLOSE UP—MELANIE

Staring.

MELANIE "—I remember nothing."

462 CLOSE UP—SCARLETT

Her eyes moving back and forth. She jumps to her feet.

463–483 BACK TO SCENE

The others follow Scarlett and run to the window to look out.

SCARLETT *(turning from window)* Melly! They're drunk!

She starts forward but Melanie stops her.

MELANIE Leave this to me, Scarlett! And please—say nothing. *(she exits scene)*

INDIA You stupid fool!

MRS. MEADE Ssh!

Melanie opens the door. The Captain and his men, Dr. Meade, and Rhett, supporting Ashley, are on the porch.

CONTINUED:

463–483 CONTINUED

RHETT *(singing)* "—in de cornfield. Here—"

CAPTAIN Will you shut up for the love of—

ASHLEY Hello, Melly—

MELANIE *(like a very annoyed wife)* So you've got my husband intoxicated again, Captain Butler! Well, bring him in.

CAPTAIN I'm sorry, Mrs. Wilkes, your husband's under arrest.

MELANIE *(quite steady)* If you arrest all the men who get intoxicated in Atlanta, you must have a good many Yankees in jail, Captain. Bring him in, Captain Butler, if you can walk yourself.

Now Rhett, weaving drunkenly himself, supports Ashley through the open door. He is still singing drunkenly as Rhett supports him into the room. Rhett is also acting like a wild drunk. Melanie follows them, and the other women stare silently.

MELANIE Put him there in that chair.

Rhett obeys and Ashley forthwith collapses, most convincingly drunk. Scarlett stares at Ashley, her eyes wide in incredulous horror. Ashley's mumbling and drunken singing continues off-screen.

Dr. Meade lurches into the room, the Yankee Captain bringing up the rear. Three or four of his men wait in the hallway. Melanie turns to Rhett:

MELANIE Now, will you leave my house, please, Captain Butler? And try to remember not to come here again.

Rhett seizes the back of the chair as though trying to steady himself.

RHETT *(somewhat drunkenly)* That's fine thanks I get for bringing him home, and not leaving him on the streets in this shameful condition!

Dr. Meade picks up the singing where Ashley's voice has dwindled off.

MELANIE As for you, Dr. Meade, I'm astonished at you!
(then, to Ashley)
Oh, Ashley, how can you do this to me?

Rhett jogs Ashley, who makes a hazy effort to look up.

ASHLEY I ain't so very drunk, Melly.

MELANIE *(she bursts into tears)* Help him into the bedroom, Mammy. Lay him out on the bed as usual.

Mammy steps forward. So does the Yankee Captain.

CAPTAIN Don't touch him! He's under arrest!
(he calls out)
Sergeant!
(the sergeant steps forward into the room)

Rhett, seemingly to steady himself, lays a hand on the Captain's arm.

RHETT Now, Tom! What do you want to arrest him for? I've seen him drunker! I've seen *you* drunker! You've seen *me* . . .

CAPTAIN He can lie in the gutter for all I care. I'm not a policeman. But he led a raid tonight on that shantytown where Mrs. Kennedy got into trouble this afternoon!

Scarlett stiffens with embarrassment and growing shame.

CAPTAIN A lot of those shanties were burned, and a couple of men were killed. It's about time you Rebels learned you can't take the law into your own hands!

Rhett begins to laugh so hard that he has to sit on the sofa and hold his head in his hands.

CAPTAIN What are you laughing at?

RHETT *(he is laughing)* This isn't your night to teach that lesson, Tom! These two have been with me tonight! Yessir!
(he roars with laughter)

CAPTAIN With you, Rhett?
(he is skeptical)
Where?

RHETT I don't like to say—in the presence of ladies.

CAPTAIN You'd better say.

RHETT Come out on the porch and I'll tell you.

MELANIE Speak out, Captain Butler! I think I have a right to know where my husband's been!

A pause for embarrassment before Rhett answers.

CONTINUED:

463–483 CONTINUED

RHETT Well, ma'am, we dropped in on a friend of mine . . . *and* the Captain's. A Mrs. Belle Watling . . . We played cards, drank champagne . . .

A gesture leaves the rest to the imagination.

DR. MEADE Now you've done it! Did you have to show me up in front of my wife?

Rhett snickers.

RHETT I hope you're satisfied, Tom! These ladies will not be on speaking terms with their husbands tomorrow!

Now it is the Yankee's turn for embarrassment.

CAPTAIN *(regretfully)* Rhett! I had no idea! . . . Look here! Will you take an oath they've been with you at—er—
(with embarrassment)
—Belle's?

RHETT *(very steadily)* Ask Belle if you don't believe me. She'll tell you, Captain.

CAPTAIN *(abashed)* Do you give me *your* word as a gentleman?

RHETT As a gentleman?
(he grins)
Why, certainly, Tom.

He extends his hand; the Yankee Captain takes it.

CAPTAIN W-well . . . If I've made a mistake, I'm sorry . . .
(sheepishly, his eyes avoiding Melanie's)
I—I hope you'll forgive me, Mrs. Wilkes. I—

MELANIE *(stiffly but with dignity)* If you'll go and leave us in peace, please.

CAPTAIN *(backing away)* Well I—I say—I'm sorry—and, well—I am sorry. Come on, Sergeant.

He backs out, his men accompanying him. Scarlett, her knees shaking, catches hold of a chair beside which she has been standing. The front door closed, Dr. Meade springs to Ashley.

RHETT *(to Mammy)* Lock that door! Pull down the shades.

(Mammy and Mrs. Meade obey)

But Dr. Meade has already opened Ashley's coat and the shirt is seen to be bloodstained.

MELANIE Oh!

DR. MEADE It's all right.

SCARLETT *(points)* Ashley! Ashley's hurt!

INDIA Did you think he was really drunk?

DR. MEADE It's all right. It's only through the shoulder. Get him on the bed where I can dress the wound.

But Ashley has revived.

ASHLEY I—I think I can walk.

He gets to his feet unsteadily, and promptly collapses. Rhett catches him and picks him up like a child.

RHETT It's not worth the effort. Which way?

MELANIE *(stands with lamp by door to hall)* In here.

Rhett carries Ashley out. Melanie snatches a water pitcher and a napkin from the table and follows. Scarlett brings up the rear. Dr. Meade turns to the others in the room.

DR. MEADE Mammy, I'll want some hot water, some boiling water, and some towels.

MAMMY *(she hurries out)* Yassuh.

DR. MEADE And lint for bandages.

INDIA I'll find them.
(she goes)

DR. MEADE Now what can I use for a probe! If I only had my bag . . . .

But Mrs. Meade is staring at him.

MRS. MEADE *(in a distracted whisper)* Were you really there? What did it look like? Does she have cut-glass chandeliers and plush curtains and dozens of mirrors?

DR. MEADE Good heavens, Mrs. Meade! Remember yourself!

484 INT. MELANIE'S BEDROOM—NIGHT

Ashley is stretched out full length on the bed. Melanie sits beside him washing his face with the napkin which she dabs in the water pitcher. Rhett stands beside her. Scarlett looks on from the foot of the bed.

MELANIE And now, Captain Butler, tell me what happened—all that happened!

RHETT I was too late. When I got to the old Sullivan place, there'd already been a skirmish with the Yankees. I found Mr. Wilkes wounded, and Dr. Meade was with him. I had to prove they'd been *somewhere,* anyplace but where they were. So I took them to—Belle's.

MELANIE And she took them in?

RHETT She's by way of being an old friend of mine.

MELANIE *(her eyes fall)* Oh, I—I'm sorry. I—

RHETT I'm sorry I couldn't think up a more dignified alibi.

Melanie's candor is never more clear or lovely as she rises to take his hand.

MELANIE This isn't the first time you've come between me and disaster, Captain Butler. It isn't likely that I'd question any device of yours. And now I—I'll go and see what Dr. Meade needs . . .
(she goes out)

SCARLETT Oh, Ashley! Ashley!

Rhett looks steadily at her across the unconscious Ashley.

RHETT Have you no interest in what's become of your own husband, Mrs. Kennedy?

Scarlet snickers nervously:

SCARLETT Humph! Did Frank go with you to Belle Watling's?

RHETT No.

The least pause.

SCARLETT Where is he?

RHETT *(quietly and without melodrama)* He's lying out on Decatur Road shot through the head. . . . He's dead.

Scarlett reacts in horror, as we

FADE OUT.

485 FADE IN:
INT. BELLE WATLING'S CARRIAGE—NIGHT

Belle in large head profile in f.g. Through the carriage door we see Melanie approaching, timidly peering toward the carriage.

MELANIE Who is it?

BELLE *(leans forward and calls)* It's . . . It's Miz Watling . . .

MELANIE Oh, Mrs. Watling! Won't you come in the house?

BELLE Oh, I couldn't do that, Miz Wilkes. You come in here and set a minute with me.

Belle makes room for her as Melanie enters.

MELANIE How can I thank you enough for what you did for us? How can any of us thank you enough?

BELLE I got your note sayin' you wuz goin' to call on me and thank me. Miz Wilkes, you musta lost your mind. I come up here as soon as 'twuz dark to tell you you mustn't even think of any sech thing. Why, I'm—why, you're—well, it wouldn't be fittin' at all.

MELANIE It wouldn't be fitting for me to call and thank a kind woman who saved my husband's life?

BELLE Miz Wilkes, there ain't never been a lady in this town nice to me like you wuz . . . about the money for the hospital, you know. And I don't forget a kindness. I thought about you being left a widder with a little boy if Mr. Wilkes got hung—He's a nice little boy, your boy is, Miz Wilkes. I got a boy myself and so I . . .

MELANIE Oh, have you? Does he live—er—

BELLE Oh, no'm! He ain't here in Atlanta! He ain't never been here. He's off at school. I ain't seen him since he was little.

MELANIE Oh.

BELLE I—well, anyway, if it'd been that Miz Kennedy's husband by hisself, I wouldn't of lifted a finger, no matter *what* Captain Butler said.

CONTINUED:

485 CONTINUED

MELANIE *(surprised)* But why?

BELLE Well, Miz Wilkes, I know a heap of things. And she ain't no good, that Miz Kennedy. She's a mighty cold woman and she kilt her husband prancin' about Atlanta by herself, same as if she shot him.

MELANIE *(interrupting, not unkindly but firmly)* You mustn't say unkind things about my sister-in-law.

BELLE Excuse me, Miz Wilkes. I forgot you liked her, and I'm sorry about poor Mr. Kennedy . . . But she just ain't in the same class with you, Miz Wilkes, and I can't help it if I think so.

Melanie is distressed at this continued attack. There is a moment's embarrassed silence.

BELLE *(assuming heartiness)* Well, anyway, I gotta be goin'. I'm skeered somebody'll recognize this carriage if I stay here longer. And that wouldn't do you no good. And, Miz Wilkes, if you ever see me on the street, you—you don't have to speak to me. I'll understand.

MELANIE I shall be proud to speak to you—proud to be under obligation to you. I hope we meet again.

BELLE No, that wouldn't be fittin'. . . . Good night, Miz Wilkes.

MELANIE *(extending her hand)* Good night.

DISSOLVE TO:

486 INT. SCARLETT'S BEDROOM AT AUNT PITTYPAT'S—CLOSE UP OF BRANDY BOTTLE

Scarlett's hand comes into shot, lifts up bottle. PULL BACK CAMERA—to see Scarlett, with a slight jag on, pouring drink into a glass. She takes a big swig—looks over at Kennedy's picture on the dresser, then takes another big swig and rises. She goes to the dresser and stares again at her late husband's picture, then turns it facedown on the dresser top. The sound of carriage wheels from outside attracts her. She runs to the window and looks out.

487 EXT. HOUSE (FROM HER ANGLE)

Rhett stepping from his elegant carriage, and walking up the path to the front door.

SCARLETT'S VOICE Great balls of fire!

(hiccoughs)
It's Rhett!

488 BACK TO SCARLETT

She runs back to the mirror—smooths her hair hurriedly—thinks of her breath—holds her hand in front of her mouth—blows on it—grimaces as she sniffs the odor on her hand from her breath—goes hurriedly to the dresser from which she takes cologne bottle—tilts it back and gargles cologne from the bottle. A knock is heard on her door.

MAMMY'S VOICE *(disgustedly)* Miss Scarlett! Cap'n Butler here to see you. I tol' him you was prostrate with grief.

Scarlett affects a tragic voice which belies her appearance and her hasty attempts to straighten herself up.

SCARLETT Tell him—tell him I'll be right down, Mammy.

489 INT. AUNT PITTYPAT'S DINING ROOM

Rhett strolls in from the hall where he has been pacing. The dining room bears evidence that Kennedy's funeral services have just been held there —chairs still arranged in rows, the coffin stand still standing, and scattered flowers on the floor.

Rhett bends down and picks up a lily of the valley, which he sticks in his lapel.

Mammy comes in the door, giving Rhett a dirty look.

MAMMY She says she's comin'. Ah don' know why she's comin', but she's a-comin'.

Rhett smiles, then looks at her reprovingly.

RHETT You don't like me, Mammy.
(Mammy snorts)
Now don't argue with me. You don't—you really don't.

Rhett laughs as Mammy exits in a huff. He hears Scarlett's descending footsteps and goes into the hall to meet her.

490 INT. HALL

Scarlett is coming slowly down the stairs. She tries to put on a great show of dignity as she sees Rhett at the foot of the stairs waiting for her, and

CONTINUED:

490 CONTINUED

extends her hand to him. He bows over it very low, starts to kiss it, and sniffs.

RHETT *(as he rises from her hand)* It's no use, Scarlett.

SCARLETT What?
(she starts guiltily)

RHETT The cologne.

SCARLETT I—I'm sure I don't know what you mean!

RHETT I mean you've been drinking.
(goes toward her to look more closely)
Brandy. Quite a lot.

SCARLETT *(bridles)* Well, what if I have? Is that any of your affair?

RHETT *(stops in doorway)* Don't drink alone, Scarlett. People always find out and it ruins the reputation.
(closes doors behind him)

He looks at her, amused, as she crosses into the living room, then follows.

491–500 INT. LIVING ROOM

Scarlett, sniffling into her handkerchief, crosses and sits on the sofa. First closing the door after them, Rhett follows and sits beside her.

RHETT What is it? This is more than losing old Frank.

SCARLETT *(she looks up pathetically)* Oh, Rhett, I'm so afraid!

RHETT *(he smiles)* I don't believe it. You've never been afraid in your life.

SCARLETT *(she insists)* I'm afraid now. I'm afraid of dying and going to hell.

He wants to laugh and rises and moves away to restrain himself. Then:

RHETT You look pretty healthy. And maybe there isn't any hell.

Scarlett looks up, shocked and injured.

SCARLETT *(very earnestly)* Oh, there is! I know there is! I was raised on it!

RHETT Well, far be it from me to question the teachings of childhood. Tell me what you've done that hell yawns before you.

SCARLETT I ought never to have married Frank to begin with. He was Suellen's beau, and he loved her, not me. And I made him miserable and I killed him! Yes, I did! I killed him! Oh, oh, Rhett, for the first time I'm finding out what it is to be sorry for something I've done!
(she dissolves into tears again)

RHETT *(he offers his handkerchief)* Dry your eyes. If you had it all to do over again, you'd do no differently. You're like the thief who isn't the least bit sorry he stole, but he's terribly, terribly sorry he's going to jail.

SCARLETT Oh, I'm glad mother's dead. I'm glad she's dead so she can't see me. I always wanted to be like her—calm and kind—and I certainly have turned out disappointing.

RHETT You know, Scarlett, I think you're on the verge of a crying jag.
(she rises, furious, but still he continues:)
So I'll change the subject and say what I came to say.

SCARLETT Say it, then, and get out!
(then, in spite of herself)
What is it?

RHETT That I can't go on any longer without you.

SCARLETT *(slowly; the great lady)* Oh—you really *are* the most ill-bred man to come here at a time like this with your filthy . . .

RHETT *(interrupting and completely disregarding her performance)* I made up my mind that you were the only woman for me, Scarlett, the first time I saw you at Twelve Oaks . . . Now you've got your lumber mill and Frank's money, you won't come to me as you did to the jail . . . So I see I shall have to marry you.

SCARLETT I never heard of such bad taste!

RHETT *(interrupting)* Would you be more convinced if I fell to my knees?
(he kneels and takes her hand. She tries to draw it back, but he holds it fast)

SCARLETT Turn me loose, you varmint, and get out of here!

RHETT *(playacting)* Forgive me for startling you with my sentiments,

CONTINUED:

491–500 CONTINUED

my dear Scarlett—I mean, my dear Mrs. Kennedy. But it cannot have escaped your notice that for some time past the friendship I have felt for you has ripened into a deeper feeling. A feeling more beautiful, more pure, more sacred . . . Dare I name it? Can it be love?

SCARLETT *(furious)* Get up off your knees. I don't like your common jokes!

RHETT This is an honorable proposal of marriage, made at what I consider a most opportune moment.
(he rises)
I can't go all my life waiting to catch you between husbands.

SCARLETT You're coarse and you're conceited, and I think this conversation's gone far enough. . . .
(afterthought)
Besides, I shall never marry again.

RHETT Oh, yes you will. And you'll marry me.

SCARLETT You! I don't love you . . . And I don't like being married.

RHETT Did you ever think of marrying just for fun?

SCARLETT Marriage *fun?* Fiddle-dee-dee! Fun for men, you mean!
(this time he does laugh heartily and she is frightened)
Hush up! Do you want them to hear outside?

RHETT You've been married to a boy and an old man. Why not try a husband of the right age, with a way with women?

SCARLETT You're a fool, Rhett Butler, when you know I shall always love another man . . .

RHETT Stop it!
(then, in a low voice, shaken, though, by the violence of his feeling)
Do you hear me, Scarlett? Stop it! No more of that talk!

He takes her in his arms, bends her head back across his arm, and kisses her hard on the mouth again and again, till she struggles for breath.

SCARLETT Rhett, don't! I shall faint!

RHETT I want you to faint. This is what you were meant for! None of the fools you've ever known have kissed you like this, have they?
(continues kissing her)

Your Charles or your Frank or your stupid Ashley?

He kisses her again and slowly Scarlett's arms go around him. At long last Scarlett O'Hara has surrendered.

Rhett draws back from the embrace.

RHETT *(hoarsely)* Say you're going to marry me! . . . Say yes! Say yes!

SCARLETT *(whispers)* Yes.

She closes her eyes, preparing for another kiss. He starts to kiss her again, then draws back and looks at her. Scarlett opens her eyes.

RHETT You're sure you meant it? You don't want to take it back?

SCARLETT No.

He puts his hand under her chin and lifts her face to his.

RHETT Look at me. And try to tell me the truth! Did you say yes because of my money?

SCARLETT *(taken aback)* Well—yes, partly.

RHETT *(looks at her sourly)* Partly!

He drops his arms and walks away from her a few steps.

SCARLETT *(floundering)* Well, you know, Rhett, money does help—and of course—I am fond of you—

RHETT Fond of me!

SCARLETT Well, if I said I was madly in love with you, you'd know I was lying. But you've always said we had a lot in common—

As she talks, Rhett bites his lip and shakes his head in despair, with which is mixed a degree of humor at what he's putting up with to get this woman. In the face of what she says he has no alternative but to control his emotions and assume as casual an attitude as hers.

RHETT Yes, you're right, my dear. I'm not in love with you any more than you are with me. Heaven help the man who ever really loves you! . . . Well, what kind of a ring would you like, my darling?

SCARLETT Ooo—a diamond ring! And—and do buy a great big one, Rhett.

CONTINUED:

491–500 CONTINUED

RHETT You shall have the biggest and the most vulgar ring in Atlanta . . . and I'll take you to New Orleans for the most expensive honeymoon my ill-gotten gains can buy.

SCARLETT Oh, that would be just *heavenly!*

RHETT And I think I'll buy your trousseau for you, too.

SCARLETT Oh, Rhett, how *wonderful!*
(on second thought)
But you won't tell anybody, will you, Rhett?

RHETT *(looking at her with slightly sour amusement)* Still the little hypocrite!
(he laughs, starts out of the room, Scarlett running after him)

501 INT. HALL

Scarlett running after Rhett, who is at the door.

SCARLETT Well, aren't you going to kiss me good-bye?

RHETT Don't you think you've had enough kissing for one afternoon?

SCARLETT Oh, you're impossible! You can go and I don't care if you never come back!

She turns and flounces toward the stairs, peering over her shoulder, expecting Rhett to come after her. But he simply opens the door and calls:

RHETT But I will come back.

He closes the door after him and we

DISSOLVE TO:

502 LONG SHOT—RIVER BOAT ON THE MISSISSIPPI

Negroes are singing off-scene and the singing continues through the next scene.

503 CLOSE UP—WEDDING RING AND ENORMOUS DIAMOND & EMERALD RING ON SCARLETT'S FINGER

CAMERA PULLS BACK, and we see that Scarlett is lying in bed in a cabin of an elegant riverboat of the period, dimly lighted. Rhett, in dressing gown, enters. Scarlett looks up at him, smiling and coy. She throws her head back luxuriously and thoughtfully on the pillow. She makes a very provocative picture.

RHETT *(softly and romantically)* What are you thinking about, Scarlett?

SCARLETT *(she closes her eyes romantically, and after a second speaks)* I'm thinking about how rich we are.

Taken aback, Rhett cannot help laughing nevertheless.

SCARLETT *(suddenly nervous)* Rhett—I can keep the lumber business, too, can't I?

RHETT *(tolerantly, as to an adored and spoiled child)* Yes, of course you can . . . if it amuses you. And now that you're so rich, you can tell everybody to go to the devil as you always said you wanted to.

SCARLETT But you were the main one I wanted to go to the devil.

DISSOLVE TO:

504 INT. NEW ORLEANS CAFE

CLOSE SHOT—A LINE OF CREOLE DANCING GIRLS, about seven-eighths covered by the smoke. The café is gas-lighted *and there are many shadows.*

PULL BACK to reveal Scarlett and Rhett in profile across from each other at a table. Rhett is smoking a long cigar.

On the table is the most elaborate possible food—an elegantly prepared dove, etc., etc. . . . wineglasses . . . two or three kinds—and buckets of wine.

Scarlett's plate is almost empty. Rhett's is half-eaten but he has finished. She is stuffing herself and scraping her plate, and in between times gobbling champagne as though it were water. She is as tight as a tick.

RHETT Don't scrape the plate, Scarlett. I'm sure there's more in the kitchen.

At this moment Scarlett sees a waiter go by with an elaborate tray of pastries.

SCARLETT Ooooh, Rhett! Can I have one of those chocolate ones stuffed with meringue?

CONTINUED:

504 CONTINUED

RHETT If you don't stop being such a glutton you'll get as fat as Mammy. Then I'll divorce you.

DISSOLVE TO:

505 INT. NEW ORLEANS HOTEL—LIVING ROOM OF SUITE—DAY

Open on CLOSE SHOT of bed and floor and chairs strewn with finery Scarlett has bought, and with boxes, wrappings, etc. There are night-gowns, chemises, evening gowns, furs, high-heeled shoes, silk stockings, etc. There is also a big box of liberally colored candies. During the scene Scarlett stuffs herself with candies while she pirouettes in front of the mirrors with all the things she has bought.

By this time CAMERA IS FULL BACK.

During the scene Scarlett holds things up in front of herself, tries on hats, etc. There is probably other business that will suggest itself for both Rhett and Scarlett during this scene with the props of the clothes.

RHETT Don't you think it would be nice if you bought something for Mammy, too?

SCARLETT Why should I buy her a present? When she called us both mules?

RHETT *(laughing)* Mules? Why mules?

SCARLETT Yes— She said we could give ourselves airs and get ourselves all slicked up like race horses, but we were just mules in horse harness, and we didn't fool anybody.

RHETT I never heard anything more true. Mammy's a smart old soul and one of the few people I know whose respect I'd like to have.

SCARLETT Why, I won't give her a thing! She doesn't deserve it!

RHETT Then I'll take her a petticoat. . . . I remember my mammy always said that when she went to Heaven she wanted a red taffeta petticoat so stiff that it would stand by itself and so rustley that the Lord would think it was made of angel's wings.

SCARLETT She won't take it from you! She'd rather die than wear it.

RHETT That may be, but I'm making the gesture just the same.

DISSOLVE TO:

506 *INT. HOTEL BEDROOM—CLOSE SHOT—SCARLETT TOSSING IN BED—NIGHT*

The room is dark, lighted only by moonlight streaming across Scarlett's face. Her eyes are closed. She is screaming. Rhett's hand comes in and shakes her. Scarlett opens her eyes. Rhett is sitting on the edge of the bed.

RHETT You were having another nightmare.

Scarlett looks about her, then turns to Rhett with little-girl terror.

SCARLETT Oh, Rhett, I was so cold and hungry . . . and so tired! I couldn't find it! I ran through the mist but I couldn't find it!

RHETT Find what, honey?

SCARLETT I don't know. I always dream the same dream and I never know! It seems to be hidden in the mist.

RHETT Darling!
(he kisses her)

SCARLETT Rhett, do you think I'll ever dream that I've found it—and that I'm safe?

Rhett shakes his head, smiling tenderly at her.

RHETT Dreams don't work that way. But when you get used to being safe and warm, you'll stop dreaming that dream . . . And, Scarlett, I'm going to see that you are safe . . .
(he holds her in his arms)

SCARLETT Oh, Rhett, will you do something for me if I ask you?

RHETT You *know* I will.

SCARLETT Take me away from here.

RHETT Don't you like New Orleans?

SCARLETT Oh, I love New Orleans, but I want to go home and visit Tara. Will you take me to Tara?

RHETT Yes, Scarlett. Of course I will. We'll go tomorrow.

As Scarlett holds herself close to him, we

DISSOLVE TO:

507 EXT. FRONT OF TARA—LONG SHOT—DAY

CAMERA PULLS BACK until Rhett and Scarlett are revealed standing in the f.g.

RHETT *(moodily)* You get your strength from this red earth of Tara, Scarlett. You're part of it, and it's part of you.

SCARLETT *(nostalgically, almost with a cry of pain and hope)* Oh, Rhett, I'd give anything to have Tara the way it was before the war!

RHETT *(kindly)* Would you? . . . Then go ahead and make it that way. Spend whatever you want to make it as fine a plantation as it ever was.

Scarlett looks at him, unbelieving.

SCARLETT Oh, Rhett, Rhett, you *are* good to me!
(she throws her arms around his neck)
And can we still have our big new house in Atlanta?

RHETT Yes.
(laughing)
And it can be as ornate as you want it . . . Marble terraces, stained-glass windows and all.

SCARLETT Oh, Rhett, won't everybody be jealous! I want everybody who's been mean to me to be *pea-green* with envy!

He laughs.

DISSOLVE TO:

508 INT. BEDROOM—TARA—SUELLEN AND CARREEN—NIGHT

SUELLEN *(sobbing in rage)* I don't care! Scarlett's hateful—building that new house just to show off! And even taking our servants!

CARREEN Darling, you mustn't think unkindly of her. She's made it possible for us to keep Tara—always—

SUELLEN *(turns)* Yes, and what good is Tara? She's had three husbands—
(screaming through her tears)
—and I'll be an old maid!

DISSOLVE TO:

509 EXT. BUTLER HOUSE (COSGROVE)

In the background through the trees we see the elegant new house. In the f.g., Pork, Mammy, and Prissy are standing agape, looking up at the house, bags in hand. Their luggage consists of old-fashioned worn leather suitcases, which had probably belonged to the O'Hara family. Pork totes a small, square leather hat trunk of the period, which he holds by its handle.

PORK Great Jehosophat! Great Jehosophat!

PRISSY *Lawzee!* We sho' is rich now.

FADE OUT

510–515 FADE IN:
INT. RHETT'S ROOM—NIGHT—SPRING, 1867

CLOSE UP RHETT'S FEET pacing the floor—surrounded by cigar butts on the fine carpet. As another is thrown down on the carpet:

RHETT'S VOICE That's ridiculous! Why can't I go in?

CAMERA HAS PANNED UP and we are now on a CLOSE SHOT of Rhett.

RHETT *(continuing)* I'm entitled to at least see what my own child looks like.

CAMERA PULLS BACK to show us that Rhett is in his room talking to Mammy. The door to the hall is open.

MAMMY You control yo'seff, Mist' Rhett—you'll be seein' it fer a long time.

Rhett continues mumbling, goes over and pours himself a drink, and drinks it during Mammy's following speech.

MAMMY Ah'd lak to 'pologize, Mist' Rhett, 'bout it's not bein' a boy.

RHETT Oh, hush your mouth, Mammy. Who wants a boy? Boys aren't any use to anybody. Don't you think I'm proof of that?

Mammy laughs uproariously at Rhett's joke. He pours a drink into another glass and hands it to Mammy.

RHETT Have a drink of sherry, Mammy.
(suddenly worried)
Mammy, she *is* beautiful, isn't she?

CONTINUED:

510–515 CONTINUED

Mammy takes the drink, peering around and looking through the open door to see no one is looking.

MAMMY *(gulps it down)* She sho' is.

RHETT *(still worried)* Did you ever see a prettier one?

MAMMY Well, suh, Miss Scarlett wuz mighty nigh that pretty when she come, but not quite.

RHETT *(his worries assuaged)* Have another drink, Mammy.

He takes the glass from her, starts pouring another drink. Mammy takes a step or two forward toward him, her skirts rustling.

RHETT *(sternly, but with twinkling eyes)* Mammy . . . what's that rustling noise I hear?

MAMMY Lawsy, Mist' Rhett, dat ain' nothin' but mah red silk petticoat you done give me.
(she giggles and swishes till her huge bulk shakes. She drinks.)

RHETT Nothing but your petticoat! I don't believe it. Let me see. Pull up your skirt.

MAMMY Mist' Rhett, you is bad! Yeah-O-Lawd!

She gives a little shriek and retreats about a yard, modestly lifting her dress a few inches to show the ruffle of her red taffeta petticoat.

RHETT *(grumbling)* You sure took a long enough time about wearing it.

MAMMY Yassuh, too long.

RHETT No more mule in horse harness?

MAMMY Mist' Rhett, Miss Scarlett wuz bad to tell you dat. You ain' holdin' dat 'gainst ol' Mammy?

RHETT No, I'm not holding it—I just wanted to know. Have another drink, Mammy—here, take the whole bottle.

Melanie appears at the door.

MELANIE Dr. Meade says you may go in now, Captain Butler.

Rhett exits as though he'd been shot.

MAMMY *(to Melanie)* Dis sho' is a happy day ter me. I done diapered three ginrations of dis fambly's girls, and it sho' is a happy day.

MELANIE Oh, yes, Mammy. The happiest days are when babies come. I wish . . .

Mammy looks at her keenly. Melanie is suddenly aware of her look.

MELANIE Oh, Mammy, she's beautiful! What do you suppose they'll name her?

As Mammy starts to answer, CAMERA STARTS TO MOVE UP CLOSER TO HER:

MAMMY Miss Scarlett done tol' me effen it wuz a girl she wuz goin' to name it *Eugenia Victoria!*

For the last words we are on a LARGE CLOSE UP OF MAMMY'S FACE, and from her big, black face, we

DISSOLVE TO:

516 CLOSE UP—THE BABY'S TINY WHITE FACE (AS IT LIES IN ITS CRIB)—DAY

Over it we hear Rhett's voice talking baby talk.

RHETT'S VOICE Yes, she's a beautiful baby, the most beautiful baby ever. Yes.
(clucks)
Do you know that this is your birthday?
(leans farther into crib—CAMERA PANS with him)
That you're a week old today? Yes.
(starts to pick her up)
I'm gonna buy her a pony the likes of which this . . .
(bent over crib; Mammy left b.g.)
. . . town has never seen. Yes, I'm gonna send her to the best
(picks her up out of cradle)
schools in Charleston. Yes.

517 INT. SCARLETT'S BEDROOM—REVERSE SHOT—RHETT

Rhett turns, still talking baby talk, moves to b.g. Mammy moves to crib in f.g., as CAMERA PANS with Rhett.

RHETT And her'll be received by the best families in the South.

CONTINUED:

517 CONTINUED

(he is crossing the room)
And when it comes time for her to marry—well—

RHETT *(cont'd.)*
(CAMERA REVEALS Scarlett in bed)
She'll be a little princess.

CAMERA PANS OVER TO SCARLETT, who lies in the nearby bed.

SCARLETT *(irritably)* You certainly are making a fool of yourself.

RHETT Why shouldn't I? She's the first person who's ever completely belonged to me.

SCARLETT Great balls of fire! I had the baby, didn't I?

A knock is heard.

MELANIE'S VOICE *(o.s.)* It's Melanie. May I come in?

SCARLETT Come in, Melly.

RHETT Yes. Come in and look at my daughter's beautiful blue eyes.

MELANIE *(crossing and laughing)* But, Captain Butler, most babies have blue eyes when they're born.

SCARLETT Don't try to tell him anything, Melly. He knows *everything* about babies.

RHETT Nevertheless, her eyes are blue and they're going to stay blue.

MELANIE *(laughingly)* As blue as the Bonnie Blue Flag.

RHETT That's it! That's what we'll call her! Bonnie Blue Butler!

518 CLOSE UP—SCARLETT

—looking at Rhett in disgust.

519 CLOSE UP—INFANT

—in Rhett's arms.

FADE OUT.

520–530 FADE IN:
INT. SCARLETT'S BEDROOM—NIGHT (ABOUT SIX WEEKS LATER)

Just as in her girlhood days at Tara, Scarlett's stays have just been laced by Mammy. The lacing completed, Mammy is pulling a tape measure tight around Scarlett's waist. Mammy looks up at her mistress.

SCARLETT Try again, Mammy.

MAMMY Twenty inches.

Scarlett's jaw drops.

SCARLETT Twenty inches! I've grown as big as Aunt Pitty! You've simply got to make it eighteen and a half again, Mammy!

MAMMY *(shakes her head)* You done had a baby, Miss Scarlett, an' you ain' never goin' to be no eighteen an' a half inches again—never. An' dere ain' nothin' to do 'bout it.

This statement provides Scarlett with the most unpleasant possible food for thought. A pause while she digests it, then:

SCARLETT There *is* something to do about it! I'm just not going to get old and fat before my time! I just won't have any more babies!

MAMMY I heerd Mist' Rhett say that he'll be wantin' a son next year.

SCARLETT Go tell Captain Butler I've decided not to go out after all. *(she picks up a wrapper from a nearby chair and slips it on)*
I'll have supper in my room.

Meditatively, Scarlett crosses the room. She sits at the dressing table and stares at herself in the mirror. Mammy goes out, sighing, and shaking her head disgustedly. Scarlett's eyes drop to a little drawer in her dressing table. She opens the drawer. Takes out a daguerreotype in its case and opens it. It is a picture of Ashley Wilkes in his major's uniform.

So absorbed is she that she does not hear Rhett's entrance. He comes toward her. Puts his hands on her shoulders tenderly. She starts and conceals the daguerreotype quickly in her lap.

RHETT I got your message. I'll have them bring my supper up here, too.

He bends to kiss her neck. She gives a sudden, quick shudder. She is on her feet. The daguerreotype slips from her lap to the rug.

RHETT *(looks at her curiously)* No objections to that, I hope?

CONTINUED:

520–530 CONTINUED

SCARLETT No. Yes. I—I mean, I don't care where you have your supper.
(she moves to the window, speaking over her shoulder)
Rhett . . .

RHETT Yes?

SCARLETT You see—well—I've decided—well—
(she blurts it out)
I hope I don't have any more children.

Startled, Rhett takes a step toward her. His foot comes into contact with the daguerreotype. He looks down, CAMERA WITH HIM. It is open. Rhett's jaw sets. He controls himself. His tone is cold.

RHETT My pet, as I told you before Bonnie was born, it is immaterial to me whether you have one child or twenty!

SCARLETT *(faces him)* No—but you know what I—
(she is embarrassed, lowers her eyes. Then looks at him again, belligerently)
Do you know what I mean?

RHETT I do . . . And do *you* know that I can divorce you for this?

SCARLETT You're just low enough to think of something like that! If you had any chivalry in you—or—or would be nice like—well, look at Ashley Wilkes! Melanie can't have any more children and he—he—

Scarlett stops, unable to explain further. Rhett looks at her silently for a moment, sees through her. His face takes on a bitter little smile.

RHETT You've been to the lumber office this afternoon, haven't you?

SCARLETT *(guiltily)* What has that got to do with it?

RHETT Quite the little gentleman, Ashley . . . Pray go on, Mrs. Butler.

SCARLETT *(she chokes with rage, realizing the futility of any future hopes)* It's no use! You wouldn't understand!

Rhett goes over and pinches her chin playfully, attempting to cover his hurt.

RHETT You know, I'm sorry for you, Scarlett.

SCARLETT *(with a sneer)* Sorry—for me?

RHETT Yes, sorry for you—because you're throwing away happiness with both hands—and reaching out for something that will never make you happy.

SCARLETT *(pushing his hand down from her chin)* I don't know what you're talking about.

RHETT If you were free, and Miss Melly were dead and you had your precious, honorable Ashley, do you think you'd be happy with him?
(a bitter little laugh)
You'd never know him, never even understand his mind—any more than you understand anything except money.

SCARLETT Never mind about that. What I want to know is—

RHETT You may keep your sanctity, Scarlett. It'll work no hardship on me.

SCARLETT You mean to say you don't care?

RHETT The world is full of many things and many people . . . and I shan't be lonely. I'll find comfort elsewhere.

SCARLETT That's fine! But I warn you, just in case you change your mind, that I intend to lock my door!

RHETT Why bother?
(he is on his way to the door)
If I wanted to come in, no lock could keep me out!

He opens the door with one savage kick, which tears the hardware out of the splintered jamb.

Scarlett gasps, staring after him. Rhett (as seen by Scarlett through the broken door) goes quickly to a table in the next room, pours himself a drink from a decanter which is on the table, drinks a portion of the liquor, notices the portrait of Scarlett on the wall, and with savage intensity hurls the drink, glass and all, at the likeness of Scarlett. Scarlett, in the next room hears this, as we

FADE OUT.

531 FADE IN:
INT. BELLE WATLING'S PLACE

CONTINUED:

531 CONTINUED

Which is a little too richly appointed. Rhett is pacing like a caged, enraged lion. CAMERA PULLS BACK to reveal BELLE, sitting at a table with her back to Rhett, moodily playing with a glass and listening to him.

RHETT *(pacing)* I always knew that most women were cheats . . . hypocritical and hard . . . but *this* one!

BELLE *(without looking at him)* Oh, Rhett, it ain't no use.

RHETT *(stopping short and looking at her angrily)* What do you mean?

BELLE I mean you're poisoned with her . . . I don't care *what* she's done to you . . .
(moodily)
. . . you're still in love with her . . . And don't think it pleasures me any to say it.

RHETT *(savagely)* Maybe so! But I'm through with her, I tell you! I'm through!

BELLE You got to think of the child. The child's worth ten of the mother.

Rhett takes this, and after a moment speaks:

RHETT
(looking at her warmly and speaking kindly)
You're a shrewd woman, Belle, and a very nice one, and . . .
(he stops)

BELLE *(looking up at him)* Yes, Rhett?

RHETT *(quietly but with a little bitterness)* I was just thinking of the difference between you and . . . You're both hardheaded business women and you're both successful . . . but—
(sincerely)
you've got a heart, Belle . . . and you're honest.

Belle doesn't look at him. There are tears in her eyes.

BELLE *(without looking up)* Good-bye, Rhett.

RHETT Good-bye, Belle.

He leaves. CAMERA MOVES to CLOSE UP of Belle. There are tears in her eyes.

FADE OUT.

532 FADE IN:
EXT. PEACHTREE STREET—LATE SUMMER—CLOSE UP THE FRONT OF A TOY HORSE—bouncing up and down as if traveling along the street.

CAMERA PULLS BACK to reveal that the horse is the front of a baby carriage (half toy, half baby carriage), and to reveal BONNIE, now about six or seven months old, sitting up gurgling in her carriage, holding the reins which extend back from the bridle of the toy horse.

RHETT'S VOICE She'll be a wonderful horsewoman . . . Look at those hands—and *that seat!*

SCARLETT'S VOICE Oh, fiddle-dee-dee!

CAMERA PULLS FARTHER BACK to a CLOSE TWO SHOT OF RHETT AND SCARLETT. Rhett is wheeling Bonnie's carriage; Scarlett walks alongside in an ill temper. Rhett is very blithe. As the scene progresses, they talk to characters off-scene, whom we do not see.

SCARLETT Just why we have to wheel the baby when we have a house full of servants . . .

RHETT *(bowing and tipping his hat with a little too much friendliness)* Good morning, Mrs. Merriwether.

MRS. MERRIWETHER'S VOICE *(coldly)* Oh, good morning, Captain Butler . . . Good morning, Scarlett.

Scarlett affects a very insincere smile and nods, then, giving Mrs. Merriwether time to get out of sight, her face goes back to its original expression.

SCARLETT Making fools of ourselves in front of these old buffaloes!

RHETT *(angrily)* If you'd thought of your position years ago, you wouldn't have to do this. But as it is, we're going to cultivate every female dragon of the old guard in this town . . .
(suddenly spots someone else off-scene)
Good morning, Mrs. Whiting.

CONTINUED:

532 CONTINUED

MRS. WHITING'S VOICE *(coldly)* Good morning, Captain Butler. Good morning, Scarlett.

Scarlett again smiles and nods insincerely and, when Mrs. Whiting has had time to get out of view, resumes her ill-tempered expression, and turns back to Rhett.

SCARLETT So the millionaire speculator's turning respectable!

RHETT All our money can't buy what I want for Bonnie. Oh, I'll admit I've been at fault, too. But Bonnie's going to have a place with *decent* people! Yes, even if we both have to crawl on our bellies to every fat old cat . . .
(he spots another, tips his hat, and smiles)
Good morning, Mrs. Meade.

MRS. MEADE'S VOICE *(also coldly)* Good morning, Captain Butler. Good morning, Scarlett.

For the third time, Scarlett affects a friendly smile and nod for the benefit of Mrs. Meade—not resuming her annoyed expression until Mrs. Meade has had time to get out of view; and as the CAMERA PULLS BACK on the domestic portrait of Rhett blithely wheeling the carriage and Scarlett by his side in a rage, we

DISSOLVE TO:

533 EXT. RESIDENTIAL PEACHTREE STREET—
CLOSE SHOT BONNIE ON HORSEBACK, shooting over horse's head. Bonnie is now two and a half. She is sucking her thumb, and her other hand grips the pommel of the saddle.

CAMERA MOVES TO A CLOSE SHOT of Rhett, who is revealed in the saddle behind Bonnie. His hat is in his hand and his arm is around Bonnie. His other hand holds the reins. As we move the Camera back, we hear his voice:

RHETT'S VOICE Mrs. Merriwether, I've always had a great regard for your knowledge, I wonder if you could give me some advice?

THE CAMERA MOVES TO INCLUDE MRS. MERRIWETHER, standing at the curb, talking up at Rhett. She is in a plumed bonnet.

MRS. MERRIWETHER *(flattered)* Why, certainly, Captain Butler.

RHETT My Bonnie sucks her thumb. I can't make her stop it . . .

MRS. MERRIWETHER *(vigorously)* You should *make* her stop it. It will ruin the shape of her mouth.

RHETT *(sadly, shaking his head)* I know, I know.
(looking at Bonnie)
And she has such a beautiful mouth, too.
(turns back to Mrs. Merriwether)
I've tried putting soap under her nails.

MRS. MERRIWETHER Soap! Bah! Put quinine on her thumb and she'll stop sucking it quick enough!

RHETT *(with exaggerated astonishment and pleasure)* Quinine! . . . I *never* would have thought of it; I can't thank you enough, Mrs. Merriwether! You've taken a great load off my mind. Good morning.

He bows and rides on with Bonnie, leaving Mrs. Merriwether looking after him with admiration and pleasure at the acceptance of her own expert advice. Mrs. Meade hurries along the street to Mrs. Merriwether.

MRS. MEADE Good morning, Dolly . . .
(with pleasure)
Wasn't that Captain Butler?

MRS. MERRIWETHER Good morning, Caroline . . . I was just thinking—there must be a great deal of good in any man who can love a child so much.

MRS. MEADE But of course there is!
(leans over confidentially)
Did I tell you, Dolly, that Fanny Elsing told Dr. Meade that Captain Butler finally admitted he was honored by the Confederate Congress for his services at the battle of Franklin?

MRS. MERRIWETHER *(in astonished pleasure, looking down the street)* No! . . . And did I tell *you,* Caroline, that Captain Butler made a stupendous contribution to the Association for the Beautification of the Graves of the Glorious Dead?

MRS. MEADE No!

Both gaze off admiringly down the street in the direction Rhett has taken with Bonnie.

CONTINUED:

533 CONTINUED

MRS. MERRIWETHER *(proudly)* My little grandbaby, Napoleon Picard, is going to give a party for Bonnie next week.

MRS. MEADE *(indignantly)* Now, Dolly Merriwether, you know right well that it was *my* idea to give a party for Bonnie Butler.

MRS. MERRIWETHER *(the old buffalo!)* Why, Caroline Meade!

And on the picture of the two women fighting as to which of them is going to entertain Bonnie, we

DISSOLVE TO:

534 EXT. BUTLER GARDEN AND LAWNS

In the foreground Rhett has had erected a very low bar.

Bonnie, now four, stands watching as Rhett teaches her pony to jump. Rhett is on his large horse and holds a guiding rope in his hand attached to Bonnie's pony.

RHETT Now watch Daddy put your pony over, Bonnie.
(guiding the pony alongside a fence in the garden, toward the jump)
Now watch!

The pony, guided by Rhett, takes a successful jump over the low hurdle. Bonnie screams in delight.

BONNIE Wheee! Daddy, let me—let me!

RHETT All right, darling. Put her on, Pork.

Rhett is still holding the guiding rope as Bonnie runs to the pony. Pork walks after her.

RHETT Whoa! Up we go!

Pork lifts her into the saddle.

RHETT Oh, there!

PORK *(overlapping)* Dere yo' is!

535 EXT. TERRACE—MEDIUM SHOT—MAMMY

Mammy comes out on the terrace. She has been picking flowers, and has a basket of flowers on one arm and some blossoms in her other hand.

MAMMY *(impatiently)* Lawsy Mercy! Dere he goes again!

536 BACK TO SCENE

RHETT Grip tightly with your legs and sit close. Lean forward and be sure you go with him. Hold your reins properly in a firm hand.

Bonnie starts down the run for the jump—Rhett riding a little off, still holding rope. Bonnie, on her pony, comes up to the jump and barely makes it.

BONNIE Wheee!
(she goes over to Rhett)

RHETT That was fine! I knew you'd do it! When you get a little older, I'll take you to Kentucky and Virginia. You'll be the greatest horsewoman in the South. Give your daddy a kiss.
(he leans down from his horse and kisses her as she sits on her small pony)

MAMMY'S VOICE Mist' Rhett! Mist' Rhett!

537 TWO SHOT—MAMMY AND RHETT

Mammy comes running across the lawn to them.

MAMMY Mist' Rhett!

RHETT Did you see her, Mammy? Wasn't she wonderful?

MAMMY *(impatiently)* Mist' Rhett, I done tol' you and tol' you it jus' ain' fittin' fer a girl chile to ride a-straddle wid her dress flyin' up!

RHETT *(propitiating)* All right, Mammy. I'll teach her to ride sidesaddle . . . and I'll buy her a blue velvet riding habit. She'll love that.

MAMMY *(grumbling)* A nice black broadcloth is whut li'l girls wear.

RHETT *(arguing plaintively)* Oh, now, Mammy, be reasonable.

MAMMY *(grumbling)* Well . . . I don't think it's fittin', but . . .

Rhett laughs, leans over and pats Mammy on the back. He turns his horse to ride off, and Mammy, still grumbling, looks after him.

MAMMY It ain' fittin'. It jus' ain' fittin'.
(she turns to go back to the house, then looks back as if in afterthought)
It ain' fittin'.

DISSOLVE TO:

538–550 INT. LUMBER MILL OFFICE—DAY—SUMMER, 1872

Ashley, very tired, is closing the ledger as we come in on the scene. He gets up and is slipping into his coat when he is suddenly aware of the presence of Scarlett, who has entered unknown to him. Though she looks no older, her face is perceptibly hardened and her whole bearing more mature.

(There has been a time lapse of several years since we have seen Scarlett.)

ASHLEY Scarlett! What are you doing downtown at this time of day?

SCARLETT Well, Ashley, I—

ASHLEY Why aren't you helping Melly get ready for my surprise birthday party?

SCARLETT *(indignantly)* Why, Ashley Wilkes, you aren't supposed to know a thing about it! Melly will be so disappointed if you're not surprised.

ASHLEY Oh, I won't let on. I'll be the most surprised man in Atlanta . . . But as long as you're here, let me show you the books so you can see just how bad a businessman I really am.
(he starts for the books)

SCARLETT Oh, don't let's fool with any books today! When I'm wearing a new bonnet all the figures I ever knew go right slap out of my head.

ASHLEY The figures are well lost when the bonnet's as pretty as that one.
(goes to her, takes her hands, and spreads them wide, looking at her dress)
Scarlett, you know, you—you get prettier all the time. You haven't changed a bit since the day of our last barbecue at Twelve Oaks when you sat under a tree, surrounded by dozens of beaux.

SCARLETT *(shakes her head, saddened by the memory of her girlhood)* That girl doesn't exist anymore . . . Nothing's turned out as I expected, Ashley! Nothing!

ASHLEY Yes, we've traveled a long road since the old days, haven't we, Scarlett? Oh, the lazy days, the warm, still, country twilights! . . . The high, soft, Negro laughter from the quarters! . . . The golden warmth and security of those days!

SCARLETT *(tears in her eyes)* Don't look back, Ashley! Don't look back! It drags at your heart till you can't do anything but look back!

He goes to her and puts his arms around her.

ASHLEY I didn't mean to make you sad, my dear.
(puts his hand under her chin and turns her face up to his)
I'd never want you to be anything but completely happy.

He kisses the tear off her cheek. Suddenly his face changes as he looks off in dismay. Scarlett, noticing the change in his expression, turns her face in the same direction in which he is looking.

WE CUT or SWING THE CAMERA to reveal the malevolent face of India staring at them triumphantly. India raises her head with a sneer and a smile, turns, and is gone.

551 TWO SHOT—SCARLETT AND ASHLEY

SCARLETT *(terrified)* Oh, Ashley!

Ashley drops his arms from around her, and his eyes fall in dismay and fright as he realizes the import of the situation and the interpretation that will inevitably be placed on it. On the portrait of Scarlett staring at him in confusion and dismay, we

FADE OUT.

552 FADE IN:
INT. SCARLETT'S BEDROOM—NIGHT

Only the lamps are lit. Scarlett is in a wrapper, stretched out full-length on the bed. A knock on the door and she sits up frightened.

SCARLETT Who is it?

RHETT *(off-scene)* Only your husband.

Scarlett gasps.

SCARLETT *(calls out in terrified voice)* Come in.

Rhett enters. He is dressed for the evening. His mood is cold and murderous.

RHETT Am I actually being invited into the sanctuary?

CONTINUED:

552 CONTINUED

He comes to the bed where Scarlett has shrunk back into the pillows, and jerks her upright.

RHETT You're not ready for Melanie's party!

SCARLETT *(terrified)* I've got a headache, Rhett. You go without me, and make my excuses to Melanie.

Rhett looks at her disgustedly for a moment, then speaks.

RHETT *(drawlingly and bitingly)* What a white-livered little coward you are!
(then:)
Get up! You're going to that party and you'll have to hurry!

SCARLETT Oh, has India dared to . . .

RHETT Yes, my dear. India has! Every woman in the town knows the story. And every man, too . . .

SCARLETT You should have killed them for spreading lies!

Her eyes search Rhett's face, but it is dark and impassive.

RHETT I have a strange way of not killing people who tell the truth. . . . There's no time to argue now. Get up.

SCARLETT I won't go! I can't go—until this—this misunderstanding is cleared up.

RHETT You're not going to cheat Miss Melly out of the satisfaction of publicly ordering you out of her house!

SCARLETT There was nothing wrong! India hates me so! I—I can't go, Rhett. I couldn't face it!

RHETT If you don't show your face tonight you'll never be able to show it in this town as long as you live . . . And while that wouldn't bother me, you're not going to ruin Bonnie's chances! . . . You're going to that party if only for her sake.
(he grabs Scarlett out of bed and pushes her across the room)
Get dressed.

He goes rapidly to the clothes closet.

553 CLOSE SHOT—SCARLETT

Reluctant and trembling she stands in the middle of the room, uncertain what he is going to do.

554 CLOSE SHOT—RHETT AT CLOSET

Searching through the dresses. Rhett takes one of the gowns from the closet.

RHETT Wear that!
(throws it at her)
Nothing modest or matronly will do for this occasion.

555 CLOSE SHOT—SCARLETT

In her chemise—trembling, frightened, picks up the dress from where he has thrown it.

556 BACK TO SCENE

RHETT Put on plenty of rouge! I want you to look your part tonight!

As Scarlett sits down in front of the dressing table, we

DISSOLVE TO:

557 INT. MELANIE'S PARLOR

Come in on birthday cake. The company, including Ashley, Melanie, Dr. and Mrs. Meade, and Aunt Pittypat, is packed around the table. Evidently Ashley has just been led up to the cake by Melanie. His manner is nervous; he is clearly under strain and clearly making all possible effort to do what is expected of him.

Someone begins to sing "For He's a Jolly Good Fellow." The company joins in. Of the three musicians, the harpist leads off. Dr. Meade chimes in with his violin and René Picard with his flute.

558 EXT. DOOR TO MELANIE'S HOUSE (SHOOTING FROM INTERIOR THROUGH OPEN DOOR)—TWO SHOT—SCARLETT AND RHETT

RHETT Good night, Scarlett.

SCARLETT But, Rhett, you're going to—

RHETT No. You go into the arena alone, Scarlett. The lions are hungry for you!

CONTINUED:

558 CONTINUED

SCARLETT Oh, Rhett, don't leave me! Don't—

RHETT You're not afraid?

Rhett bows and goes, leaving Scarlett standing in the doorway alone, looking inside.

559 BACK TO SCENE

The chorus is no sooner under way than Ashley takes a deep breath to blow, but he does not blow because he sees Scarlett standing in the doorway. The startled look on his face attracts Mrs. Meade's attention. Her singing stops. Then, as each one of the rest of the company turns, the song dies out. Only the harpist continuing uncertainly until she also stops.

In the meanwhile, Melanie is the last to see Scarlett. She brushes quickly through the tense silence of her guests, goes to Scarlett. She slips an arm about her waist.

MELANIE *(very clear)* What a lovely dress, Scarlett, darling! India wasn't able to come tonight. Will you be an angel? I do need you to help me receive my guests.

Sensation!

MELANIE Mrs. Meade, here's our darling Scarlett.

MRS. MEADE *(stiffly)* Good evening.
(she shakes Scarlett's hand reluctantly)

SCARLETT *(just as stiffly)* Good evening.

Melanie and Scarlett continue through the room, the guests greeting Scarlett as she and Melanie pass. Scarlett returns the greetings, her head high.

AD LIB Good evening, Scarlett.
Good evening.

They finally reach Ashley.

MELANIE Ashley, aren't you going to get our Scarlett a glass of punch?

As Ashley and Scarlett look at each other

DISSOLVE TO:

560 INT. SCARLETT'S BEDROOM—SAME NIGHT

CLOSE SHOT the gown Scarlett has worn to Melanie's party. It is on the floor where Scarlett has stepped out of it. Mammy is picking it up, also a few other articles of clothing which Scarlett has dropped—and is talking sleepily as she does:

MAMMY Did you have a good time tonight at Miss Melly's party, chile?

During above line CAMERA HAS PULLED BACK and now reveals Scarlett sitting in her red dressing gown at her dressing table.

SCARLETT *(impatiently)* Yes, yes! . . . Now you be sure and leave word . . .
(nervously)
If Captain Butler asks for me when he comes back, I'm asleep.

MAMMY Yas'm.

She gives Scarlett a suspicious look as she exits, and we

DISSOLVE TO:

561 INT. BUTLER HALL—NIGHT

It is lit with simply one, or at the most two, of the elaborate lighting fixtures. We see long shadows of Scarlett as she comes tremblingly down the stairs. Near the bottom of the flight she stops short as she sees light coming from the dining room. She is dressed in negligee and her hair down.

562 INT. DINING ROOM—(FROM SCARLETT'S ANGLE)

A candle is burning on the dining table in the otherwise dark room.

563 CLOSE SHOT—SCARLETT

She descends a few more steps, stealthily and nervously.

RHETT'S VOICE *(thickly)* Come in, Mrs. Butler.

Scarlett reacts in fright, pauses irresolutely, saying nothing.

564 INT. DINING ROOM—(FROM SCARLETT'S ANGLE)

Rhett's face moves into the light of the candle. He is without a coat and his cravat hangs down on either side of his open collar. His shirt is open and his hair rumpled. He is drunk. On the table is a silver tray bearing a

CONTINUED:

564 CONTINUED

decanter with cut-glass stopper out, surrounded by glasses. The glass from which Rhett has been drinking is on the table.

RHETT *(motions roughly)* Come here!

565 TRUCKING SHOT WITH SCARLETT

Scarlett has never seen him drunk before, does not know quite what to do —but she draws a deep breath, clutches her wrapper closer to her, and goes down the remaining steps and into the dining room, her head up, her heels clacking.

Rhett stands up and approaches the door with mock gallantry. He bows to her as she passes him and enters the dining room.

566 INT. DINING ROOM

As Scarlett enters. Monstrous shadows are thrown by the candle on the high-ceilinged room, making the massive furniture look like huge crouching beasts. Rhett follows her into the room.

RHETT *(curtly)* Sit down.
(Scarlett is frightened)
There's no reason why you shouldn't have your nightcap, even if I *am* here.

SCARLETT I didn't want a drink. I heard a noise and—

RHETT You heard nothing of the kind. You wouldn't have come down if you'd thought I was here. You must need a drink badly . . .
(he picks up the decanter and sloppily pours her a drink)

SCARLETT *(protesting)* I do not . . .

RHETT Take it!
(shoves the drink into her hand)
Don't give yourself airs. I know you drink on the quiet and I know how much you drink . . . Do you think I care if you like your brandy?

Scarlett looks at him a moment doubtfully, then bolts down the drink, making an unbecoming grimace. She notices, as she does, that Rhett has seen the grimace and that he is smiling sneeringly.

SCARLETT *(coldly)* You're drunk. And I'm going to bed.

RHETT I'm very drunk, and I intend getting still drunker before the evening's over. But you're not going to bed—not yet. Sit down!

Scarlett sits.

"His voice still held a remnant of its wonted cool drawl but beneath the words she could feel violence fighting its way to the surface, violence as cruel as the crack of a whip. She wavered irresolutely and he was at her side, his hand on her arm in a grip that hurt. He gave it a slight wrench and she hastily sat down with a little cry of pain. Now, she was afraid, more afraid than she had ever been in her life. As he leaned over her, she saw that his face was dark and flushed and his eyes still held their frightening glitter. There was something in their depths she did not recognize, could not understand, something deeper than anger, stronger than pain, something driving him until his eyes glowed redly like twin coals. He looked down at her for a long time, so long that her defiant gaze wavered and fell, and then he slumped into a chair opposite her and poured himself another drink. She thought rapidly, trying to lay a line of defenses. But until he spoke, she would not know what to say for she did not know exactly what accusation he intended to make."

RHETT *(finally)* So she stood by you, did she? How does it feel to have the woman you've wronged cloak your sins for you?

She makes no comment.

RHETT You're wondering if she knows all about you and Ashley. You're wondering if she did it just to save her face. You're thinking that she's a fool for doing it, even if it did save your hide.

SCARLETT I will not listen!

RHETT Yes, you'll listen. Miss Melly's a fool, but not the kind you think. It's just that there's too much honor in her to ever conceive of dishonor in anyone she loves. And she loves you—though just why she does, I'm sure I don't know.

SCARLETT If you were not so drunk and insulting I could explain everything.
(she rises, recovering some of her dignity)
As it is, though—

RHETT *(threateningly)* If you get out of that chair once more . . .
(Scarlett sits)
Of course, the comic figure in all this is the long-suffering Mr. Wilkes! Mr. Wilkes—who can't be mentally faithful to his wife—and *won't* be unfaithful to her technically.

CONTINUED:

566 CONTINUED
(takes a drink)
Why doesn't he make up his mind?

Scarlett springs to her feet with a cry. Rhett lunges from his seat, laughing softly. He is in back of her and presses her down into the chair.

567 TWO SHOT—SCARLETT AND RHETT—LARGE HEADS, ONE ABOVE THE OTHER

SCARLETT Rhett, you—

Scarlett sits tensely as Rhett stands behind her. He puts his hands in front of her face, flexing them.

RHETT Observe my hands, my dear. I could tear you to pieces with them—and I'd do it, if it'd take Ashley out of your mind forever. But it wouldn't. So I'll remove him from your mind forever, this way . . . I'll put my hands so, one on each side of your head . . .
(he fits the deed to the word)
And I'll smash your skull between them like a walnut . . . and that'll block him out.

His hands are under her flowing hair, caressing and hard. There is a moment of silence. Scarlett is frightened, but she has never been without animal courage, which supports her now.

568 TWO SHOT—SCARLETT AND RHETT

Scarlett narrows her eyes and speaks coldly and slowly:

SCARLETT Take your hands off me, you drunken fool!

To her surprise he does so, slowly removing them, and seating himself on the edge of the table, he pours himself another drink.

RHETT Well, I've always admired your spirit, my dear. Never more than now, when you're cornered.

She draws her wrapper close about her body. She rises, but without haste so as not to reveal her fear—tightens the wrapper across her hips, and throws her hair back from her face.

SCARLETT *(cuttingly)* I'm not cornered. You'll never corner me, Rhett Butler—or frighten me! You've lived in dirt so long you can't understand anything else. And you're jealous of something you can't understand. Good night.

(she starts casually toward the door)

There is a burst of laughter from Rhett. She stops and turns. He sways across the room toward her, still laughing. He puts his hands heavily upon her and pins her shoulders to the wall.

RHETT Jealous, am I? Yes, I suppose I am—even though I know you've been faithful to me all along. How do I know? Because I know Ashley Wilkes and his honorable breed. They're gentlemen—and that's more than I can say for you—or for me. We're not gentlemen and we have no honor—have we?
(he releases her, laughs, and starts for the decanter)

Scarlett stands a second, then runs swiftly out into the dark hall.

568A INT. DARK HALL

Out of the darkness comes Rhett after Scarlett. He seizes her and roughly turns her around to him, holding her close.

RHETT It's not that easy, Scarlett.
(he kisses her violently)
You turned me out while you chased Ashley Wilkes—while you dreamed of Ashley Wilkes. This is *one* night you're not turning me out!

He swings her off her feet into his arms. He starts up the stairs with her, her head crushed against his chest. She cries out, frightened, but the sounds are muffled against his chest.

He carries her up the stairs—up and up, into the increasing darkness, their shadows on the stairs.

THE CAMERA DRAWS BACK as he goes further and further up the stairs, Scarlett's cries diminishing. Then they are lost in the darkness at the top of the stairs and Scarlett's cries cease.

For a moment THE CAMERA HOLDS THE EMPTY STEPS, lit only by the hall light, then we

SOFTLY FADE OUT.

569 FADE IN:
INT. SCARLETT'S BEDROOM—NEXT MORNING

Scarlett in bed, just finishing her breakfast, which is on a tray. She is in a very happy mood. She stretches luxuriously. She hears someone ap-

CONTINUED:

569 CONTINUED

proaching the door; quickly arranges herself as becomingly as possible and looks anxiously at it. But it is Mammy who comes lumbering in to remove Scarlett's tray.

SCARLETT *(very gaily)* How you feeling this morning, Mammy?

MAMMY Well . . . this mizry in mah back ain' so good.

Scarlett, paying no attention to Mammy's complaints, starts to hum happily the first bars of "Ben Bolt."

MAMMY Yo' ack' mighty happy this mornin', Miss Scarlett.

SCARLETT I am, Mammy! I am!

She picks up the song, singing softly from "Ben Bolt" as Mammy waddles out with the tray, pulling the door to but leaving it ajar.

570 CLOSE SHOT—SCARLETT

SCARLETT *(singing)* "She wept with delight when you gave her a smile,
"And trembled with fear at your frown."

As she sings, she adjusts her bedjacket more fetchingly over her shoulders, bites her lips, and pinches her cheeks in a quick, almost forgotten gesture to bring color to them. She stops singing and lies back on her pillow, thinking of the night before. Suddenly she is embarrassed—giggles like a girl and pulls the covers up tight around her neck.

RHETT'S VOICE *(casually)* Hello . . .

Scarlett looks up, startled and delighted.

571 BACK TO SCENE

As Scarlett looks up she sees a very nonchalant Rhett. He is extremely offhand and anything but the ardent lover she had expected. He is sober and very quietly dressed.

RHETT *(very insincerely)* I—uh—I'd like to extend my apologies for my conduct of last night.

SCARLETT *(sitting up in disappointment)* Oh, but, Rhett—

RHETT *(satiric)* I was very drunk and—quite swept off my feet by your charms.

572 CLOSE UP—SCARLETT

Her expression changes. As far as she is concerned, this is the old Rhett.

SCARLETT *(bitterly)* Well, you needn't bother to apologize. Nothing you ever do surprises me.

573 TWO SHOT

Rhett approaches her.

RHETT *(with a change of tone)* Scarlett, I've been thinking things over, and I really believe that it would be better for both of us if we admitted we'd made a mistake and got a divorce.

SCARLETT *(amazed and hurt)* A divorce?

RHETT Yes. There's no point in our holding on to each other, is there? I'll provide for you amply. You've plenty of grounds. Just give me Bonnie and you can say what you please and I won't contest it.

SCARLETT *(really angry now)* Thank you very much, but I wouldn't dream of disgracing the family with a divorce!

RHETT *(who has been quite simple and serious now becomes angry at her hypocrisy)* You'd disgrace it quick enough if Ashley were free! It makes my head spin to think how quickly you'd divorce me!

Scarlett doesn't answer. She is hurt and furious. Rhett looks at her, "the old, puzzling, watchful glint in his eyes—keen, eager, as though he hangs on her next words hoping they would be—"

RHETT Wouldn't you, Scarlett?
(she doesn't answer)
Well, answer me. Wouldn't you?

SCARLETT Will you please go now, and leave me alone?

RHETT Yes, I'm going. That's what I came to tell you. I'm going on a very extended trip—to London. I'm leaving today.

SCARLETT *(stunned)* Oh!

RHETT And I'm taking Bonnie with me. So you'll please get her little duds packed right away.

SCARLETT You'll never take my child out of this house!

RHETT She's my child, too, Scarlett. And you're making a mistake if

CONTINUED:

573 CONTINUED

you think I'm leaving her here with a mother who hasn't the decency to consider her own reputation!

SCARLETT You're a fine one to talk! Do you think I'll let that child get out of this house, when you'll probably have her around with people like—like that Belle—

Rhett strides across the floor to her furiously.

RHETT If you were a man I'd break your neck for that! As it is, I'll thank you to shut your stupid mouth. Do you think I don't love Bonnie —that I'd take her any place where— And as for you giving yourself pious airs about your motherhood, why, a cat's a better mother than you are!
(Scarlett is terrified by his outburst)
You have her things packed and ready for me in an hour or I warn you . . . I've always thought a good lashing with a buggy whip would benefit you immensely!
(he turns on his heel and storms out of the room)

574 INT. UPPER HALL

Rhett striding out of Scarlett's room and crossing the hall in a rage. He passes Pork and almost knocks him over.

575 CLOSE UP—PORK

PORK S'cuse me, Mistah Rhett.

He looks after Rhett—startled and frightened.

576 INT. BONNIE'S NURSERY—(SHOOTING FROM HALL)

Rhett throws open the door—revealing Bonnie and her cousin, Beau Wilkes, playing on the floor in the nursery. Beau sees him first.

BEAU Hello, Uncle Rhett.

As Bonnie looks up and runs to Rhett:

RHETT Hello . . . Hello, Beau.

BONNIE Daddy! Daddy! Where have you been? I've been waiting for you all morning!

RHETT Well, I've been hunting for a rabbit skin to wrap my little Bonnie in . . . Give your best sweetheart a kiss.

(she kisses him)
Uhm-hmmm—Bonnie, I'm going to take you on a long trip to Fairyland.

CAMERA STARTS TO MOVE IN TO A CLOSE TWO SHOT OF BONNIE AND RHETT.

BONNIE Where? Where?

RHETT I'm going to show you the Tower of London where the little Princes were . . . and London Bridge . . .

BONNIE London Bridge? Will it be falling down?

RHETT Well, it will if you want it to, darling.

DISSOLVE TO:

577 THE THAMES—LONDON—(AUTUMN, 1872)

Big Ben striking a late hour. As the chimes end, the CAMERA IS DRAWING BACK through a hotel window, and as the chimes end we hear a baby's voice, terrified, screaming over them. As we get back in the INTERIOR of the HOTEL ROOM we discover Bonnie in the completely dark room—absolutely dark except for the light from outside on the child's terrified face. We hear Rhett's muffled voice from outside as Bonnie screams.

BONNIE'S VOICE *(screaming)* Daddy, dark! Dark! Daddy!

RHETT'S VOICE *(overlapping)* Bonnie! Bonnie! Bonnie! It's all right, Bonnie.

CAMERA SWINGS TO THE DOORWAY, through which Rhett enters. He wears evening clothes and a light overcoat. He crosses the dark room, the light hitting his face as he crosses.

BONNIE *(screaming)* Dark! Dark!

RHETT *(angrily, as he crosses)* Who put out that light? Nurse! Nurse!

Bonnie continues screaming until Rhett puts on a light.

BONNIE Daddy, dark! Dark!

RHETT There . . . shh . . . shh . . . shh . . .

CONTINUED:

577 CONTINUED

Rhett goes to her, tenderly lifts her from her bed, and holds her in his arms.

BONNIE Daddy, dark!

RHETT Yes, yes, yes . . . What's the matter with my Bonnie?

BONNIE A bear!

RHETT Oh, a bear? A big bear?

BONNIE Dretfull big! . . . And it sat on my chest.

RHETT Well, well, I'll stay here and shoot him if he comes back! Hmm?
(Bonnie's tears subside)
That's better.

He kisses the child and strokes her hair tenderly. She puts her arms around his neck. He looks at her adoringly, then puts her back into her bed. Now the nurse enters from the next room, rubbing her eyes. She has obviously been asleep and is startled at seeing Rhett.

NURSE Oh, good evening, Mr. Butler.

Rhett advances toward her, CAMERA PANNING WITH HIM.

RHETT *(angrily)* Haven't I told you you're never to leave this child alone in the dark?

NURSE If you'll pardon me, sir, children are often afraid of the dark, but they get over it. If you just let her scream for a night or two—

RHETT *(interrupting)* Let her scream! Either you're a fool or the most inhuman woman I've ever seen!

NURSE *(stiffly)* Well, of course, sir, if you want her to grow up nervous and cowardly—

RHETT Cowardly! There isn't a cowardly bone in her body! You're discharged.

He leaves her and goes to sit on Bonnie's bed or on the chair near the bed.

NURSE *(coldly)* As you say, sir.

The nurse turns on her heel and exits. Bonnie opens her eyes.

BONNIE Where's mother?

RHETT *(leaning over her tenderly)* Bonnie, aren't you happy here in London with me?

BONNIE I want to go home.

Bonnie's eyes close again, she drops off to sleep, her hand around Rhett's finger. Rhett looks at her thoughtfully, leans over, kisses her on the forehead, makes a tentative attempt to release his finger, finds it caught tight. He smiles sadly, prepares for a long stay. AS CAMERA MOVES UP TO CLOSE UP of the thoughtful, depressed Rhett, we

FADE OUT

578 FADE IN:
INT. BUTLER HOUSE—HALL—DAY—(AUTUMN, 1872)

Mammy is running up the stairs, holding her back, which is giving her a bit of trouble with the years. (In the course of the scene the labor of running up the stairs also tells on her. The troubled years of the war and the Reconstruction, and the effort of them, have told on her. There is grey in her eyebrows and she hasn't her old spryness.)

MAMMY Miss Bonnie! An' Cap'n Butler!
(calling back through door)
Miss Scarlett!

BONNIE Hello, Mammy . . .

MAMMY Honey chile . . .

BONNIE *(starting up the stairs)* Mummy . . . Mummy . . .

MAMMY *(calling)* Miss Scarlett! Dey's back! Dey's back, Miss Scarlett!

Bonnie's little figure is seen galloping up the stairs in back of Mammy, as quick as its little legs will take it. She clutches a kitten to her breast.

Scarlett appears, quite beside herself with joyous excitement. She runs down a few steps.

579 CLOSE SHOT—SCARLETT

SCARLETT Bonnie! Bonnie! Bonnie! Bonnie, baby!

580 REVERSE SHOT—(SCARLETT IN F.G., SHOOTING DOWN THE STAIRS)

Bonnie galloping up the stairs and Rhett below in the hall.

CONTINUED:

580 CONTINUED

Rhett looks up at Scarlett, sweeps off his hat in a wide gesture.

581 CLOSE SHOT—SCARLETT

She reacts to this—looks back at him in chagrin. But in a second Bonnie is in her arms and Scarlett is embracing her frantically.

SCARLETT Darling, baby! Are you glad to be home?

BONNIE *(showing her mother the kitten)* Daddy gave me a kitten!

SCARLETT Oh, a little, lovely kitten. What a lovely kitten.

BONNIE London's a horrid place.

SCARLETT Oh, my darling!

BONNIE Where's my pony? I want to go out and see my pony!

SCARLETT You go out and see your pony.

Rhett has come up the stairs to the scene. Scarlett meets his steady, resentful look. Her eyes fall.

SCARLETT You run along with Mammy . . . Go with Mammy.

Mammy drops a curtsy and leads Bonnie out of the scene.

582 TWO SHOT—RHETT AND SCARLETT

Rhett comes to the top of the stairs.

RHETT Mrs. Butler, I believe.

SCARLETT *(smiling, glad to see him)* Mammy said you'd come back.

RHETT But only to bring Bonnie. Apparently any mother, even a bad one, is better for a child than none.

SCARLETT *(dismayed)* You mean you're going away again?

RHETT What perception, Mrs. Butler. Right away. In fact, I left my bags at the station.

SCARLETT *(her face betraying her great disappointment)* Oh . . .

Rhett stands casually, his hand on his hip, and looks her over appraisingly from head to toe, and then back again to her face.

RHETT You're looking pale. Is there a shortage of rouge? Or can this wanness mean you've been missing me?

Scarlett flinches under the first word. Now she steps in, angry.

SCARLETT If I'm pale it's your fault—not because I've been missing you —but because—
(she can't go on)

RHETT Pray continue, Mrs. Butler.

SCARLETT *(blurting it out)* It's because I'm going to have a baby.

In spite of himself, Rhett is startled and for a moment his supercilious expression drops. He takes a step forward as though to put his hand on her arm, but she twists away from him and his former mood returns. Only for a moment has the shell disappeared.

RHETT Indeed! And who's the happy father?

Scarlett clutches the banister.

SCARLETT *(her voice shaking with sick rage)* You know it's yours! I don't want it any more than you do! No woman would want the child of a cad like you! I wish it were—I wish it were anybody's child but yours!

Rhett's expression changes suddenly into an expression of violent anger. He is silent for a moment, then the old impassive mask is back again.

RHETT Cheer up. Maybe you'll have an accident!

Scarlett stands appalled. Her fists clenching in rage as Rhett looks at her coolly. Then, after a moment, she lunges for him swift as a cat—but with a startled movement he sidesteps her, throwing up his arm to ward her off. And as her arm, with the whole weight of her body behind it, strikes his outthrust arm, she loses her balance, makes a wild clutch for the banister, and misses it. She rolls down the stairs backward.

583 LARGE CLOSE UP—RHETT'S FACE

He is aghast as he sees what has happened.

584 LONG SHOT—(SHOOTING DOWN THE STAIRS PAST RHETT)

As Scarlett rolls over and over to the bottom of the flight.

585 CLOSE SHOT—SCARLETT'S FACE

Distorted in torture as it rolls down the final steps.

586 LONG SHOT

THE CAMERA ZOOMS down to Scarlett's unconscious form.

DISSOLVE TO:

587 INT. HALL—EXT. SCARLETT'S DOOR—MORNING

Rhett is waiting in the hallway outside the door as Aunt Pittypat comes out from Scarlett's room.

RHETT *(looking up anxiously)* Is she better?

Aunt Pittypat doesn't answer, just lowers her head. Rhett reacts desperately to this.

RHETT *(pitifully)* Has she asked for me?

AUNT PITTYPAT *(avoiding his eyes)* I wish you'd understand . . . she's delirious.

Rhett controls his deep emotion and turns away.

DISSOLVE TO:

588 INT. SCARLETT'S BEDROOM—CLOSE SHOT—SCARLETT —NIGHT

In bed, delirious, dimly lit by one lamp in the room. She can barely be heard in her delirium.

SCARLETT *(very weakly whispering)* Rhett! I want Rhett!

The door opens, and she turns slightly, eagerly, but in agony. Mammy enters the room and approaches to her.

MAMMY *(very gently)* What's the matter, honey? Did you call somebody, chile?

SCARLETT It's no use . . . it's no use . . .

Mammy places a cold cloth on Scarlett's forehead, and as Scarlett lapses back into semi-consciousness, we

DISSOLVE TO:

589 INT. RHETT'S ROOM—BEDROOM WINDOW—RAINY NIGHT—CAMERA INSIDE

Against the window frame outside a loose shutter bangs methodically in the wind. The window is partially open and rain enters the room. CAM-

ERA PANS to the bedroom wall, showing the shadow of the gas chandelier swaying back and forth. CAMERA PANS FARTHER to the table, where Rhett is seated with a whiskey bottle and a glass in front of him. He has been drinking and shows it. From the hall door, now in b.g., comes the sound of someone knocking gently. He pays no attention. The knock is repeated. The sound at last penetrates his consciousness. Unsteadily he rises and opens the door. Melanie stands there.

MELANIE Dr. Meade's left.

RHETT *(after a moment's silence, heavily, in a dead tone)* Scarlett's dead.

MELANIE *(with a gentle, sympathetic smile)* Oh, no, she's much better—really she is.

CAMERA MOVES WITH MELANIE as she goes to Rhett. As she moves to him, she realizes that he is completely broken.

MELANIE *(comforting him)* There, there, Captain Butler, you're beside yourself. She'll very soon be well again. I promise you.

He lifts his head pitifully, and we see that there are tears in his eyes. When he speaks it is the voice of a man who has been through a torture of self-accusation, and whose mind is clouded with liquor. His voice betrays the struggle he is going through to keep from crying. Melanie is at first utterly uncomprehending and utterly maternal, but as the scene progresses, she is shocked in spite of herself by the revelation of secret things.

RHETT No—no—you don't understand. She never wanted this baby and—

MELANIE Not want a baby? Why, every woman wants a baby—

RHETT Yes, you want children. But she doesn't. Not my children! She told me she didn't want any more children—and I wanted to hurt her because she had hurt me! I wanted to—and I did—

MELANIE Hush, Captain Butler. You mustn't tell me these things. It's not fit.

RHETT *(continuing, heedless of her interruption)* I didn't know about this baby until the other day—when she fell. If I'd only known, I'd have come straight home—whether she wanted me home or not.

MELANIE Well, of course you would.

CONTINUED:

589 CONTINUED

RHETT And then when she told me—there on the steps—what did I do? —What did I say? I laughed and I said—
(he breaks)

MELANIE But you didn't mean it. I know you didn't mean it.

RHETT But I did mean it! I was crazy with jealousy! She's never cared for me! I thought I could make her care. But I couldn't!

MELANIE You're so wrong. Scarlett loves you a great deal—much more than she knows.

RHETT *(pitifully hopeful)* If that were only true, I could wait forever. If she'd only forgive me! Forget this ever happened . . .

MELANIE *(stroking his hair)* She will. You must be patient . . .

RHETT *(his momentary hope vanishes as he suddenly recollects)* No, no! . . . It's not possible! You don't understand . . . If you only knew who she really loved—but you wouldn't believe it . . .
(looks into her eyes)

MELANIE *(after a moment's silence, meeting his gaze squarely)* Surely, you haven't listened to idle gossip? . . . No, Captain Butler . . .
(she shakes her head)
. . . I wouldn't believe it.
(he lowers his eyes. She strokes his hair)
There, there. Scarlett's going to get well. And there can be other babies.

RHETT No, no. She couldn't . . . Even if she wanted to . . . after what she's been through . . .

MELANIE But of course she could. *I'm* going to—

Rhett looks at her, amazed.

RHETT No, Miss Melly. You mustn't risk it! It's too dangerous.

MELANIE Children are life renewing itself, Captain Butler . . . And when life does that, danger seems very unimportant.

RHETT *(looking up at her slowly—moved, touched, comforted, quieted)* I've never before known anyone who was really brave! I pray God things go well with you, Miss Melly, and I want to thank you for all you've done for me, and for Scarlett. From my heart I thank you.

He takes her hand and kisses it. She lays her other hand on his head as though in benediction.

FADE OUT.

590 *FADE IN:*
EXT. BUTLER TERRACE AND GARDEN—LONG SHOT—DAY—(COSGROVE)

Scarlett, dressed in a blue negligee, is stretched out in an easy chair with blankets around her and pillows at her back. Rhett enters from the house.

MAMMY Miss Scarlett's feelin' a heap bettah today, Mist' Rhett.

RHETT Thank you, Mammy.

591 *CLOSE TWO SHOT—RHETT AND SCARLETT*

Scarlett is pale and drawn from the agonies of the miscarriage from which she is recuperating. She gives Rhett one look as he approaches her, turns her face, and shrinks away from him. A moment of silence, then:

RHETT I've come to ask your forgiveness. In the hope that we can give our life together another chance.

He is contrite, simple, serious—completely without any affectation of cynicism or any distrust of Scarlett. He is the simplest and most sincere he has been in his whole life.

SCARLETT *(without looking at him, sarcastically)* Our life—together? When did we ever have a life together?

Rhett lowers his eyes. He is determined to take full blame and not to let anything Scarlett may say to him upset his final hopes.

RHETT Yes, you're right. But I'm sure if we could only try again—we could be happy.

SCARLETT What is there to make us happy now?

RHETT *(simply)* Well, there's—there's Bonnie . . . and . . .
(quietly and simply)
I love you, Scarlett.

SCARLETT *(jeeringly)* When did you discover that?

CONTINUED:

591 CONTINUED

RHETT I've always loved you, but you've never given me a chance to show it . . .

During his speech Scarlett has been moved just a shade, despite her will not to be moved.

SCARLETT *(after a moment, not so bitterly)* Well—just what do you want me to do?

RHETT To begin with . . . give up the mill, Scarlett. We'll go away. We'll take Bonnie with us, and we'll have another honeymoon.

SCARLETT *(indignantly, her momentary softness exploded)* Give up the mill! But why should I? It's making more money than it ever did!

RHETT *(patiently)* Yes—I know. But we don't need it. Sell it. Or better still, give it to Ashley. Melanie's been such a friend to both of us—

SCARLETT Melanie! Always Melanie! If you'd only think a little more about *me*—

RHETT I am thinking of you. And I'm thinking that—well—maybe it's the mill that's taking you away from me—and from Bonnie.

SCARLETT *(blowing up)* I know what you're thinking. And don't try to bring Bonnie into this. You're the one that's taking her away from me.

RHETT But she loves you—

SCARLETT *(not listening)* You've done everything possible to make her love you and not me. Why, she's so spoiled now that—

BONNIE'S VOICE Mommy! Daddy! Watch me!

They look off.

592 EXT. GARDEN AND TERRACE

Bonnie, on her pony, calls to them from the garden. She is riding sidesaddle now, and wears a blue velvet riding habit with long, flowing skirt and a plumed hat.

SCARLETT We're watching, darling.
(she looks at Bonnie admiringly)
You're mighty pretty, precious.

BONNIE *(generously)* So are you. . . . I'm going to jump. Watch me, Daddy!

RHETT I don't think you ought to do much jumping yet, Bonnie. Remember, you've just learned to ride sidesaddle.

BONNIE I will so jump! I can jump better than ever 'cause I've grown. And I've moved the bar higher—

almost simultaneously

SCARLETT *(alarmed)*
Don't let her do it, Rhett.

RHETT *(tolerantly)*
No, Bonnie you can't.

But Bonnie, unheeding, gallops away toward the jump.

RHETT *(with a laugh; calling after her)* Well—if you fall off, don't cry and blame me.

593 CLOSE SHOT—BONNIE

Sticking her heels into the pony's ribs and starting across the grounds, emitting a terrific yell.

594 CLOSE SHOT—SCARLETT AND RHETT

SCARLETT *(rising and protesting as strongly as her condition permits)* Rhett, stop her!

Rhett looks at Scarlett, realizes she is seriously concerned, turns, and shouts:

RHETT Bonnie!
(more insistently)
Bonnie!

595 CLOSE UP—BONNIE

Her eyes blazing delightedly in anticipation of the thrill she is about to get from the jump.

BONNIE Watch me!

596 CLOSE SHOT—SCARLETT

She sinks back in her chair.

SCARLETT *(with annoyance)* Just like Pa!

Suddenly terror comes into her face as she realizes the parallel. Instinctively she knows what is about to happen.

CONTINUED:

596 CONTINUED

SCARLETT *(terrified)* Just like Pa!

But it is too late. We hear Rhett's terrified voice:

RHETT'S VOICE Bonnie! Bonnie! Bonnie!

Scarlett screams.

597 ANGLE AT THE HURDLE

As the pony runs up to the hurdle, he stops short and Bonnie is thrown over his head, her little body hitting the ground flat on its back. The pony turns and gallops off in panic, kicking up splinters from the shattered bar with his hooves.

598 CLOSE SHOT—NEAR THE JUMP

Bonnie's body lies in front of the jump, splinters of wood from the hurdle beside her. Her face is cut and scarred, her eyes are closed. She is dead. As Rhett runs in and picks up the little body, saying:

RHETT Bonnie! Bonnie!

FADE OUT.

599 FADE IN:
EXT. DOOR TO BUTLER HOUSE—CLOSE SHOT—SMALL SPRAY OF WHITE ROSEBUDS WITH WHITE CREPE STREAMERS—NIGHT

CAMERA PULLS BACK to reveal Melanie standing waiting nervously outside the door. The door opens and she is admitted by Mammy, who is dressed entirely in black, her face puckered in sad bewilderment.

MAMMY Lawsy, Miss Melly, Ah sho is glad you've come!

600 INT. HALL

As Melanie enters and Mammy closes the door behind her. She helps Melanie shed her wrap and gloves, Melanie talking the while:

MELANIE *(sadly, looking around)* Oh, Mammy, this house won't seem the same without Bonnie . . . How's Miss Scarlett bearing up?

MAMMY Miss Melly, dis yere done broke her heart. But Ah din' fetch you here on Miss Scarlett's account. Whut dat chile got ter stand, de good Lawd give her strength ter stand. It's Mist' Rhett Ah's worried 'bout.

(tears flow down her face; she lifts the hem of her black skirt and dries her eyes)
He done lost his mind dese last couple o' days.

MELANIE Oh, no, Mammy! No!

Mammy starts toward the stairs and Melanie accompanies her, CAMERA FOLLOWING WITH THEM.

MAMMY Ah ain' never seed no man, black or white, set sech a store by any chile. When Doctah Meade say her neck broke . . .
(she stops at the memory of the awful moment)
. . . Mist' Rhett grab his gun and run out dere an' shoot dat po' pony —an' fer a minit Ah think he gwine shoot hisseff.

Tears fall again but this time Mammy doesn't bother to wipe them away. Tears come to Melanie's eyes also.

MELANIE Oh, poor Captain Butler!

MAMMY Yas'm. An' Miss Scarlett, she call him a murderer fer teachin' dat chile to jump. She say, "You give me mah baby whut you killt." And den he say Miss Scarlett ain't neber keered nuthin' 'bout Miss Bonnie . . . It lak ter turn mah blood cold de things dey say ter one 'nother.

MELANIE Stop, Mammy! Don't tell me any more!

MAMMY An' dat night, Mist' Rhett, he lock hisseff in de nuss'ry wid Miss Bonnie an' he wouldn' even open de do' when Miss Scarlett beat on it an' hollered ter him. An' dat's de way it's been fer two whole days.

MELANIE *(horror-stricken)* Oh, Mammy!

MAMMY *(nods ominously and shivers)* An' den dis evenin' Miss Scarlett, she shout through de do' an' she say dat de fune'l set fer termorrer mawnin' an' he say, "You try dat an' Ah kills you termorrer. Do you think Ah's gwine put mah chile in de dahk when she's so skeered of it?"

Mammy and Melanie have reached the head of the stairs, and the scene continues on the landing.

MELANIE *(distracted and grief-stricken herself)* Mammy, Mammy, he *has* lost his mind!

CONTINUED:

600 CONTINUED

MAMMY Yas'm, it's de Gawd's truff . . . He ain't gwine let us bury dat chile. You gotter help us, Miss Melly.

MELANIE But I can't intrude.

MAMMY Ef you cain' help us, who kin? Mist' Rhett always set great store by yo' 'pinion. Please, Miss Melly.

Melanie steels herself, terrified at the prospect of what she has to do, but realizing that she must do it. She stands a moment while Mammy looks at her pleadingly.

MELANIE I'll do what I can, Mammy.
(she goes to the door of Rhett's room and knocks softly)

RHETT'S VOICE Get away from that door and leave us alone!

MELANIE *(she knocks again)* It's Mrs. Wilkes, Captain Butler. Please let me in. I've come to see Bonnie.

A pause, then the door is opened quickly from within and the drunken bulk of Rhett's figure, his face unshaven, haggard, looks huge and dark against the blazing forest of candles around Bonnie's bier. Grotesque shadows play on the gaily decorated walls of the nursery. Mammy shrinks back into the window recess of the landing as Rhett looks down on Melanie for a moment; then grasps her arm and pulls her into the room, shutting the door. Mammy emerges, watches a second, and then slowly, ponderously, sinks down on her knees, raising her hands and her eyes in prayer.

MAMMY Oh, Lawd, please he'p Mist' Rhett in dis hour of his grief. He'p him, Lawd!

DISSOLVE TO:

601 INT. HALL—CLOSE SHOT—NURSERY DOOR—LATER THAT NIGHT

It opens and Melanie slips out. Before she closes the door quietly behind her, we see Rhett's figure in the background in the nursery, seated next to the bier, his head resting on his arm. Mammy steps forward to Melanie from where she has been sitting in the recess. Melanie stands swaying a little, supporting herself on the doorknob. She speaks steadily, but seemingly with a little difficulty.

MELANIE Mammy, I want you to go and make a good deal of strong coffee and bring it up to Captain Butler. I'll go and see Miss Scarlett . . .

MAMMY *(eager for news of what has happened)* But—?

MELANIE Captain Butler is quite willing for the funeral . . . to take place . . . tomorrow morning . . .

The steadiness of her voice has not wavered, but the volume has diminished.

MAMMY *(raising her eyes)* Hallelujah! Ah 'specks de angels fights on you' side, Miss Melly. Hallelujah!

She lowers her eyes just in time to see Melanie struggle to avoid collapsing. Melanie falls forward on the floor.

MAMMY *(terrified)* Miss Melly! Miss Melly! Miss Melly! Miss Melly! Miss Melly!

She quickly stoops down and puts her arm around Melanie for support.

602 CLOSE TWO SHOT

Melanie opens her eyes. Even now her competence asserts itself.

MELANIE Send for Doctor Meade, Mammy. And try—try to get me home.
(she closes her eyes again)

MAMMY Miss Melly! Miss Melly!

DISSOLVE TO:

603 INT. MELANIE'S PARLOR—NIGHT

Aunt Pittypat, Scarlett, and India sit at the table. Aunt Pittypat dabs her eyes. India is rigid. Rhett sits apart. There is a fire in the grate. A moment of silence, then Ashley walks out from Melanie's room carrying his sobbing son.

BEAU Where is my mother going away to? And why can't I go along, please?

ASHLEY We can't always go along, Beau, much as we want to. You're going back to bed now.

CONTINUED:

603 CONTINUED

He starts across the room to take Beau back to his bed. Scarlett turns to Rhett.

SCARLETT *(a whisper)* Oh, Rhett, she can't be dying! She can't be!

RHETT *(low)* She hasn't your strength. She's never had any strength. She's never had anything but heart.

ASHLEY *(looks back over his shoulder, to Rhett)* You knew that, too.

BEAU Why do I have to go back to bed? It's morning.

ASHLEY It isn't really morning yet.
(he exits)

Dr. Meade enters from the bedroom.

DR. MEADE You may come in now, Scarlett.

INDIA *(goes to the doctor and puts her hand on his sleeve)* Doctor, please let me see her. I've been waiting for two whole days and I've got to tell her—that I was wrong about something.

DR. MEADE She knows you were wrong.
(turns to Scarlett)
She wants to see Scarlett.
(he leads Scarlett into the hallway)

604 HALLWAY

As Dr. Meade and Scarlett enter.

DR. MEADE Miss Melly's going to die in peace. I won't have you easing your conscience telling her things that make no difference now! You understand?

Scarlett stops him with a gesture. Dr. Meade gives her a little push into the bedroom and closes the door after her.

605 INT. MELANIE'S BEDROOM

Melanie is lying very still on the bed. Her closed eyes are sunken in twin purple circles. Her face is a waxy yellow. Scarlett tiptoes across the room to the quiet figure and stands over her.

SCARLETT It's me, Melly.

The eyes open, then close again.

MELANIE Promise me?

SCARLETT Anything!

MELANIE Look after my little son! I gave him to you once before, remember? The day he was born?

SCARLETT Oh, Melly, don't talk this way! I know you'll get well!

MELANIE Promise me . . . College . . . ?

SCARLETT Yes! Yes! And Europe. And a pony. Whatever he wants! But, Melly! Do try . . .

MELANIE Ashley . . .
(Scarlett's eyes go wide, but Melanie continues)
Ashley and you . . .

Scarlett bows her head in sudden prayer. Melanie's fingers reach out to touch her.

SCARLETT *(almost voiceless)* What about—Ashley, Melly?

MELANIE Look after him for me. Just as you looked—looked after me for him.

SCARLETT I will, Melly.

MELANIE Look after him. But never let him know.

Scarlett is almost on the point of breaking. She rises, abruptly sinking her teeth into her thumb to regain control. The door opens slightly. Dr. Meade stands in the threshold, beckoning imperiously. She bends over the bed, takes Melanie's hand, and lays it against her cheek.

SCARLETT Good night.

MELANIE *(very faint)* Promise . . .

SCARLETT What else, Melly?

MELANIE Captain Butler. Be kind to him . . .

SCARLETT *(surprised)* Rhett?

MELANIE He loves you so.

SCARLETT *(sobs)* Yes, Melly.

MELANIE Good-bye.

CONTINUED:

605 CONTINUED

SCARLETT Good-bye.

She bends over and kisses Melanie's forehead, then draws back. The eyes are closed again. A last look at Melanie, then Scarlett goes. Dr. Meade follows her to the door.

606 INT. PARLOR

Scarlett and Dr. Meade enter. India and Aunt Pittypat are standing now. Ashley sits at the table. Rhett looks on from the hall.

DR. MEADE *(to the others)* You ladies may come in now.

They go in. The women hold their skirts close to their sides to keep them from rustling.

SCARLETT *(calls to Ashley)* Oh, Ashley! Ashley!

Ashley displays a worn glove.

ASHLEY I don't know where the mate to this is. She must have put it away.

SCARLETT *(crying)* Oh, stop it.
(drops to her knees beside him)
Hold me—I'm so frightened! I'm so frightened!

Ashley clutches Scarlett, pressing his head against her heart.

607 CLOSE SHOT—RHETT

He looks at Scarlett in Ashley's arms. Then, with an expression of mixed distaste and resignation, picks up his hat and coat and leaves.

608 TWO SHOT—ASHLEY AND SCARLETT

ASHLEY *(breaking their embrace)* Oh, Scarlett! What can I do? I can't live without her! I can't! Everything I ever had is—is going with her.

She looks at him, then the truth of things as they are comes clear to her.

SCARLETT Oh, Ashley! You really love her, don't you?

ASHLEY She's the only dream I ever had that didn't die in the face of reality.

SCARLETT *(with a flash of her usual spirit)* Dreams! Always dreams with you! Never common sense.

ASHLEY Oh, Scarlett, if you knew what I've gone through—

SCARLETT Oh, Ashley, you should have told me years ago that you loved her, not me, and not left me dangling with your talk of honor. But you had to wait till now—now when Melly's dying to show me I could never mean anything more to you than . . . than this Watling woman does to Rhett!

"Ashley winces at her words, but his eyes still meet hers, imploring silence, comfort. Every line of his face admitted the truth of her words. The very droop of his shoulders showed that his own self-castigation was more cruel than any she could give. He stood silent before her, clutching the glove as though it were an understanding hand and, in the stillness that followed her words, her indignation fell away and pity, tinged with contempt, took its place."

SCARLETT *(continuing)* And I've loved something that—that doesn't really exist. Somehow I don't care. Somehow it doesn't matter. It doesn't matter one bit.

Ashley bends his head, sobbing. She takes him in her arms and smooths the back of his hair.

SCARLETT Oh, Ashley, Ashley, forgive me! Don't cry. She mustn't see you've been crying!

Dr. Meade enters.

DR. MEADE Ashley!

Ashley starts up. Dr. Meade only snaps his fingers. Ashley goes in quickly. The door is left open. Scarlett stands listening. A cry of real anguish:

ASHLEY *(o.s.)* Melly! Melly!

Just the least sound from the motionless Scarlett. India comes out of the bedroom, sobbing in the most uncontrollable grief. She goes past Scarlett to throw herself on the sofa. Aunt Pittypat follows and goes apart, crying. Then Dr. Meade comes and closes the door after him. Scarlett looks at the three, then suddenly comes to life.

SCARLETT Rhett! Rhett!
(she looks for him and sees that the hall is empty. She goes to the hall)
Rhett! Where are you?
(she goes out through the open door)

609 EXT. DOOR TO MELANIE'S HOUSE—MIST

SCARLETT *(as she throws open the door)* Rhett! Wait for me!

It is grey and there is a heavy mist. Scarlett enters into the mist and is almost completely enveloped by it, so that we see only her face and part of her black dress in it. We hear her voice:

SCARLETT'S VOICE Rhett! Wait for me! Rhett! Rhett! Rhett! Rhett!

610 TROLLY SHOT—IN FRONT OF SCARLETT GOING UP THE HILL

The most we ever see of her through the mist is a bit of her dress and her face, and even these are lost occasionally as we trolly before her, up, up, up the hill.

INTERCUT with this is a REVERSE ON HER BACK.

In these angles she peers through the mist, attempting to see through it. She is frantic, eager to get home. Her tempo accelerates as she gets higher on the hill. Her hair becomes slightly awry, and she becomes increasingly breathless as she nears the top of the hill.

ALSO INTERCUT WITH THIS should be a LARGE CLOSE UP of her, also trollying in front of her.

611 EXT. DOOR TO BUTLER HOUSE—CLOSE SHOT

The mist is lifting. The door is slightly ajar. Scarlett pushes it open eagerly and as the CAMERA goes behind her, she calls:

SCARLETT Rhett! Rhett!

She looks from right to left and moves around the great hall. But there is no answer. She starts up the stairs, calling:

SCARLETT Rhett! Rhett!

612 SIDE ANGLE

Scarlett halfway up the stairs.

SCARLETT Rhett!

613 ANGLE SHOOTING DOWN THE STAIRS

Scarlett has reached the top of the stairs.

SCARLETT Rhett!

She goes to the door to Rhett's room and throws it open without knocking. She stops short.

614 INT. RHETT'S ROOM

Rhett is sitting morosely in a chair. Beside him is a decanter and a glass, but the glass is unused and the stopper is in place. He turns slowly and looks at her steadily. There is no mockery in his eyes. His emotion is that of a man who is saddened, first by the passing of Melanie for whom he has had deep feeling, and second by the realization that an important phase of his life is ended.

RHETT *(quietly)* Come in.

SCARLETT Rhett—Rhett!

RHETT Melanie . . . she is . . . ?

Scarlett nods. She enters slowly and uncertainly. Without rising, Rhett pushes back a chair with his foot. She sinks into it.

RHETT *(heavily)* Well . . . God rest her. She was the only completely kind person I ever knew . . . A great lady . . . a very great lady.

Scarlett shivers slightly. It is difficult for her to say what is in her heart. Rhett's eyes come back to her. He speaks again. This time his voice is changed and he is now light and cool, more like himself.

RHETT So she's dead? That makes it nice for you, doesn't it?

Scarlett is stunned and tears come to her eyes.

SCARLETT Oh, how can you say such a thing! You know how I loved her really!

RHETT No, I don't know that I do. But at least it's to your credit that you could appreciate her at the end.

SCARLETT Of course I appreciated her! She thought of everybody except herself—why, her last words were about you.

Rhett turns to her. There is genuine feeling in his eyes.

RHETT *(after a moment, quietly; he again drops his mockery)* What did she say?

SCARLETT She said, "Be kind to Captain Butler. He loves you so."

CONTINUED:

614 CONTINUED

Rhett drops his eyes. Suddenly he rises and goes to the window.

RHETT Did she say anything else?

SCARLETT She said—she asked me to look after Ashley, too.

He is silent for a moment, and then he laughs softly.

RHETT It's convenient to have the first wife's permission, isn't it?
(he walks out of the shot)

SCARLETT What do you mean?
(suddenly she sees something)
What are you doing?

615 RHETT—IN ANOTHER PART OF THE ROOM

He is standing over a partly packed bag in a part of the room which we have not yet photographed in this sequence, and which Scarlett has not yet seen in this sequence. He is throwing into the bag toilet articles and a few other small things. Scarlett rises to her feet, frantically.

RHETT *(continuing with his packing)* I'm leaving you, my dear . . . All you need now is a divorce—and your dreams of Ashley can come true.

SCARLETT Oh, no! No!
(she runs to him)
You're wrong! Terribly wrong! I don't want a divorce—
(following Rhett's steps as he packs)
Oh, Rhett, when I knew tonight that I—when I knew I loved you I ran home to tell you—Oh, darling—darling—

RHETT Scarlett, please don't go on with this. Leave us some dignity to remember out of our marriage. Spare us this last.
(he continues packing)

SCARLETT "This last?" . . . Rhett, do listen to me! I must have loved you for years, only I was such a stupid fool I didn't know it. Please believe me! You *must* care! Melly said you did.

RHETT I believe you. But what about Ashley Wilkes?

SCARLETT I—I never really loved Ashley—

RHETT You certainly gave a good imitation of it—up till this morning.
(he stops packing, laughs a bit, rather bitterly)

No, Scarlett, I tried everything, and if you'd only met me halfway, even when I came back from London . . .

SCARLETT Oh, I was so glad to see you! I *was,* Rhett! But—but you were so nasty!

RHETT *(he starts to put things in bag again)* And then when you were sick and it was all my fault, I hoped against hope that you'd call for me, but you didn't.

SCARLETT I wanted you—I wanted you desperately! But I didn't think you wanted me.

RHETT It seems we've been at cross purposes, doesn't it? But it's no use now. As long as there was Bonnie there was a chance we might be happy. I liked to think that Bonnie was you, a little girl again, before the war and poverty had done things to you. She was so like you—and I could pet her and spoil her, as I wanted to spoil you. . . . When she went, she took everything.
(finished packing, he closes his bag)

SCARLETT *(crying frantically)* Oh, Rhett! Rhett, please don't say that! I'm so sorry—I'm so sorry for everything—

RHETT My darling, you're such a child. You think that by saying "I'm sorry," all the past can be corrected . . . Here, take my handkerchief. Never, at any crisis of your life, have I known you to have a handkerchief.

She takes the handkerchief, blows her nose, and sits down. Rhett picks up his bag, goes to the door, and exits. Scarlett leaps up and runs after him.

616 INT. HALL

Scarlett runs out to Rhett on the landing, crying:

SCARLETT Rhett! Rhett! Where are you going?

RHETT I'm going to Charleston, back where I belong.

SCARLETT Please—*Please*—take me with you!

RHETT No. I'm through with everything here.
(he sets down his bag, stops, looks at Scarlett. With a faraway look; it is a new Rhett—new to us and new to him)

CONTINUED:

616 CONTINUED

I want peace . . . I want to see if somewhere there isn't something left in life of charm and grace . . .
(with just a trace of amusement)
Do you know what I'm talking about?

SCARLETT No. I only know that I love you.

RHETT *(picking up his bag)* That's your misfortune.
(goes down stairs)

SCARLETT *(going downstairs after him)* Oh, Rhett! Rhett! Rhett! Rhett! Rhett!
(she reaches the front door)
But, Rhett, if you go, what shall I do? Where shall I go?

RHETT *(at the door, opens it)* Frankly, my dear, I don't give a damn!

He goes out into the mist, Scarlett looking after him.

617 CLOSE SHOT—SCARLETT

She is left stunned. She looks around, crushed by this blow, and speaks aloud:

SCARLETT I can't let him go! I can't! I won't think about losing him now! I'll go crazy if I do! . . . I'll think about that tomorrow . . .

She closes the door and goes back into the hall, moving jerkily and without design. But the thought of it will not stay down. She throws herself on the stairs, defeated, and with nothing to look forward to. She lies facedown with her head on her hands. CAMERA MOVES UP to a CLOSE UP of Scarlett sobbing and HOLDS for a moment.

SCARLETT But I must think about it! I must think about it! What is there to do? What is there that matters?

Suddenly on the sound track we hear Gerald's voice:

GERALD'S VOICE Do you mean to tell me, Katie Scarlett O'Hara, that Tara doesn't mean anything to you?

Scarlett's sobbing quiets. She starts to lift her tearstained face slowly.

GERALD'S VOICE *(continues)* Why, land's the *only* thing that matters—it's the only thing that lasts.

ASHLEY'S VOICE Something you love better than me, though you may not know it—Tara!

RHETT'S VOICE It's this from which you get your strength—the red earth of Tara.

Scarlett's face lifts a little higher as she listens.

GERALD'S VOICE Why, land's the *only* thing that matters—it's the only thing that lasts.

ASHLEY'S VOICE Something you love better than me, though you may not know it—Tara!

RHETT'S VOICE It's this from which you get your strength—the red earth of Tara.

Once again we hear the three voices repeating the same lines. The volume is still louder, the space between them still less, the speed of their repetition still faster:

GERALD'S VOICE Why, land's the *only* thing that matters—

ASHLEY'S VOICE Something you love better than me—

RHETT'S VOICE The red earth of Tara.

CAMERA MOVES SLOWLY UP to a LARGE CLOSE UP of SCARLETT'S FACE as we hear:

GERALD'S VOICE Tara!

ASHLEY'S VOICE *(louder than Gerald's)* Tara!

RHETT'S VOICE *(louder than either)* Tara!

A beautiful smile of hope crosses Scarlett's face as the realization comes to her that she still has Tara.

SCARLETT *(lifting her face)* Tara! Home! . . . I'll go home—and I'll think of some way to get him back.

She lifts her chin higher. We see the stuff of which Scarlett O'Hara is made, and we thrill with the knowledge that she won't be defeated for long.

SCARLETT After all, tomorrow is another day!

As the speech progresses, we see and hear her strength return—her voice

CONTINUED:

617 CONTINUED
accelerates in power and volume and we must believe completely that what Scarlett O'Hara wants to do, she can do.

SLOW DISSOLVE TO:

618 FULL SHOT—TARA LANDSCAPE—SUNSET

With the huge tree where Gerald has spoken to Scarlett. From behind the hill comes the silhouetted figure of Scarlett until she stands outlined along the sky. She turns halfway and stands looking over the broad acres. Wind blows her skirts slightly.

CAMERA DRAWS BACK as we once did on Scarlett and Gerald, until the tiny silhouetted figure of Scarlett is outlined against Gerald's Tara.

FADE OUT

THE END